Jaguar Books on Latin

Series Editors

WILLIAM H. BEEZLEY, Professor of History,
  University of Arizona
COLIN M. MACLACHLAN, Distinguished Professor of History,
  Tulane University

Volumes Published

John E. Kicza, ed., *The Indian in Latin American History: Resistance,
  Resilience, and Acculturation* (1993; rev. ed., 2000).
  Cloth ISBN 0-8420-2822-6 Paper ISBN 0-8420-2823-4

Susan E. Place, ed., *Tropical Rainforests: Latin American Nature and
  Society in Transition* (1993). Cloth ISBN 0-8420-2423-9
  Paper ISBN 0-8420-2427-1

Paul W. Drake, ed., *Money Doctors, Foreign Debts, and Economic
  Reforms in Latin America from the 1890s to the Present* (1994).
  Cloth ISBN 0-8420-2434-4 Paper ISBN 0-8420-2435-2

John A. Britton, ed., *Molding the Hearts and Minds: Education,
  Communications, and Social Change in Latin America* (1994).
  Cloth ISBN 0-8420-2489-1 Paper ISBN 0-8420-2490-5

David J. Weber and Jane M. Rausch, eds., *Where Cultures Meet: Frontiers
  in Latin American History* (1994). Cloth ISBN 0-8420-2477-8
  Paper ISBN 0-8420-2478-6

Gertrude M. Yeager, ed., *Confronting Change, Challenging Tradition:
  Women in Latin American History* (1994). Cloth ISBN 0-8420-2479-4
  Paper ISBN 0-8420-2480-8

Linda Alexander Rodríguez, ed., *Rank and Privilege: The Military and
  Society in Latin America* (1994). Cloth ISBN 0-8420-2432-8
  Paper ISBN 0-8420-2433-6

Darién J. Davis, ed., *Slavery and Beyond: The African Impact on Latin
  America and the Caribbean* (1995). Cloth ISBN 0-8420-2484-0
  Paper ISBN 0-8420-2485-9

Gilbert M. Joseph and Mark D. Szuchman, eds., *I Saw a City Invincible:
  Urban Portraits of Latin America* (1996). Cloth ISBN 0-8420-2495-6
  Paper ISBN 0-8420-2496-4

Roderic Ai Camp, ed., *Democracy in Latin America: Patterns and Cycles* (1996). Cloth ISBN 0-8420-2512-X   Paper ISBN 0-8420-2513-8

Oscar J. Martínez, ed., *U.S.-Mexico Borderlands: Historical and Contemporary Perspectives* (1996). Cloth ISBN 0-8420-2446-8 Paper ISBN 0-8420-2447-6

William O. Walker III, ed., *Drugs in the Western Hemisphere: An Odyssey of Cultures in Conflict* (1996). Cloth ISBN 0-8420-2422-0 Paper ISBN 0-8420-2426-3

Richard R. Cole, ed., *Communication in Latin America: Journalism, Mass Media, and Society* (1996). Cloth ISBN 0-8420-2558-8 Paper ISBN 0-8420-2559-6

David G. Gutiérrez, ed., *Between Two Worlds: Mexican Immigrants in the United States* (1996). Cloth ISBN 0-8420-2473-5 Paper ISBN 0-8420-2474-3

Lynne Phillips, ed., *The Third Wave of Modernization in Latin America: Cultural Perspectives on Neoliberalism* (1998). Cloth ISBN 0-8420-2606-1   Paper ISBN 0-8420-2608-8

Daniel Castro, ed., *Revolution and Revolutionaries: Guerrilla Movements in Latin America* (1999). Cloth ISBN 0-8420-2625-8 Paper ISBN 0-8420-2626-6

Virginia Garrard-Burnett, ed., *On Earth as It Is in Heaven: Religion in Modern Latin America* (2000). Cloth ISBN 0-8420-2584-7 Paper ISBN 0-8420-2485-5

Carlos A. Aguirre and Robert Buffington, eds., *Reconstructing Criminality in Latin America* (2000). Cloth ISBN 0-8420-2620-7 Paper ISBN 0-8420-2621-5

Revolution and Revolutionaries

Revolution and Revolutionaries
Guerrilla Movements in Latin America

Daniel Castro
Editor

Jaguar Books on Latin America
Number 17

A Scholarly Resources Inc. Imprint
Wilmington, Delaware

© 1999 by Scholarly Resources Inc.
All rights reserved
First published 1999
Printed and bound in the United States of America

Scholarly Resources Inc.
104 Greenhill Avenue
Wilmington, DE 19805-1897
www.scholarly.com

Library of Congress Cataloging-in-Publication Data

Revolution and revolutionaries : guerrilla movements in Latin America /
    Daniel Castro, editor.
        p.   cm. — (Jaguar books on Latin America ; no. 17)
    Includes bibliographical references.
    ISBN 0-8420-2625-8 (cloth : alk. paper). — ISBN 0-8420-2626-6
(paper : alk. paper).
        1. Guerrillas—Latin America—History.   2. Insurgency—Latin
America—History.   3. Latin America—History—19th century.
4. Latin America—History—20th century.   I. Castro, Daniel, 1945–   .
II. Series.
F1413.R475   1999
322.4'2'098—dc21
                                                    99–12775
                                                        CIP

Acknowledgments

No book is ever an individual endeavor, but, rather, the result of a collective willingness to create. This undertaking might never have materialized without the patience, cooperation, and understanding of many people. I have contracted a profound debt of gratitude with the editors of the Jaguar series, Colin MacLachlan and Bill Beezley and Richard Hopper, for suggesting that I put together this book and for seeing it through. I also want to thank Linda Pote Musumeci for her editorial assistance, suggestions, support, and, above all, patience.

In the process of putting together this book, I am grateful for the help of many people across the country and abroad, including Richard Greenleaf, Trudy and Gene Yeager, Steve Davidson and Jan Dawson, Alejandro Delfos, Greg Freeman, Sue Stephens, Carol Wolff, Carol Segina, Len Pudelka, and Ann Koblitz. Part of the research was made possible through a Scholar-in Residence grant at Cornell University where I received invaluable support from Billie Jean Isbell, Mary Jo Dudley, and the Center for Latin American Studies.

Last, but not least, I want to dedicate this modest effort to Mariella Ruiz-Castro, my companion, best friend, and wife. Words will never capture my gratitude to her for her unqualified support through the years, for always being there with the right question and the right word. I dedicate this book to her because of her sense of justice and her support for those who struggle for a better life.

About the Editor

Daniel Castro is an assistant professor of history at Southwestern University in Georgetown, Texas. He holds a Ph.D. in Latin American history from Tulane University and has authored several articles on the struggles of women in Peru. He is currently working on a book about Spanish missionary and historian Bartolomé de Las Casas and ecclesiastical imperialism in the sixteenth century.

Contents

Preface

The Cuban Revolution shook the world like a seismic wave, ushering in a new era of revolutionary upheavals throughout the Americas. Although guerrilla warfare had been the preferred praxis of Latin American insurgents for nearly five centuries, it was only in 1959 that a handful of Cuban *guerrilleros*, under the leadership of Fidel Castro and Ernesto "Che" Guevara, overthrew dictator Fulgencio Batista, demonstrating the viability of guerrilla warfare as a vehicle of revolutionary transformation.

Prior to the victory of the July 26 Movement (M-26) in Cuba, the only other case in which guerrilla warfare had contributed to the success of a Latin American revolution had been Mexico. Twenty years later, Nicaragua joined the revolutionary ranks following the overthrow of Anastasio Somoza after years of guerrilla-driven struggle. With the exception of Mexico, Cuba, and Nicaragua, however, most Latin American guerrilla movements have ended in failure and death for the revolutionaries. Nevertheless, on the eve of the twenty-first century guerrilla movements of varying duration and ideological orientation continue to be active in Colombia, Mexico, and Peru.

The success of the Cuban Revolution rekindled the rebellious spirit of revolutionaries throughout the Americas, and also revived the interest of the world in Latin America. A result was to create the mistaken impression that guerrilla warfare was a relatively new addition to the Latin American political process, instead of being one of the oldest manifestations of rebellion and resistance on the continent.

The significance of guerrilla movements often has been politically and historically overlooked. It is as if their importance could be measured only by the degree of success that they achieved, without taking into consideration the fact that from the Dominican Republic to Patagonia, directly or indirectly, guerrillas have played a significant role in shaping and transforming the social and political landscape of every country in which they have been active for the last five centuries.

With rare exceptions, most of the available literature on guerrillas is limited to either a particular region or a specific period. The following selection of articles is intended to provide a perspective on various aspects of the character and historical evolution of Latin American guerrilla movements from colonial times to the present. Given the innumerable instances of guerrilla outbreaks over the past five centuries, realistic considerations of cost, time, and space take primacy over wistful expectations and thus limit the size of this volume to a fraction of what it might be.

This brief anthology attempts to provide an introduction to the history of Latin American guerrillas over the past two hundred years. Whenever possible, I have tried to allow the participants to speak in their own voices. In addition to a brief introductory overview of guerrillas in Indoamerica, the anthology includes nineteen selections arranged in loose chronological order. The first two documents provide insights into two of the most important Amerindian uprisings in Latin America, the rebellion of Tupac Amaru in 1780 and the Caste War of Yucatán in the nineteenth century. Selections 3 and 4 are dedicated to two of the earliest and most significant leaders in the first guerrilla movements of this century, Emiliano Zapata and Augusto César Sandino.

The years of revolutionary fervor inspired by the Cuban Revolution are presented in Selections 5 through 11. Che Guevara's rationale for guerrilla warfare constitutes Selection 5. The sixth document is Régis Debray's call "to free the present from the past" through armed struggle. Selection 7 is an examination of the activities and the leaders involved in one of the earliest uprisings in Guatemala. Selection 8 is a brief anthology of the writings of Colombia's revolutionary priest Camilo Torres. The ninth is a now famous speech by Peruvian guerrilla leader Luis de la Puente announcing in 1965 the inevitability of armed struggle. The next selection is a summing up of the 1965 Peruvian guerrillas by Héctor Béjar, one of the leaders. The eleventh document, written by Inti Peredo, one of the surviving participants in the ill-fated Bolivian *foco* that cost Che his life, describes the final days of the insurgency.

Selections 12 through 14 provide a glimpse into the ideological underpinnings of some of the most important urban guerrilla movements in the seventies. Selection 12 attempts to define the position of Brazil's urban guerrillas in the words of one of their leaders, Carlos Marighella; the next two documents attempt to do the same for Uruguay and Argentina.

The final five articles are dedicated to examining different aspects and perceptions of the repositories of guerrilla tradition in Latin America. Selection 15 looks at the evolution of Peru's Shining Path. The next selection examines the role of women in Peruvian insurgencies. The selection by Claribel Alegría and Darwin Flakoll sheds some light on the activities of the lesser known Tupac Amaru Revolutionary Movement. The penultimate document explores the ramifications of the uprising by the Zapatista National Liberation Army, while the last, authored by Herbert

Braun, captures in poignant terms the decline of revolutionary movements in Colombia.

The articles included in this reader encompass a little more than two hundred years in the history of guerrilla movements in Latin America and represent an attempt to tell the story of the guerrillas from a multitude of perspectives that will lead, I hope, to a greater understanding of the revolutionary phenomenon in Latin America.

We are partisans of principles and not of men!
—*Emiliano Zapata*
"Plan de Ayala"

At the risk of seeming ridiculous, let me say that the
true revolutionary is guided by feelings of love.
—*Ernesto "Che" Guevara*
"Man and Socialism in Cuba"

Violence against violence. The only solution is what we
are doing now: using violence against those who used it
to attack the people and the nation.
—*Carlos Marighella*
For the Liberation of Brazil

There also exist some slight contradictions
something like a dialectics of opprobrium.
For instance, there is a prison named Freedom
so if they proudly say:
the citizen here lives in Freedom,
it means that he is serving a ten-year sentence.
—*Mario Benedetti*
"Otra noción de patria"
La casa y el ladrillo

What an interminable century!
We ask:
When will it fall? When will it fall on its face
to the compact, to the void,
to the idolized revolution,
or the definitive patriarchal lie?
—*Pablo Neruda*
"La puerta"
Fin de mundo

Introduction—The Interminable War: Guerrillas in Latin American History

Daniel Castro

Guerrilla warfare, the proverbial "little war," has been inextricably linked to the vicissitudes of Latin American history from the time of the earliest native uprisings to the guerrilla movements active in Mexico, Peru, and Colombia as this century comes to an end. Despite a storied past, guerrilla-driven revolutionary movements, with rare exceptions, have failed to accomplish their aims of replacing traditional governments representing the interests of a dominant class with revolutionary ones. In the two decades following the Cuban Revolution of 1959, countless revolutionary guerrilla *focos* ("nuclei") attempted to transform the Latin American political landscape but met with failure. The sole exception was the Sandinista National Liberation Front (FSLN), which succeeded, with the support of a multiclass alliance, in overthrowing the dictatorship of Anastasio Somoza but failed to consolidate a revolutionary system.

In the Americas, guerrillas trace their origins to the rebellion of the cacique Enriquillo, who in reaction to the abuses of Spanish colonizers established a stronghold in the hills of Hispaniola in 1519. For fourteen years Enriquillo and his followers demonstrated that, under certain conditions, a small irregular band of ill-equipped rebels was capable of harassing and holding off a well-armed, well-supplied, well-trained, and numerically superior professional army lacking the mobility of irregular troops. But despite the rebels' relative military success, the long years of struggle without a decisive final victory forced them to sign a peace accord with the authorities.

As Spanish domination spread to the mainland, so did popular resistance. In almost every instance, the rebels' choice of guerrilla warfare was dictated more by the conditions prevailing at the time of the insurgency than by the exigencies of a preconceived strategy. This truth became evident in Peru when Manco Inca and his descendants, operating from their hideout in the Andes, harassed the Spanish occupying forces for thirty-five years, patiently nibbling at their lines of defense. The rebellion ended in 1571 when viceroy Francisco de Toledo captured and executed Manco Inca's last surviving son, Tupac Amaru I.

Toward the end of the century, the epicenter of rebellion shifted from Peru to New Spain. The insurgents, led by a runaway African slave named Yanga, kept the Spanish army in check for twenty-nine years beginning in 1579. Ultimately, time eroded the rebels' ability to continue fighting, and in 1608, to safeguard his surviving followers, Yanga signed a peace accord.[1]

During colonial times the highest incidence of armed rebellion occurred in the countryside, in response to the predatory behavior of estate owners and government authorities. The juxtaposition of terrain and social conditions, particularly in places with large concentrations of Indians, slaves, mestizos, and poor whites, made the pairing of rural insurgencies and guerrilla warfare unavoidable. In 1780 the opprobrious conditions endured by Andean natives set the stage for the Great Andean Rebellion led by Tupac Amaru II in Peru and Tupac Katari in Bolivia. Characterized as the bloodiest conflict in colonial America, the revolt sought justice for the Indians while attempting to vindicate the aspirations of native Andeans to overthrow the Spanish yoke and re-create the ancient Incan state.[2] In "The Rebellion of Tupac Amaru" (Selection 1), Alberto Flores Galindo examines some of the most salient characteristics of the conflict between the Spaniards and the rebels, who relied on guerrilla war to keep their struggle alive until the waning years of the conflict, by which time most of their leaders had been captured and executed.

The Spanish word *guerrilla* ("little war") was coined in the nineteenth century to identify and define the irregular war waged by small groups of Spanish patriots against Napoleon's occupying army. In Indoamerica, from New Spain to Buenos Aires, what began as a protest against the French invasion of Spain soon turned into an all-out war between American patriots and imperial Spain. While the Spaniards enjoyed the advantage of well-equipped militias, the patriots' limited resources forced them to rely only on guerrilla warfare.

After independence, Latin America was a continent divided along class lines. As Terry Rugeley points out in "The Caste War: Rural Insurgency in Nineteenth-Century Yucatán" (Selection 2), the most "successful and largest rebellion in Latin America" originated more as a protest against taxes and exploitation than over the question of race. While the peasants' successful application of guerrilla warfare kept the struggle alive, the lack of unity among the rebels and the lack of a clearly determined objective undermined their original impetus.

The Mexican Revolution transformed the character and nature of guerrilla warfare. In the hands of the legendary Emiliano Zapata, guerrilla war became one of the most powerful instruments in the revolutionaries' struggle for power. But as Robert Millon contends in "The Struggle of the Zapatistas" (Selection 3), the military accomplishments of Zapata were insufficient to survive his death and fulfill the aspirations of the masses of workers and peasants he had led.

In the aftermath of the Mexican Revolution, the winds of rebellion in the 1920s shifted to Brazil. Groups of junior officers (*tenentes*) attempted to topple the oligarchy-dominated government. Under the leadership of Captain Juan Carlos Prestes, the rebel forces participated in what can only be described as the Brazilian Long March. Originally initiated by a thousand people, the column's march across Brazilian territory, from north to south and east to west, had as an objective to mobilize people while trying to find a suitable base of operations in the interior. In 1927, three years and sixteen thousand miles later, 640 members of the column crossed the border into the safety of Bolivia. Although militarily undefeated, the Prestes column had failed to mobilize the people of Brazil.

In Central America, the Nicaraguan patriot Augusto César Sandino, a nationalist fighter more than a revolutionary socialist, waged a successful guerrilla campaign against occupying U.S. troops. In early 1928 the U.S. armed forces, overwhelmed by the evidence of Sandino's fighting capacity, stopped referring to him as a bandit and recognized him as a guerrilla. Sergio Ramírez, in "The Kid from Niquinohomo" (Selection 4), characterizes the incident as "a promotion won by bullets." After the recovery of Nicaragua's sovereignty, Sandino laid down his arms and was murdered by Anastasio Somoza's national guard in 1934.

The years between Sandino's death and the onset of the Cold War constituted a time of political realignment for all political camps in Latin America. New political parties, of the right and left, were created and consolidated, and the middle class was thrust into prominence. In Guatemala, a middle-class-inspired revolt overthrew the dictator Jorge Ubico in 1944. In Bolivia, the largely middle-class National Revolutionary Movement (MNR) came to power in 1952 after years of civil war and political turmoil. The Bolivian Revolution attempted to emulate its Mexican counterpart, but the country lacked the cohesiveness of Mexico. Eventually the revolution fell victim to its own limitations: isolation, a monocultural economy, lack of preparation, and lack of capital.

Following closely on the heels of the Bolivian Revolution and the overthrow of Guatemalan president Jacobo Arbenz in 1954, a group of Cubans, exiled in Mexico and far from the reach of the dictator Fulgencio

Batista, began preparing an invasion of the island and the overthrow of the dictator. On December 2, 1956, a group of eighty-two recruits, members of the July 26 Movement, landed on Cuban soil after an eventful journey from Mexico.[3] After an initial bloody encounter with Batista's troops, a small group of twenty survivors under the leadership of Fidel Castro and the then-unknown Argentine physician Ernesto "Che" Guevara sought refuge in the Sierra Maestra. From their stronghold in the mountains, the rebels galvanized the support of the Cuban people and the world behind their guerrilla campaign. Buoyed by peasant support, they began to win important tactical victories over the regular armed forces, demoralizing them while increasing the popularity of their cause. On New Year's Day 1959, Batista fled the island, leaving the rebels in control. As Che Guevara points out in his remembrances of the war, the dictator failed to take into consideration the rebels' capacity to survive, endure, and adapt to the rigors of guerrilla warfare while winning enough popular support to overthrow his regime.

In two short years, the Cuban *guerrilleros* had validated the axiom that under certain conditions a small group of determined combatants can defeat a well-armed and well-supplied, combat-tested regular army. After repelling an invasion at Playa Girón (the Bay of Pigs) staged by CIA-trained Cuban refugees,[4] the new revolutionary government of Cuba informed the world of its willingness to share its revolutionary experience with other Latin American nations. The Cubans further exacerbated tensions with the United States by offering to provide training facilities for aspiring guerrilla movements across Latin America.[5] For Castro, "the Andes remained the Sierra Maestra of the continent."

In addition to the tactical support extended by the Cuban government, Che Guevara's writings provided a blueprint for guerrilla war while emphasizing the importance of human commitment to the success of a revolutionary struggle (Selection 5). More than any other revolutionary figure, Guevara inspired people of diverse political affiliations to take up arms against oppressive regimes. At the core of Guevara's revolutionary strategy rested the *foco* theory, which maintained that in any country in which class contradictions were intolerable it was possible for a small nucleus of well-armed individuals to begin a guerrilla campaign that would act as a catalyst to mobilize the population at large to topple the existing system.

First suggested in 1960 and later revised in 1963, the *foco* theory was warmly embraced by revolutionaries throughout the Americas. The theory was popularized and disseminated throughout the world by French intellectual Régis Debray, who extolled its virtues in several of his writings (among them, Selection 6). The Cuban Revolution—and Che Guevara, in particular—added an ideological component to guerrilla warfare. After the Cuban success, it was no longer possible to be a successful *guerrillero* without an ideological foundation, and more often than not a Marxist ideology.

A scarce three months after the fall of Batista, a group of would-be Panamanian revolutionaries staged an invasion of their country, but they were quickly exterminated. In June of the same year a group of anti-Somoza rebels attempted an invasion of Nicaragua but met the same fate as the Panamanians. In the same month, opponents of the dictator Rafael Trujillo landed in the Dominican Republic, but, unlike the Cuban experience, there were no survivors to carry the fight into the mountains. In August there were reports that thirty men had invaded Haiti, allegedly led by an Algerian who had fought in Castro's army, but they too were eliminated. The last attempt by a rebel group to initiate a revolution during the first year of the Cuban Revolution occurred in Paraguay, when a group of eighty guerrillas crossed over from Brazil in November but were exterminated by the army and the police during their first week of operations.[6]

Despite considerable barriers erected by the United States and cooperating Latin American governments, within a few short years rebel *focos* of considerable strength had burst into prominence in Guatemala, Venezuela, Colombia, Peru, and Bolivia. As described by Richard Gott (Selection 7), in Guatemala a group of army officers organized a revolt on November 13, 1960. They demanded that Cuban refugees training in their country in preparation for the invasion of Cuba be removed from Guatemalan soil. Among the junior officers supporting the revolt were two young lieutenants, Marco Antonio Yon Sosa and Luis Antonio Turcios Lima, both graduates of the School of the Americas. In 1962, in an attempt to ignite a nationwide revolution, members of the November 13 Revolutionary Movement (MR-13), named in commemoration of the officers' revolt, joined forces with the Guatemalan Workers Party (PGT) and founded the Rebel Armed Forces (FAR). The FAR was unable to survive factional infighting and grew weaker after the deaths of Turcios Lima and Yon Sosa in 1966 and 1970, respectively.

Surviving segments of the FAR served as the foundation for the Organization of the People in Arms (ORPA), which joined still another group, the Guerrilla Army of the Poor (EGP). In 1982 the EGP, the FAR, the ORPA, and a faction of the PGT came together under the umbrella of a united front representing all groups, the Guatemalan National Revolutionary Unity (URNG). By the mid-1990s guerrilla activity had become an irritant to the government and a justification for repression. Together with the activities of right-wing paramilitary death squads, the actions of the government resulted in the deaths of more than 140,000 people. Finally, the government and the rebels negotiated a peace agreement in the waning days of December 1996. The agreement put an end to decades of fighting but did not resolve the contradictions that had prompted the rebellion thirty-six years earlier.

Like the Guatemalans, many of the Venezuelan guerrillas were disenchanted members of the military and middle-class centrist parties. In early 1961 members of the Venezuelan Communist Party (PCV) and the Movement of the Revolutionary Left (MIR) began exploring the possibilities of initiating armed struggle in the countryside. By the end of the following year, the guerrillas had come perilously close to elimination. This forced them to re-evaluate their tactics, and in February 1963 the PCV, the MIR, and some disgruntled military officers founded the National Liberation Armed Forces (FALN). After long years of fighting, President Luis Herrera Campins, in an attempt to end the conflict, promised to free more than a hundred political prisoners and offered amnesty to Comandante Douglas Bravo, leader of the FALN and the most recalcitrant of the guerrillas. Bravo's acceptance of Herrera's offer in 1979 effectively marked the end of seventeen years of fighting without having realized the aspirations of the FALN to bring "the people [of Venezuela] to redemption."

Unlike their Venezuelan counterparts, the Colombian guerrillas traced their origins to 1948 and the beginning of a unique Colombian genocidal cycle known simply by the name *la violencia* ("the violence"). It was from among veterans of *la violencia* and urban intellectuals that Antonio Larotta recruited, in 1960, the members of the first Colombian *foco*, the Worker-Student-Peasant Movement (MOEC).

Three important guerrilla groups emerged in the Colombian countryside after Larotta's death in 1961 and the demise of the MOEC: the Revolutionary Armed Forces of Colombia (FARC), affiliated with the orthodox Colombian Communist Party (PCC); the Popular Liberation Army (EPL), identified with a pro-Chinese line; and the National Liberation Army (ELN), an offspring of the MOEC, identified as a Castroite movement.[7] The ELN's reputation was enhanced by the recruitment of Camilo Torres, a Catholic priest, who abandoned the pacifist ways of the Church and joined the guerrillas instead (Selection 8). After his death, Camilo acquired a revolutionary stature comparable only to that of Che. As Richard Gott indicated, in death [Camilo] "was a more potent symbol than he had been when alive, especially outside his own country."[8]

In 1968, as guerrilla violence became endemic, Colombia's army was increased threefold in an attempt to put an end to the war once and for all. Despite the government's effort, the guerrillas almost miraculously re-emerged from the verge of extinction. Six years later, the equation was further complicated when a fourth group, the April 19 Movement (M-19), led by Jaime Bateman Cañón, a former law student and former member of the FARC, joined the fight. The newcomer was primarily an urban group that gained prominence through kidnappings and attacks on various private and public entities.

In the early eighties, the government began amnesty talks with the rebels while stepping up military pressure. In 1984 the M-19, despite levying charges against the FARC, signed a cease-fire agreement in May but in June accused the government of reneging on the pact and went back to fighting. On November 7, 1985, M-19 guerrillas stormed the Palace of Justice, taking the chief justice and other members of the court hostage. They demanded to negotiate with the president, but the army moved on the guerrillas and demolished the building with artillery fire. When the army took over what remained of the palace, the chief justice and eleven members of his court were dead. All the guerrillas and an additional thirty-three judges also had been killed. All told, more than one hundred people had died.[9] Five years later, the M-19 laid down its arms in a much publicized ceremony celebrating peace.

As the century winds down, Colombian guerrillas still remain active, but little is left of the original idealism that sparked their participation in the revolutionary struggle almost a half-century before. Unlike M-19, the FARC, the ELN, and the EPL never expected to participate in the electoral process, and many of them are still unable to readapt to the complexities of political life. Survival for the guerrillas at this point means becoming allied with and protecting drug-traffickers throughout the country. The FARC is still the largest of the groups, with a purported seven thousand members. The ELN and its four thousand members is estimated to have a net worth in the neighborhood of $12.5 million, generated from kidnappings and protection quotas. As Herbert Braun explains in "End of an Era" (Selection 19), little of the original revolutionary idealism remains among the guerrillas. The EPL has regrouped and claims one thousand members, and some dissidents of the M-19 have abandoned electoral politics and renewed hostilities. In the meantime, masses of rural folk, uprooted from their traditional way of life, continue to flock into the cities to an even more uncertain life than the one they previously led.[10]

The other two South American countries where guerrillas attempted to spark revolutions through rural *focos* were Peru and Bolivia. In both countries the guerrillas aimed to accomplish their objectives by making common cause with the aspirations of the indigenous peasants to recover their land and dignity.[11]

The first Peruvian guerrilla movement originated in the Cusco region, led by a young native of the area, Hugo Blanco, a member of the Trotskyite Revolutionary Workers Party (POR). In late 1962, Blanco shot and killed a policeman in a political confrontation. For months he managed to elude capture by retreating to the mountains, where he attempted to establish a guerrilla base, but he found himself increasingly isolated from peasants mistrustful of supporting his revolutionary movement for fear of reprisals.

Shortly after the capture of Blanco, a group of would-be guerrillas returning from Cuba were savagely annihilated at Puerto Maldonado by members of the Special Forces. Among those killed was the young prize-winning poet Javier Heraud. Two years after the killing of Heraud and his companions, the National Liberation Army (ELN)—founded by Héctor Béjar, a survivor of Puerto Maldonado—and the Movement of the Revolutionary Left (MIR), led by Luis de la Puente, began a guerrilla campaign against the government of Fernando Belaúnde.

The Peruvian MIR, like the one in Venezuela, pursued a more revolutionary line than the orthodox Communist Party of Peru, which advocated an electoral solution. As Luis de la Puente proclaimed, "The revolutionary path is the only path open to our people" (Selection 9). In May 1965 the leaders of MIR, who had spent several months setting up their bases of operation, met on the barren Andean plateau of Mesa Pelada in Cusco, and after long discussions they prepared a Revolutionary Proclamation announcing the initiation of armed struggle.[12]

In June the guerrilla front "Tupac Amaru," led by MIR leader Guillermo Lobatón, began operations in the region between the eastern slopes of the Andes and the rain forest. After some initial success against the army, they found themselves accosted by large army battalions backed by the air force and two branches of the police. In the last confrontation between the armed forces and the column, on January 7, 1966, Lobatón and other leaders of the front were killed.[13]

The army, already forewarned of guerrilla activity, moved into the area of Mesa Pelada even before de la Puente and his column, "Pachacutec," began their campaign. Inexorably, the army forced the guerrillas upward into the inhospitable reaches of the barren mountain, where the rebels' position became untenable. The final confrontation between the armed forces and the guerrillas took place in late 1965, resulting in the death of de la Puente and his supporting staff. At about the same time of the MIR's campaign, the ELN's "Javier Heraud Front," led by Béjar, was forced into action. Hunted down by the same troops that had finished off de la Puente, Béjar was captured in December 1965, tried, and sentenced to prison.

The failure of the 1965 Peruvian guerrillas illustrated some of the most prominent weaknesses of the *foco*. It demonstrated that even in the face of glaring contradictions in any given country, the commitment and sacrifice of a reduced group of fighters were not sufficient to bring about a revolution. In his summation of the events of 1965, "Some Final Notes [on a Guerrilla Experience]" (Selection 10), Héctor Béjar recognizes his own shortcomings and those of his fellow guerrillas. He points to the rebels' lack of a "coherent ideological framework and not offering the masses a structured program" as the main sources of their failure. The Peruvian guerrillas of 1965 failed to assess the real strength of the opposition and paid a heavy price: more than eight thousand peasants killed, thousands of peasants left homeless and jailed indefinitely, and thousands of acres burned by bombs and napalm.

Shortly after the Peruvian debacle, a new *foco* began operations in Bolivia in late 1966. The Bolivian *foco* had the distinction of being led by none other than the heroic commander of the M-26 guerrillas in the campaign against Batista, the former minister of industry in postrevolutionary Cuba, the paradigmatic guerrilla leader and strategist Ernesto "Che" Guevara, who had just arrived in the country. From the beginning, the Bolivian venture was plagued by political and tactical problems. The same year that Guevara arrived in Bolivia, Mario Monje, the secretary general of the Bolivian Communist Party (PCB), visited Havana twice. The first time was during the Tricontinental Conference in January. He returned in May to assure Fidel Castro of his support for a still, by his own account, unspecified revolutionary project in South America.[14] Monje's backing, never too forthcoming, began to waver even before Guevara arrived in Bolivia, but its true weakness was revealed when Che confronted him on December 31, 1966, as to who should be in charge of the military direction of the operation. Che left no doubt that he had come to Bolivia to take military control of the operation. As a result, Monje tried, unsuccessfully, to convince the PCB cadres remaining with Guevara to defect. When this failed, he divorced himself from the undertaking. Tension between Che and the leaders of the PCB had been evident from the beginning. Despite the PCB's "monopoly on political and material support from Havana, it failed to provide more than token backing for Guevara."[15]

Three months later, events began unfolding with vertiginous speed after some of the guerrilla recruits defected and informed the army of the exact location of the guerrillas' hideaway and of Guevara's presence in Bolivia.[16] Severely handicapped by the premature discovery of their position, guerrillas began military operations under the name of the National Liberation Army (ELN) on March 26. Their ability to fight and move freely was further hampered by the presence among them of Régis

Debray, Argentine journalist Ciro Bustos, and the German-Argentine citizen Tamara Bunke (Tania), in charge of support groups in the cities. In the meantime, the United States sent military advisors to train the Bolivian army as well as an undisclosed number of CIA agents to participate in an all-out hunt for Guevara.

On April 17 the force split into two columns, a rear one headed by Cuban commander Juan Vitalio Acuña (Joaquín) and a vanguard column led by Che (Ramón). From that moment until the end of the campaign, with the exception of the daring occupation of the town of Samaipata in July, most of the guerrillas' energy was spent attempting to reunite both columns. The turning point came on August 31, when Joaquín's column was ambushed by the army and all of its members were killed.

Abandoned by the PCB and without support of any kind from the city or their Cuban allies, Guevara's column wandered aimlessly through the countryside in an effort to stay alive. Finally, on October 8, at Quebrada del Yuro, Che divided the remaining seventeen men of the column into two groups, one of which was intended to serve as a "suicide" vanguard, led by the Bolivian Guido (Inti) Peredo, to take the army head-on, while the other tried to get away (Selection 11). Ironically, it was the suicide squad that broke through, while a wounded Guevara was murdered soon after being captured with three of his companions. The news was broadcast to the farthest corners of the world in a terse dispatch: "Guevara was captured on October 8, 1967. He was held overnight in a mud-floor schoolhouse in the hamlet of La Higuera, about 30 miles from Vallegrande, and the next day, on the orders of Bolivia's president, Gen. René Barrientos, he was executed."[17]

The death of Che Guevara closed one of the most intense revolutionary periods in the history of Latin America. It was precisely because of Guevara's belief in the international character of the continental revolution that he and his companions had chosen Bolivia as their center of operations. He died as he had lived, true to his revolutionary principles, but he had failed to create a "second and third Vietnam," as he had expected to do. After Guevara's death the mantle of guerrilla warfare was passed from the countryside to the cities of the Southern Cone, just as military dictatorships began to replace elected civilian governments in Brazil (1964), Argentina (1966), and Uruguay and Chile (1973).

In Brazil one of the most ardent advocates of armed struggle was veteran communist Carlos Marighella. After attending the 1967 Organization of Latin American Solidarity (OLAS) Conference in Havana, Marighella broke away from the orthodox Communist Party and co-founded the Revolutionary Communist Party of Brazil (PCRB) in 1968. After the PCRB, Marighella went on to found the group Action for National Liberation (ALN), which struck the first blow against the government in 1968.

In 1969 the ALN was joined by the People's Revolutionary Vanguard (VPR), the Revolutionary Movement October 8 (MR-8), the National Liberation Command, and many other groups ready to start a revolution in Brazil's cities. Marighella's advocacy of urban guerrillas did not preclude the existence of a rural front, nor did it make light of the importance of a party (Selection 12). The death of Marighella in 1969 did not signify the end of Brazilian urban guerrillas, but within three years most of the leaders of the movement had been killed, imprisoned, or exiled, while the military dictatorship had become institutionalized.

Like the Brazilian guerrillas, Uruguay's Movement of National Liberation-Tupamaros (MLN-Tupamaros) chose the cities as their staging ground. When the guerrillas went into action in 1965, they had little choice as to where their center of operations would be located. Over half of the population of 2.6 million lived in the capital, Montevideo; 30 percent lived in other urban centers; and only 20 percent lived in the countryside.[18] Founded in 1963 by a group of disenchanted members of the Socialist Party, the guerrillas of the MLN-Tupamaros, under the leadership of Raúl Sendic, spent their first few years recruiting members, "expropriating" funds from banks, and creating an urban support network and a base of operations. From the beginning, the organization placed more emphasis on praxis than on evolving a complex political theory (Selection 13). In its formative period, the MLN was more concerned with exposing the weakness of the government than with trying to overthrow it.

As guerrilla activities increased so did repressive violence by the government, causing further retaliation by the Tupamaros, and vice versa. One of the critical points of the war was the kidnapping of U.S. Agency for International Development official Daniel Mitrione. After negotiations to exchange him for captured guerrillas failed, partially as a result of the capture of the Tupamaro leadership, Mitrione was charged by the rebels with being a CIA agent responsible for training the Uruguayan police in repressive tactics. Tried by a "people's court," he was found guilty and killed on August 9, 1970. In July of the following year, 38 women guerrillas escaped from prison, and in September 106 male guerrillas tunneled to freedom.[19] For the next two years, the country witnessed an unprecedented escalation in the activities of death squads supported by the police and the army, backed by U.S. aid. Early in 1973, President Juan María Bordaberry, faced with a military coup, worked out a deal to remain in power as the figurehead while relinquishing power to the military to rule dictatorially.

Although the military in Uruguay did not achieve particular distinction in terms of numbers of people tortured or eliminated, as did their Chilean and Argentine counterparts, it nevertheless did resort to torture and intimidation to forestall any possibility of the MLN's increasing its sphere of influence. By 1979 it was estimated that at least one in fifty Uruguayans had been through some sort of imprisonment.[20] In 1984, Uruguayans went to the polls and elected Julio María Sanguinetti, its first civilian leader in eleven years. Two years later the newly elected president declared a general amnesty that included the guerrillas. Upon their release from jail, many of the Tupamaros integrated themselves into the electoral process. They reasoned that the state of democracy in the eighties in Uruguay was radically different than it had been during the period in which they had initiated their war.

Like its neighbor, Argentina enjoyed great economic prosperity in the first half of this century, but by the early sixties, as the economy stagnated and popular discontent mounted, the military took it upon itself to chart a new course. In 1966 civilian president Arturo Illia was overthrown by the military and replaced by army general Juan Carlos Onganía. Students and workers expressed their discontent, and the government answered with increasing violence. In May 1969 one student was killed and some twenty-four injured in a demonstration in Corrientes. A general strike was called for the end of the month. Students and workers, once again, were savagely repressed in Cordoba, fourteen demonstrators being killed and hundreds wounded. A month after the incident, known as *el cordobazo*, the National Revolutionary Army (ENR), a newly created urban guerrilla group, executed labor leader Augusto Vandor for his cooperation with the military. A year later a Peronist group, identifying itself as Montoneros, kidnapped and killed army general Pedro Aramburú, the man responsible for dismantling the Peronist edifice after Perón's fall. After 1969 the number of guerrilla organizations continued to expand. In addition to the Montoneros, General Roberto Marcello Levingston, Onganía's successor, had to deal with the Peronist Armed Forces (FAP), the Liberation Armed Forces (FAL), the Revolutionary Armed Forces (FAR), and the Trotskyite People's Revolutionary Army (ERP) (Selection 14 by James Petras).

After a prolonged political crisis, the military agreed to allow former strongman Juan Domingo Perón to return to Argentina to rein in his followers. Perón arrived in Argentina in 1973 and was elected president, with his wife, María Estela Martínez Perón (Isabelita), as vice president. After his death a year after being elected, he was replaced by his wife. The incoming president appointed José López Rega—a bizarre member of the Peronist right wing nicknamed *El Brujo* (Sorcerer) for his penchant for the occult—as her minister of social welfare. López Rega personally oversaw the creation of right-wing death squads to "dispose" of suspected terrorists but was forced to resign as the economic and political crises reached new heights.[21]

Under Isabelita Perón the country slipped further into chaos. Inflation ballooned to 335 percent, political assassinations, on the right and left, became commonplace, and once again the armed forces stepped in, on March 24, 1976, deposing President Perón. The new junta, with army general Juan Rafael Videla at the helm, swore to uphold the Statute for the Process of National Reorganization (*el Proceso*), calling for the reorganization of the country along the traditions of Christianity and the Western world.

While the insurgents expected increased armed confrontations, the military gained absolute control of the country through an unprecedented system of state terror, and by 1978 those suspected subversives who had not left the country had been either imprisoned or executed.[22] For the duration of the "Dirty War," as the period is known, anyone suspected of being a subversive was a candidate for kidnapping, torture, murder in the streets, being "disappeared" in prison, or being thrown alive from aircraft into the sea. Estimates of the number of *desaparecidos* (the "disappeared") range from a low of five thousand to a high of forty-five thousand. While these events unfolded in Argentina the majority of the world remained strangely silent, and silence also became pervasive in Argentina. The military defended the fact that although they had fought a dirty war against the guerrillas, they had won.

In the aftermath of the Southern Cone's nightmare, the locus of insurgence shifted to Nicaragua and El Salvador. Twenty years after the Cuban Revolution, the Sandinista National Liberation Front (FSLN), a revolutionary movement that relied on widespread popular response and guerrilla warfare, came to power. Founded in 1961 by Tomás Borge, Carlos Fonseca Amador, and Silvio Mayorga, the Sandinistas survived a difficult first decade of existence, gaining momentum in the 1970s when they garnered peasant support in the north central region of Nicaragua.

In addition to the support of the peasantry, the Sandinistas' position as a viable opposition movement was given credence by the abuses committed by dictator Anastasio Somoza and his cohorts in the wake of the 1972 earthquake. Popular discontent was encouraged and sustained with successful military strikes against the regime. In December 1974, thirteen Sandinista guerrillas took hostage numerous prominent Nicaraguan and foreign business and political leaders. In exchange for their release, the FSLN demanded, and obtained, $5 million and the release from prison of important members of their organization; they also demanded and received free passage to Cuba. Somoza declared a state of siege and ordered the assassination of hundreds of peasants, but his actions only contributed to strengthening the people's resolve to fight.[23]

The growth in popular support and external pressure greatly benefited the Sandinistas. Despite ideological rifts, the rebels overcame their factional differences and accepted the leadership of the most moderate, mainstream faction, the *Terceristas*.[24] In 1977, thanks largely to the pressure of American president Jimmy Carter, the state of siege was lifted, allowing the Sandinistas some breathing room. Building upon their mounting success, the FSLN once again dealt the dictatorship a powerful blow when a group led by Edén Pastora (Comandante Cero) occupied the National Legislative Palace and took hostage most of the legislators, including some of Somoza's relatives. As on the previous occasion, the FSLN made a list of demands that the government had to meet. This action alone helped increase the numbers of the movement almost tenfold.

The FSLN, unlike the ill-fated *focos* of the rest of Latin America, accomplished its objectives through the creation of a multiclass alliance that coalesced to overwhelm the resistance of an entrenched dictatorship. On July 19, 1979, Anastasio Somoza Debayle fled the country, and a provisional Government for National Reconstruction (GRN) came to power. But the Nicaraguan revolutionaries who had so successfully fought against the internal enemy were not prepared for the onslaught of the reorganized counterrevolutionary forces (*contras*) supported by the United States. After winning the first open presidential elections held in almost a half-century, the Sandinistas lost the following two elections to powerful conservative candidates.[25]

While the Sandinistas were busy protecting their revolution and their sovereignty, in El Salvador revolutionaries from different factions attempted to consolidate their forces into one common front to overthrow a government bent on perpetuating a system serving the interests of the privileged elite and its backers. In the early sixties, El Salvador had been a showcase for the much-vaunted Alliance for Progress. But at the end of the decade, declining coffee and cotton prices in the world markets reduced the profits of the latifundists and forced them to revert to staple crops. Life for the less privileged became a struggle for survival, and one in eight Salvadoreans was forced to seek better fortune in neighboring Honduras. In July 1969 a war with Honduras broke out, and El Salvador won. In retaliation, Honduras repatriated all Salvadoreans then living there. The massive return of workers aggravated the difficult conditions already present, and in 1970 guerrilla groups started emerging. One of the most prominent was the Farabundo Martí Popular Liberation Forces (FPL) led by Cayetano Carpio, a former member of the Communist Party who traded the party for armed struggle. The FPL was followed by the People's Revolutionary Army (ERP) and the Armed Forces of National Resistance (FARN), a splinter group, created after the execution of poet Roque Dalton by the ERP on charges of being a "Cuban-Soviet-CIA agent."[26] Unable to join in a united front, the guerrillas and their supporters became easy prey for the army and the death squads terrorizing the country by kidnapping, torturing, and "disappearing" social activists.[27]

The need for unity produced the Democratic Revolutionary Front (FDR), born out of the merger of sixteen different organizations, including the relatively ineffective Salvadoran Communist Party. Five guerrilla groups agreed to come together under the banner of the Farabundo Martí Front for National Liberation (FMLN). In early 1981 the guerrillas initiated a wistful "final offensive" against the military government, but they failed to unite the peasantry behind them, while in the major cities government forces resorted to terrorist tactics to cow potential supporters of the guerrillas into submission. Various human rights groups reported that more than ten thousand civilians were killed by various right-wing death squads in 1980 alone.

In the face of growing civilian casualties, President Napoleon Duarte offered to negotiate with the FMLN in October 1984. Negotiations collapsed after the guerrillas presented a three-point plan demanding a new government and a reorganized army, points that the military and the United States overwhelmingly rejected. By the end of the decade, civilian casualties had mounted while the country found itself adrift in a flood of organized violence against progressive elements perceived to pose a threat to the system.[28] Despite some important victories, the guerrillas were feeling the strain of accumulated years of fighting and repression. When Duarte's successor, Alfredo Cristiani, began peace talks, the guerrillas were willing to listen. By the end of 1991 one of the leaders of the FMLN, Joaquín Villalobos, announced that the struggle was entering a new phase, its "Marxist phase" having given way to a negotiated settlement agreed upon and signed by both sides in the closing hours of December 31, 1991.[29]

Unlike in El Salvador, where several revolutionary groups fought for hegemony, in Peru the initiative for armed struggle was assumed by a single group, the Communist Party of Peru (PCP), better known by its nickname Sendero Luminoso ("Shining Path"). As Daniel Masterson indicates (Selection 15), this was a totally different type of revolutionary movement, one whose ideological orientation purportedly blended the teachings of Karl Marx, V. I. Lenin, Mao Tse-tung, José Carlos Mariátegui, and its leader, Abimael Guzmán (Chairman Gonzalo) into an ideology applicable to the unique Andean context of the country. The uniqueness of Sendero's character was further defined by the significant role played by women in the rank and file and the leadership of the organization (Selection 16).

The beginning of armed struggle in May 1980 "was like a thunderbolt on a clear sky." Although the PCP had announced its intention to engage in armed struggle as early as 1964, no one had expected the timing of the war to coincide with a time when the country was returning to a system of electoral politics after twelve years of military rule. The response of the newly elected president, Fernando Belaúnde, was to increase the number of elite police units in the emergency zone, and it was only in December 1982 that he called on the armed forces to take charge of anti-subversive activities.

The accelerated growth of a national crisis characterized by three- and four-digit inflation, political repression, and the end of government subsidies of staple goods provided the insurgents with a ready-made constituency. As contradictions became more acute, the frequency of violent acts increased exponentially.[30] The sanguinary nature of the war caused Americas Watch to characterize Sendero Luminoso as "the most brutal and vicious guerrilla organization that has yet appeared in the western hemisphere,"[31] although other observers pointed out that it was necessary to "recognize that the army and the police have surpassed guerrillas in violence against civilians."[32]

After twelve years of concentrated activity in rural areas, Sendero set out to accomplish its much vaunted "strategic equilibrium," the qualitative jump forward that would have allowed it to field a semiregular guerrilla army to begin encircling the cities from the countryside, leading, in their own words, "to generalized chaos and the collapse of the government." As Sendero stepped up its campaign of political violence so did the government of Alberto Fujimori. On April 5, 1992, the president dissolved the congress and assumed virtually dictatorial powers.[33] A month later Fujimori ordered a raid against the penal establishment of Miguel Castro Castro (Canto Grande), where most imprisoned members of Sendero were being held. As a result of the confrontation, it is estimated that between 35 and 50 members of Sendero were killed. In response to the prison killings, Sendero placed a powerful bomb in one of Lima's richest neighborhoods, Miraflores, destroying several buildings and killing 25 people and wounding 140.

As Sendero continued its campaign of violence, rumors of an impending military coup began circulating with increasing frequency as the rebels targeted the capital. But on the evening of September 12, with Lima still under a state of siege decreed to curb the violence, Abimael Guzmán and other members of the PCP's Central Committee were arrested in an affluent suburb of the city. For all intents and purposes, Sendero Luminoso had been decapitated.[34] The capture of Guzmán and his subsequent conciliatory moves split the organization into two factions, those willing to sue for peace and those regrouped under the leadership of Oscar Ramírez (Feliciano), who chose to continue the war in the countryside and the cities.[35]

Despite Sendero's claim to revolutionary hegemony, another group, the Tupac Amaru Revolutionary Movement (MRTA), born as a coalition of several splinter revolutionary organizations, began its war against the Peruvian state in 1983. From the beginning, the MRTA, unlike Sendero, advocated the combination of rural and urban warfare in addition to participating in electoral politics. Ideologically, MRTA members identified themselves as anti-imperialist Marxist followers of José Carlos Mariátegui, Che Guevara, and the Cuban Revolution.

The MRTA, like the Tupamaros in Uruguay, relied on the propaganda value rather than the tactical value of its actions. As a result, the organization engaged in kidnappings, bank "expropriations," the bombing of U.S.-owned businesses—Kentucky Fried Chicken, Kodak, and Citibank, among others—and the taking of churches during services and foreign news agencies (such as UPI), as well as other visible guerrilla activities.[36]

In 1990 and again in 1996, the MRTA staged two highly publicized and daring operations. The first was the escape of forty-eight of its top members, including the cofounder and leader of the organization, Victor Polay Campos (Comandante Rolando), from the high-security prison of Miguel Castro Castro in July 1990, just as the country was preparing to inaugurate Alberto Fujimori as president. The imprisoned guerrillas escaped through a three-hundred-meter tunnel dug by their comrades from the outside over a period of more than three years (Selection 17). The second operation began on December 17, 1996, when a group of fourteen guerrillas, commanded by Nestor Cerpa Cartolini, seized the residence of the Japanese ambassador, taking an estimated six hundred hostages and demanding the liberation of nearly four hundred comrades and safe passage for the guerrillas to a remote location in the Peruvian jungle.

From the beginning, the government of Fujimori was adamant in its refusal to meet the MRTA's demand to free its imprisoned members. Over a period of four months, the guerrillas released most of the hostages, retaining only seventy-two government officials, foreign diplomats, and businessmen. Faced with the government's refusal to meet its main demand, Cerpa and his followers contemplated the possibility of reducing their demand and began negotiating safe passage out of the country and the payment of several million dollars to the rebels. However, after 126 days, the impasse came to a tragic end. On April 22 a group of army commandos took the ambassador's residence by assault, freeing all the hostages relatively unharmed, save for one who died of a heart attack. In the action, two soldiers and all the guerrillas were killed. In the aftermath of the military operation it was rumored that some of the guerrillas had been executed after surrendering.[37] Fujimori's government used the success of the operation to boost its sagging popularity, while the MRTA struggled to salvage whatever was left of its organization.

Beyond South America, the latest two guerrilla movements to surface have done so in Mexico. The Zapatista National Liberation Army (EZLN) operates in the state of Chiapas. The other, the shadowy People's Revolutionary Army (EPR) operates in Guerrero. The EZLN went into action on New Year's Day 1994, when it occupied four of the most important cities in the highlands of Chiapas. The EZLN demanded better living conditions and justice for the state's large Indian majority. The rebels hit their targets and almost immediately withdrew when the army began to mount a counteroffensive.

The EZLN's demands were contained in the plainly but effectively worded Declaration of the Lacandon Jungle, which explained Chiapas's long tradition of struggle—against Spain, France, the United States, and the dictator Porfirio Diaz. The organization seems to be made up mostly of members of Chiapas's Indian majority. Nevertheless, during its first raid, the fighters were led by a Spanish-speaking mestizo, Subcomandante (Subcommander) Marcos, who, with the indigenous Comandante Ramona, is the most visible and articulate member of the organization. As the repositories of a long revolutionary tradition, the Zapatistas have managed greater longevity than the *focos* of Jenaro Vásquez and Lucio Cabañas almost thirty years before in Guerrero.[38] Contrary to widely held misconceptions, the EZLN's struggle has the characteristics of a class conflict rather than a purely ethnic one. The indigenous population of Chiapas constitutes an integral part of the vast numbers of workers and peasants who have been pauperized by the move toward a free-market economy pursued by the Mexican government and the capitalist elite over the past twelve years (Selection 18).[39]

Although in their declaration they had asked for the overthrow of the regime of then-president Carlos Salinas de Gortari, faced with mounting repression and given that they had accomplished their immediate goal of calling attention to their plight, they agreed to negotiate a settlement with the government. The negotiations began in 1994 and concluded in February 1996, resulting in a settlement only partially satisfactory to both sides.

The syncretic nature of the ideology of the EZLN has given rise to speculation over whether its insurgency and ultimate objectives are in fact revolutionary. Mexican scholar Jorge Castañeda maintains that the EZLN's movement is not revolutionary, insofar as it has not attempted to gain territory or control of the government by violent means. He does not see the EZLN as an armed movement in the mold of the Sierra Maestra's heroic guerrillas but as a political movement that rode the wave of world opinion to get the government to negotiate.[40] Castañeda's point was somewhat strengthened when, in January 1996, the EZLN announced the creation of the Zapatista Front for National Liberation (FZLN) as their political arm, leaving open the possibility of its participation in electoral politics.

Unlike the EZLN, details about the EPR are rather sketchy, and little is known about its membership and ideology outside of the information available in the mass media or in scarce communiqués issued by the organization. It began operations in mid-1996, claiming to represent the revolutionary aspirations of the people of Mexico. So far its activities have been primarily staged in the rural areas of the states of Guerrero and Oaxaca, in the southern region of the country. Despite increased governmental repression of the peasants there, the EPR seems to have gained few converts.

In Latin America, the contradictions pitting opposing classes in constant conflict have changed little since colonial times, and guerrilla movements have been a constant in the region's history. The scope of conflicts that guerrillas have attempted to resolve range from the resolution of an individual grievance, as in the case of Enriquillo, to the overthrow of a dictator and the radical transformation of a whole country and its society, as exemplified in Cuba, Mexico, and Nicaragua.

In assessing the significance of guerrilla warfare in the Latin American context, it is important to keep in mind that the use of this type of war by a group of insurgents does not necessarily ascribe a revolutionary character to the movement. As Che Guevara indicated in his seminal work on the subject, "guerrilla warfare has been employed on innumerable occasions throughout history in different circumstances to obtain different objectives,"[41] and the objectives have not been necessarily revolutionary in every case. Historical evidence supports the contention that the choice of guerrilla warfare as a tactical weapon is dictated by the conditions at the time of the insurgency; a desirable outcome for the insurgents is dependent, in most cases, on timing and the existing relations of power in the location where the insurgency takes place.

Although in the past half-century most guerrilla movements in Latin America have been defeated because of lack of unity, lack of popular support, or U.S. intervention paired with the *guerrilleros'* ignorance of local conditions, the impact of modern-day guerrillas has nevertheless been significant, at least on a superficial level. Throughout Latin America, the memory of guerrilla movements still evokes a measure of popular respect and the romantic veneration of its participants. In other instances, the repressive tendencies of many governments are hampered by the memory of guerrilla movements and their impact on the population.

Despite the failures of the past five hundred years, the successes of the Mexican Revolution, the overthrow of Somoza in Nicaragua, the Cuban Revolution, and the wave of global support received by the newest guerrilla-inspired revolutionary movements in Mexico seem to argue against sounding the death knell for guerrilla warfare as a revolutionary alternative for resolving the contradictions afflicting Latin America as we march inexorably into the new millennium.

Notes

1. As did Enriquillo, who died one year after signing the peace agreement, Yanga committed suicide four years after the agreement.
2. Leon G. Campbell, "Ideology and Factionalism during the Great Rebellion, 1780–1782," in *Resistance, Rebellion, and Consciousness in the Andean Peasant World, 18th to 20th Centuries*, ed. Steve J. Stern (Madison: University of Wisconsin Press, 1987), 110–39.
3. The name of the movement commemorated the first attempt to overthrow Batista on July 26, 1953.
4. The Bay of Pigs (Playa Girón) invasion of April 17, 1961.
5. James DeFronzo, *Revolutions and Revolutionary Movements* (Boulder, CO: Westview Press, 1991), 177.
6. Richard Gott, *Guerrilla Movements in Latin America* (London: Thomas Nelson and Sons, 1971), 14–16.
7. Bynum E. Weathers, *Guerrilla Warfare in Argentina and Colombia, 1974–1982* (Maxwell Air Force Base, AL: Maxwell Air Force Base, 1982), 19.
8. Gott, *Guerrilla Movements in Latin America*, 224.
9. Bernard Diederich, "Betancur's Battles: The Man of Peace Takes up the Sword," *Caribbean Review* 15, no. 1 (1986): 10–11.
10. James Brooke, "Colombia's Rebels Grow Rich from Banditry," *New York Times*, July 2, 1995.
11. Leon Campbell, "The Historiography of the Peruvian Guerrilla Movement, 1960–1965," *Latin American Research Review* 14, no. 1 (Spring 1979): 45.
12. Rogger Mercado, a biographer of the guerrillas, claimed that the guerrillas had acted contrary to the principles of secrecy that must surround a guerrilla operation, and by proclaiming their intentions they had allowed the military to take the upper hand. See pertinent comments in Campbell, "Historiography," 54; and Gott, *Guerrilla Movements*, 355.
13. Although the Peruvian army claims that Lobatón died in the encounter, his body was never recovered. For an account of the day-to-day activities, refer to the guerrilla documents cited in Gott, *Guerrilla Movements*, 351–65. For a dia-

metrically different version, see the publication prepared by the Peruvian Ministry of War, *Las guerrillas en el Perú y su represión* (Lima, 1966), 54–64.

14. Daniel James, ed., *The Complete Diaries of Che Guevara and other Captured Documents* (New York: Stein and Day, 1968), 28; Mario Monje cited in Gott, *Guerrilla Movements*, 410. Despite Monje's claim to the contrary, an entry in the diary of Harry Villegas Tamayo (a Cuban fighting under the pseudonym of Pombo) pointed out that Monje had received twenty-five thousand dollars to support the Bolivian movement. See *Pombo's Diary* in James, *The Complete Diaries*, 284.

15. James Dunkerley, *Rebellion in the Veins: Political Struggle in Bolivia, 1952–1982* (London: Verso Editions, 1984), 137.

16. All information containing dates and events is provided by Guevara's diary, *The Bolivian Diary of Ernesto Che Guevara*, ed. Mary-Alice Waters (New York: Pathfinder Press, 1994), 123–295.

17. John Lee Anderson, "Where is Che Guevara Buried? A Bolivian Tells," *New York Times*, November 21, 1995.

18. Arturo C. Porczecanski, *Uruguay's Tupamaros: The Urban Guerrilla* (New York: Praeger Publishers, 1973), 15.

19. María Esther Gilio, *The Tupamaro Guerrillas*, trans. Anne Edmonson (New York: Saturday Review Press, 1970), 184–91.

20. Martin Weinstein, *Uruguay: Democracy at the Crossroads* (Boulder, CO: Westview Press, 1988), 54.

21. He has been identified as the coordinator of a paramilitary terrorist group known as Coordinación Federal and a supporter of the right-wing death squad known as the Triple A: Argentine Anti-Communist Alliance.

22. Don Clark Hodges, *Argentina's "Dirty War": An Intellectual Biography* (Austin: University of Texas Press, 1991), 154.

23. De Fronzo, *Revolutions and Revolutionary Movements*, 201.

24. The organization was divided into three separate ideological factions, Guerra Popular Prolongada (Prolonged People's War), emphasizing the creation of a revolutionary army based on the rural element; Tendencia Proletaria (Proletarian Tendency), placing reliance on industrial workers' organizations and the participation of urban folk in staging massive strikes and popular demonstrations to bring down the regime; and, finally, the more numerous Terceristas (Third Stream) and the Christian Wing, advocating the formation of a less ideological (Marxist) and more broad-based coalition open to all those opposed to Somoza regardless of class or political affiliation.

25. Despite the reversals suffered by Nicaragua since the triumph of the revolution, it is hard not to agree with the old woman from León who, in an interview with Eric Selbin, told that before the revolution the rich used to have parties at which ropes were used to keep out the poor. After gaining a new consciousness fostered by the revolution, the woman adamantly expressed her profoundly held belief that "this could never happen again. We would never allow this. We know now that we are not cattle . . . and we will never be their cattle again." Eric Selbin, "Interview, León, Nicaragua (1989)," cited in Eric Selbin, *Modern Latin American Revolutions* (Boulder, CO: Westview Press, 1993), 58, n116.

26. There has never been a clear explanation of the real reasons behind Dalton's execution. On the formation of guerrilla groups in El Salvador, see Philip Berryman, *Inside Central America: The Essential Facts Past and Present on El*

Salvador, Nicaragua, Honduras, Guatemala, and Costa Rica (New York: Pantheon Books, 1985), 24; Walter LaFeber, *Inevitable Revolutions: The United States in Central America*, 2d ed. (New York: W. W. Norton, 1993), 244–45; Timothy P. Wickham-Crowley, *Guerrillas and Revolution in Latin America: A Comparative Study of Insurgents and Regimes since 1956* (Princeton, NJ: Princeton University Press, 1992), 211.

27. Members of paramilitary death squads were responsible for the assassination of three American nuns and one lay religious worker in 1980, the same year in which Archbishop Arnulfo Romero was assassinated by members of one of the most active and vitriolic right-wing terrorist organizations (ORDEN), with the implicit support of a former trainee of Washington's International Police Academy, Major Roberto d'Abuisson.

28. In 1989 six Jesuit priests, their housekeeper, and her daughter were murdered by members of the army. When the United States demanded an investigation, Cristiani's government informed Washington that the records had been lost.

29. For an analysis of events after the peace accord, refer to Dean Brackley, "Beyond Elections in El Salvador," *America* 171, no. 7 (September 17, 1994): 4–7.

30. In the first year of fighting, there were 219 reported acts of political violence; by the end of the second year the number had increased to 715, and by 1988 the police reported 2,802 politically related acts of violence.

31. Americas Watch Report, *Abdicating Democratic Authority: Human Rights in Peru* (New York, 1984), 1.

32. Ronald H. Berg, "Peasant Responses to Shining Path in Andahuaylas," in *The Shining Path of Peru*, 2d ed., ed. David Scott Palmer (New York: St. Martin's Press, 1994), 102.

33. Up to that point, the war had cost $25 billion and more than twenty-six thousand lives. Nathaniel C. Nash, "Shining Path Reeling in Wake of Chief's Capture," *New York Times*, November 20, 1992.

34. James Brooke, "The Snaring of Guzmán: 'Bingo—We Got Him,' " *New York Times*, September 15, 1992.

35. For details on the splits within the party and the emergence of the new leadership, see Angel Páez, " 'Feliciano' acuerda seguir 'guerra popular,' " *La Republica*, April 28, 1994.

36. Nathaniel C. Nash, "Peru under Challenge by Another Insurgency," *New York Times*, February 27, 1991; Michael Radu and Vladimir Tismaneanu, *Latin American Revolutionaries* (Washington, DC: Pergamon-Brassey's International Defense Publishers, 1990), 340–42.

37. For details about the end of the hostage crisis, see Calvin Simms, "A Signal and Peru Hostages Opened Door to Raid," *New York Times*, April 24, 1997; Diana Jean Schemo, "For Peru Rebel's Bones, Back to Poverty's Roots," *New York Times*, April 29, 1997; Empresa editora *El Comercio*, ed., *La crisis de los rehenes en el Peru* (Lima, 1997).

38. The *focos* of Vásquez and Cabañas were quickly annihilated by superior military forces. See Jaime López, *10 años de guerrillas en México, 1964–1974* (Mexico D.F.: Editorial Posada, 1974).

39. Michael Powelson, "We Have All Been Here Before: Peasant Rebellion in Chiapas from the Colonial Period to NAFTA," paper presented at the XI Southern Labor Studies Conference, University of Texas at Austin, October 29, 1995.

40. Jorge Castañeda, *The Mexican Shock* (New York: New Press, 1995), 85–86.

41. Ernesto Che Guevara, "Guerrilla Warfare: A Method," in Ernesto Che Guevara, *Guerrilla Warfare*, ed. Brian Loveman and Thomas M. Davies, Jr. (Lincoln: University of Nebraska Press, 1985), 182.

1

The Rebellion of Tupac Amaru

Alberto Flores Galindo

The rebellion started in the highlands of Peru by Tupac Amaru II in 1780 hit the American world with staggering force, and, for a few months, threatened to bring down the whole colonial edifice. The Great Andean Rebellion was a response to the onerous demands made on native Peruvians by the predatory practices of the crown's representative, the corregidor, *and to the onerous demands brought about by the Bourbon Reforms. The Peruvian historian Alberto Flores Galindo, author of* Searching for an Inca, Apogee and Crisis of the Aristocratic Republic, *and* The Agony of Mariátegui, *among other studies of Peru, was preoccupied with examining the question of identity and conflict in Andean Peru. In this excerpt from* Searching for an Inca, *he examines the difficulty and complexity of Tupac Amaru's attempt to turn the colonial edifice upside down and generate an indigenous Andean utopia while trying to wage an unsuccessful guerrilla campaign against the Spanish occupier.*

On November 4, 1780, the Indian leader Tupac Amaru II captured the Spanish *corregidor*, or administrator, Antonio de Arriaga; he would execute him two days later. This took place in Peru's southern Andes in a village called Tinta with a population of about two thousand. It was in Tinta that Indian rebel leaders from Cuzco, Puno, and other villages in the region would gather to come up with a plan not only to end exorbitant taxation by the Spaniards, but to drive out the Europeans and restore an Inca monarchy.

Tupac Amaru's decrees and proclamations would reach across Peru's highland cities. Later, his followers would destroy Spanish estates (*haciendas*) and textile mills (*obrajes*) all the way to Cuzco itself. Nevertheless,

From *The Peru Reader*, ed. Orin Starn, Carlos Iván Degregori, and Robin Kirk (Durham, NC: Duke University Press, 1995), 147–52, 154–56. Figure omitted. © 1995 Duke University Press. Reprinted by permission of Duke University Press.

five months after Arriaga's execution, the rebel chief and eight other leaders would be arrested and put to death in Cuzco's main square.

But the Great Rebellion—as the colonial authorities called it—did not end with their deaths. It continued in Puno under the leadership of Diego Cristóbal Tupac Amaru, and in parts of present-day Bolivia, northern Argentina, and Chile. The city of La Paz was taken twice by Julián Apasa Tupac Katari (first for 109 days, then for 64 days). Confronted with the difficulty of subduing the revolt and the tremendous cost of mobilizing troops (against Tupac Amaru alone they sent 17,500 soldiers), the Spaniards negotiated peace with the rebels. Still, conflicts continued. In June 1781, Felipe Velasco Tupac Inca, who regarded himself as Tupac Amaru's brother, tried to organize a rebellion in the mountains of Huarochirí, near the capital of the viceroyalty in Lima. Only the execution of Diego Cristóbal in August 1783 ended this convulsive period of Andean rebellion, which lasted more than three years.

The upheaval covered the entire southern Andes, roughly 200,000 square miles of strategically vital territory. At the very center of Spain's South American dominion, this area included cities such as Arequipa, Cuzco, and La Paz, mining centers such as Potosí, and ports such as Arica, an expanse that cut across key lines of communication between Lima and Buenos Aires. With a dense indigenous population, it was economically varied. Coca was grown in both the upper Amazon valley of Cuzco and the Bolivian lowlands, or *yungas*. Abancay had sugar; Arequipa, wines and liquor; Cochabamba, wheat; Ollantaytambo, corn. Textile mills operated in Cuzco's upper provinces. Trade knit these cities with mule trains, trading posts, and great annual markets like Copacabana, Tungasuca, and Cocharcas.

According to historian Boleslao Lewin, about 100,000 Indians participated in the rebellions, some 40,000 rebels in La Paz alone.[1] If we take into account that insurgent peasants were usually accompanied by their entire families, and if we add to this the people living in rebel-controlled areas, then the number is even higher. To be sure, one should not exaggerate. In Cuzco, for example, there were both rebel and loyalist towns. Divided allegiances sometimes fractured even neighborhoods within towns, as appears to have been the case in Chucuito. The reasons for disunity are complicated. Although there were earlier plans for a rebellion dating from 1770 and the leaders appear to have known each other (Tupac Amaru and Tupac Katari, both muleteers and traders, traveled from one extreme of the southern Andes to the other), the events were not synchronized and each revolt had its own character.

Everyone referred to Tupac Amaru as the Inca. But while in Cuzco, his proclamations were interpreted to call for respect for the property and lives of mixed-bloods (*mestizos*) and creoles (*criollos*); in La Paz it was believed that the Inca wanted all non-Indians put to death in a kind of ethnic cleansing. Some leaders in Atacama held the same opinion. In Arequipa in 1789 and in Oruro in 1781, by contrast, rebel leaders were actually creoles with urban followers composed of a mix of Indians and mixed bloods. There was not just one, in short, but many faces to the rebellion.

At the moment when these rebels attempted, by one way or another, to transform their world, the Bourbon dynasty under the reign of Charles III (1759–1788) was looking for a way to reorganize the imperial state and to streamline an antiquated colonial system. Andean colonial rule in the mid-eighteenth century followed the same model as that employed in other parts of the hemisphere by both the British and the Spanish. The metropolitan center siphoned off colony surpluses through commercial monopolies, the mining of precious metals, and heavy taxes. It was a system, as one observer has concluded, set up "to obtain the greatest amount of precious metals with the smallest investment possible."[2]

The distinction between colonizers and colonized, at first strictly drawn around the concept of separate "republics" of Spaniards and Indians, blurred with time. After all, unlike the Portuguese colonists in Africa and Asia, the Spaniards did not stay on the coast. To the contrary, they made their way into the interiors of the American continent. There they established mining centers, cities, and estates. Along with colonial administrators came merchants, landlords, and people who simply wanted to "do the Americas." These Spaniards often intermarried with Indians, creating the racial category of *mestizos*. There were also the creoles, of Spanish descent yet born in the Americas. As the lines between colonizers and colonized became less clear, so did the colonies' relation to Madrid. Initially, both Spaniards and creoles could occupy public office. By the first half of the eighteenth century, however, creoles were the majority in municipalities, religious orders, and even in the viceregal administration. Peru was part of the Spanish polity, just like any other imperial province. Together with its European aristocracy, a parallel aristocracy—that of the supposed descendants of the Incas—helped to maintain an illusory image of Peru's equal status within the empire.

To understand Spain's American rule, historian Richard Morse has adopted Max Weber's concept of "patrimonial society."[3] The king occupied the apex of multiple hierarchies whose counterbalances checked secessionism, yet muddled the system's operation. His authority was based on a civil supremacy sealed by church backing. In Peru, this political demarcation divided territory into parishes (*curatos*), magistries (*corregimientos*), and chieftainships (*curacazgos*). Thus Indians had over them a magistrate (*corregidor*), a priest (*cura*), and a chief (*curaca*), and none of them had clearly defined functions. A magistrate might also be a merchant and a priest own lands, the same as a chief, who also might be a merchant. Not surprisingly, conflicts were frequent—often ending in a crossfire of accusations about who exploited Indians worst.

But the advent of the Bourbon dynasty to Spain's crown in the eighteenth century threw the patrimonial system into crisis. Divided was the immense viceroyalty of Peru. The viceroyalties of New Granada (1740) and then Río de la Plata (1776) were created. The Jesuits, who had achieved economic autonomy through their numerous estates and urban properties, were expelled in 1767. The state seized their holdings. In addition, the Bourbons tried to regulate access to public office to streamline bureaucracy. New administrators came from the Iberian peninsula. Creoles began to be displaced from government positions. Crown-appointed inspectors (*visitadores*) were sent to the colonies to limit the power of the viceroys. New taxes were instituted, including a 12.5 percent tax on alcohol. Other taxes increased. The sales tax (*alcabala*) on produce and merchandise, for example, jumped from 2 percent in 1772 to 6 percent in 1776. Customs controls were established, and the accounting system reformed. The government also clamped down on contraband and, in general, on the corruption so common under the patrimonial system. Historian John Lynch calls the Bourbon reforms a "second conquest" of America.[4] Indeed, this was how they must have been viewed by local merchants, artisans, and even Indian tributaries, subjected to a new head count to crack down on tribute evasion. The reforms affected everyone. "Finally," writes historian Timothy Anna, "Spain was exercising a classic commercial imperialism."[5]

The reforms opened an irreparable breach between colonial society and the Crown. Understanding the outbreak of rebellion, however, requires an attention to the particularities of the southern Andes. Among other transformations, mining in Potosí had begun to recuperate in 1740 after a long decline. Together with the development of other mining centers and a gradual demographic recovery after the cataclysmic conquest, trade intensified across the southern Andes, reflected in the growing number of muleteers. A number of cases illustrate this process. For example, the Cuzco estates of Pachaca, which produced sugar, and Silque, which produced corn, stepped up production. So did textile mills. Increased production and commerce, however, soon overwhelmed the markets of a society ill-equipped to absorb new wealth because of continuing poverty. Between 1759 and 1780, as historians Enrique Tandeter and Nathan

Wachtel explain, "the Indians found themselves in a flooded market and had difficulties in obtaining the money needed to pay taxes and for repartos (forced purchases of commodities from the government)."[6]

Fully a third of the viceroyalty lived in the southern Andes, and the region's indigenous population was more concentrated than in other colonial territories. Depending on the place, Indians were anywhere from 60 to 100 percent of the population. By the 1780s, as we have seen, they were left to face the ill-fated encounter of economic crisis and political changes. All of this occurred in a space articulated in a manner that almost guaranteed a regional response. The mines of Potosí and cities like Cuzco and La Paz were not just scattered points on the long route between Lima and Buenos Aires. To the contrary, the mercantile economy fostered regional interdependence. Together with peasants and artisans were local merchants like the Ugartes, the La Madrids and the Gutiérrezes as well as Indian traders, some as prosperous as Tupac Amaru and others as poor as Tupac Katari. Many of these traders' names surface in the trials opened against the rebels in 1780. Listed in these records as among Tupac Amaru's closest collaborators, for example, were eight other muleteers. So, too, were some government administrators in Chuquisaca and Cuzco, among them some of the creoles who accompanied the rebels as scribes.

In short, conditions allowed an alternative to colonial domination to emerge in the southern Andes. For this to happen, however, the image of the absolute authority of the Spanish king and the monarchy had to shatter. Inadvertently, the Bourbons had prepared the way for the break-up of Spanish authority through their rapid reforms, but in the southern Andes the process occurred faster than in other places because this was precisely the region where a major sector of the population held to the concept of continuity with a different dynasty: the Incas, not the Bourbons. As the mixed-blood Ramón Ponce, one of Tupac Amaru's main commanders, declared in his confession: "He said that the kingdom belonged to him, because in the titles and decrees he was the fourth grandson of the last Inca."[7]

At the start of the rebellion, Tupac Amaru had his portrait painted holding the symbols of Inca royalty. Peasants who came to see him treated him as an Inca; and he was received under a canopy in the towns he visited, supervised by a Spanish priest in Andahuaylillas. His orders were to be obeyed because he was the heir to the Inca empire and thought by some even to possess divine powers, like the ability to resurrect those who died in his service.

From the beginning, Tupac Amaru was surrounded by a clique of close followers, including his wife Micaela Bastidas, their children, and cousins. This made up the core of an authority structure to supplant the Spaniards. Within the hierarchy were colonels and captains around whom Tupac Amaru hoped to organize an army like that of the Spanish, though various difficulties were to develop with this effort.

The Indians drafted for this new army were summoned by Tupac Amaru himself, or through the intermediacy of his chiefs or newly appointed authorities. As they arrived, sometimes with their wives and children, two immediate problems arose: how they were to be armed and how they would be fed. In addition, according to the European model, soldiers were to be paid a salary as well as provided with coca and alcohol. But the uprisings interrupted trade routes and blocked roads. As months passed, these logistical problems led to desertions, which were severely punished. At one point, León Ponce—Tupac Amaru's lieutenant—was told "to return to his province and bring back as many deserters as could be found there, Indians and Spaniards alike."[8]

Tupac Amaru's army replicated the hierarchy of colonial society. In fact, this restoration of the "authentic" Inca monarchy demonstrated the influence of European concepts on the indigenous aristocracy. Besides the regular army, however, there were also spontaneous uprisings and a multitude of small confrontations. These became more common with the passing months, as the revolution spread south, becoming widespread in the high moors, or *altiplano*. When the followers of Tupac Amaru arrived in Pucara near Lake Titicaca, for instance, they found that an insurrection had already erupted. In places like this, there was a local dynamic to organizing and decision making.

The Spaniards found it difficult to believe that someone like Tupac Katari would assume the title of viceroy without possessing aristocratic blood, all the more so since he was poor, dressed in worn clothes, and spoke no Spanish. Truly, the world seemed to have turned upside down. They were, however, better able to understand Tupac Amaru. Some colonial officials were certain that the name of the Incas was itself enough to unite the multitudes. During the rebellion, royal treatment was afforded Tupac Amaru not just by Indians, but also by the Spaniards who followed him. This treatment makes it easier to understand the particular cruelty of the final sentence against the rebel leader. The executions of Tupac Amaru and eight of his followers—the "show," according to a document from the time—lasted from 10:00 A.M. to past 5.00 P.M. on the afternoon of May 18, 1781. The spectacle was meant as a lesson to the Indians. It was supervised by the Crown's new representatives, including Visitor General (Visitador General) José Antonio de Areche and Judge Benito de la Mata Linares, the same people who wanted to reform the region's bureaucracy and increase revenues. The execution occurred within a society where rule would be increasingly based on brute coercion. From 1780 onward, military budgets increased as did the number of soldiers and militiamen. From 4,200 in 1760, the militia in particular grew to 51,467 immediately after the rebellion and finally to 70,000 by 1816. The militarization of the colonies resulted from Tupac Amaru's uprising."[9]

In justifying the sentence, José Antonio de Areche not only mentioned the "horrendous crime" of plotting against the monarchy, but also condemned the fact that many, especially Indians, had treated Tupac Amaru as "his excellence, highness, and majesty." This is why his execution had to be public and the remains spread across the mountains to prove Tupac Amaru was really dead, countering "the superstitions that led the people to believe that it was impossible to kill him because of the nobility of his character, which made him the inheritor of the Incas."[10]

For those who viewed Tupac Amaru as an Inca, however, the body was not that of a prisoner. Rather, it stood for the Indian nation. To quarter and then burn Tupac Amaru's body was to destroy symbolically the Inca empire. Years later, when Diego Cristóbal made peace with the Spaniards, Cristóbal assembled the supposed remains of Tupac Amaru and with great pomp buried them in Cuzco's San Francisco church. Shortly thereafter, however, the Spanish judge Mata Linares had Cristóbal arrested and condemned him to be hanged. After the execution, his body was also quartered and his houses sacked and destroyed.

On Tupac Amaru's death, the colonial authorities prohibited Inca nobility from using titles, ordered the destruction of paintings of the Incas, and forced the Indians to dress in Western clothes. According to Areche, these practices would eventually wipe out hatred toward things European. But the effect was the opposite: the measures accentuated the division between Spaniards and Indians. For Areche, the rebellion's defeat was part of the reorganization of the colonial system. Inca nobility and the Quechua language obstructed political centralization. Yet the rebellion had destabilized hopes for a return to the integration of the Andean population under Spanish rule. The massacres of Spanish immigrants, especially of those who had lived among the Indians, further widened the gap between the colonizers and the colonized. Old images of imperial authority and king had begun to dissolve.

The German baron Alexander von Humboldt journeyed across America about twenty years after the rebellion of Tupac Amaru. From the northern extreme of the viceroyalty, Humboldt made his way to Lima, remaining for several days. There, the renowned biologist and traveler spoke with local aristocrats and both creole and Spanish intellectuals. Interested in colonial government and ethnic relations, he was fascinated by the Great

Rebellion of 1780. Humboldt felt sympathy for the Indians and was critical of the Spanish magistrates. Yet after careful study—he even claimed to possess documents signed by Tupac Amaru—he ended up backing the Spaniards' position in the conflict.

Humboldt believed that Tupac Amaru's initial aim of Inca restoration had devolved into a vicious caste war with no middle ground. The battle of Americans against Europeans, in other words, slid into a struggle of Indians against whites. Spaniards and Americans of Spanish descent were ultimately brought together on the same side, supported by Humboldt because, he believed, they stood for "civilization" against "barbarism."

Civilization and barbarism. These terms also appeared in the "Report of the Government of Viceroy Jáuregui," which sought an explanation for the rebellion deeper than a hatred of colonial magistrates. Ultimately, the report attributed colonialism's failure to the fact that "it is common among the Indians to have an inclination toward their ancient barbarous customs and also to venerate the memory of the Incas."[11] The same language appears in another report that recommended Spanish schooling for the children of the revolt's "principal Indians" in order to "civilize them." An entire literature by intellectuals and colonial functionaries writing in a mix of self-reflection and defense of the system grew up after the rebellion.

In the juxtaposition of civilization and barbarism, historian Charles Minguet sees the entire problem of the colonial world, where Western minorities dominated an indigenous and mixed-blood majority, looking down on their traditions.[12] Imagining history in terms of European superiority characterized the Spanish response to the rebellion of Tupac Amaru and would stubbornly recur even after independence from Spain in the early eighteenth century, into the modern history of Latin America.

Notes

1. Boleslao Lewin, *La revolución de Túpac Amaru y los orígenes de la independencia americana* (Buenos Aires: Editorial Américas, 1967), p. 102.

2. Tulio Halperin Donghi, *Historia contemporánea de América Latina* (Madrid: Alianza Editorial, 1967), p. 58.

3. Richard Morse, "The Heritage of Latin America," in *The Founding of New Societies: Studies in the History of the United States, Latin America, Canada and Australia*, edited by Louis Hartz (New York: Harcourt, Brace and World, 1964), pp. 201–236.

4. John Lynch, *Las revoluciones hispanoamericanas* (Barcelona: Ariel, 1984), p. 13.

5. Timothy Anna, *España y la independencia de América* (Mexico: Fondo de Cultura Económica, 1986), p. 37.

6. Enrique Tandeter and Nathan Wachtel, *Precios y producción agraria: Potosí y Charcas en el siglo XVIII* (Buenos Aires: CEDES, n.d.), p. 91.

7. Comisión Nacional del Bicentenario de la Rebelión de Tupac Amaru, *Colección documental del bicentenario de la rebelión emancipadora de Tupac Amaru*, vol. 3, no. 1 (Lima, 1980), p. 594.

8. Ibid., p. 650.

9. Leon Campbell, *The Military and Society in Colonial Peru, 1750–1810* (Philadelphia: American Philosophical Society, 1978), p. 17.

10. Ibid., p. 269.

11. Agustín de Jáuregui, *Relación de gobierno* (Madrid: Consejo Superior de Investigaciones Científicas, 1982), p. 193.

12. Charles Minguet, *Alexandre von Humboldt, l'historien et géographe de l'Amérique espagnole, 1799–1804* (Paris: Institut des Hautes Etudes de l'Amérique Latine, 1969), p. 25.

2

The Caste War: Rural Insurgency in Nineteenth-Century Yucatán

Terry Rugeley

Despite the promise of a better world for everyone, the wars of indepen-dence of the nineteenth century brought relief only to the members of the American-born (Creole) elite, while Indians across Latin America saw no change in the conditions of their existence. In Yucatán, class conflict sim-mered throughout the peninsula and finally exploded in 1847 in the re-gion close to Belize. Within a year the natives controlled four-fifths of the peninsula, and the conflict known as the Caste War ran well into the mid-1850s. As the author of Yucatán's Maya Peasantry and the Origins of the Caste War, *historian Terry Rugeley points out that the rebellion was moti-vated by profound socioeconomic disparity rather than ethnic issues. He comes to this conclusion after studying the historical background of the rebellion and the reasons that made the Caste War one of the most impor-tant rural uprisings in the history of Latin America and one of the most outstanding examples of rural guerrilla war.*

The nineteenth century was a time of crisis, mobilization, and vio-lence for Mexico's indigenous peasantry. And nowhere was this more true than in Yucatán, the nation's southeast peninsula. Beginning in 1847, Yucatecan society descended into a massive rural rebellion known as the Caste War. Unquestionably the largest and most colorful of Mexico's many peasant insurgencies, it was also the most successful: after some twenty years of conflict, the rebels carved out a separatist territory that would endure for half a century.[1]

Background

Spanish colonialism arrived in Yucatán in the mid-1500s. The conquista-dor Francisco de Montejo found a collection of bitterly divided tribes that required individual and often brutal subjugation. But the spoils of this land proved disappointing. There were no precious minerals here, no lush soils awaiting commercial agriculture. For over a century the Spaniards contented themselves to live by tribute, while indigenous society reconstituted itself at the local community level. Throughout the eighteenth century, however, haciendas began to make their appearance: relatively modest-sized properties producing corn and cattle for urban markets. By 1800, Yucatán's rural world was a socioeconomic spectrum with Maya and Spanish extremes and every conceivable degree of mixture to be found between the two.[2]

The decades preceding the war are the least understood of all Yucatecan history. It was not a time of pure polarization—Hispanic dominance versus Maya submission—but rather a time of rapid change where rural peace was maintained through a complex and changing network of "middlemen" who negotiated between the highs and the lows of society. This network included petty officials, lawyers, and low-ranking priests. But its most important elements were the Maya elites, particularly the *batabs* or caciques. Their status came not from pre-Columbian lineage but rather from wealth and family connections. They also profited from their role as tax collectors for both church and state. And they aggressively seized the new opportunities brought by commercial agriculture, particularly in the sugar boom which gathered momentum throughout the first half of the nineteenth century.[3]

Meanwhile, Mayas of all levels of society continued to take advantage of legal and economic opportunities to defend themselves. Surviving records suggest an enormous willingness on the part of peasants to bring complaints of any sort, and against anybody, to the forefront. The notion of the docile Maya who kissed his master's hand was a mere facade. Peasants were learning to mobilize around the issue of tax resistance, first during the crisis of the Spanish constitution in 1812–1814, and later through many smaller acts of resistance and defiance. However, interests of the Maya elite and the peasant masses remained divided for the moment, an obstruction to concerted rural initiatives.[4]

The first two decades following independence (1821) were a time of incremental change. The state made only limited headway toward privatizing Yucatán's traditional system of public lands. Much of the growth at this time did not involve sprawling haciendas, but rather the smaller and less oligarchic *ranchos*, something within the reach of the ambitious Maya entrepreneur as well. The post-1821 regimes also perpetuated many of the colonial privileges of the church and the indigenous town governments (*repúblicas de indígenas*).[5]

The Imán Revolt and Its Aftermath

In the late 1830s, Yucatán entered a time of troubles. Angry with central Mexico's commercial restraints and army conscriptions, the peninsulars won a separatist revolt in 1840. The caudillo of this revolt, Santiago Imán, was a merchant, property owner, and reserve officer from north-central Yucatán. His army consisted largely of peasants whom he had recruited on the promise of tax abolition.[6]

There was something profoundly representative in Imán's strategy. The half-century following independence was a time when elites still found it useful and necessary to build alliance with peasants. All of the great caudillos followed this strategy: Rafael Carrera of Guatemala and Juan Alvarez of Guerrero come to mind. In the case of Yucatán, however, elite control over peasants was paper-thin. Imán's recruitments quickly gave rise to popular initiatives that the original caudillos could not control.

Imán's revolution had numerous consequences. First, it brought on a new drive toward economic liberalism. Under the new government, Yucatecan elites now began an accelerated program of privatizing public land. The regime also imposed a cultivation tax on peasants, and began a new drive to force the Mayas to learn Spanish. These measures sowed conflict throughout rural society.[7]

The second effect was a climate of political violence. In the newly independent Yucatán, various factions now struggled for supremacy at the municipal level. They had learned from Imán's success that mobilizing armed peasant support was the key to victory. After 1840, then, we begin to see an outbreak of small-scale rebellions throughout Yucatán, as multiethnic gangs tried to overthrow local officials and overturn disputed elections. Many of these took place in towns that would later become cradles of the Caste War. As one eyewitness put it, "Things are to be found here which probably have not taken place even among the wild Indians of the Californias."[8]

A third effect was heightened peasant activism. Mayas, too, understood that their participation had become central to local and even national political success. Inspired by Imán's promises, peasants once more began a heightened tax resistance. The government vacillated in its response, which merely antagonized the peasants and destabilized the whole tax structure, which was one of the backbones of rural stability. But by now tax resistance had become the language of peasant mobilization, and it remained the most commonly voiced peasant grievance throughout the entire early national period.[9]

Fourth, and finally, the post-Imán changes antagonized the peasant elites who had made their living by overseeing the old system. It was impossible to satisfy the demands of poor peasants without lowering the status of these elites. Prominent figures such as the *batabs* now found themselves confronted with heightened economic competition, a tax collection system now more unworkable than ever. As the political upheavals continued, they also found themselves confronted with physical violence, even assassination.[10] It was not surprising, then, that a small minority would begin to form popular alliances.

The Caste War

The Caste War erupted on July 30, 1847. Its source points were a string of towns that stretched from Belize to the eastern provincial capital of Valladolid. These towns had acquired something of a regional identity through the sugar and contraband trades. They had also witnessed considerable mobilization during and after the Imán revolt. Indeed, the war itself grew out of a series of local revolts which eventually escaped the control of their Creole instigators. Rural society's middle sectors, especially the *batabs* of these key towns, threw off their old patrons and assumed leadership for themselves.

This revolt had all the hallmarks of rural rebellion. There was no real unity amid the various factions, but rather a loose confederation of independent and often contentious caudillos.[11] Even these had little real control over the men who took up arms under their banners. The rebel forces were ethnically diverse as well; chiefly Maya, they also contained a large number of non-Mayas. The leadership in particular included numerous mestizos who had come to understand peasant culture and grievances.[12] Over time ethnic lines hardened, however, and the presence of these earlier caste warriors tended to pass from memory.

The aims of the war were murky and inconsistent. Despite the traditional romantic vision of an Indian rebellion aimed at driving the whites into the sea, it now appears that the leaders had more limited aims of tax adjustments and local or provincial autonomy.[13] And although historians typically identify land as the key grievance, the subject is rarely mentioned in Caste War documents. Above all, peasants wanted to end taxes, the principal mechanism used to extract their surplus wealth. One caudillo spoke to popular sentiment when he said, "We are prepared to wade through fire and blood to liberate ourselves from the payment of any tax as long as we live."[14] The chiefs' inability to raise taxes to support their own efforts was a weak spot, and those who ignored this prohibition risked being assassinated by their own followers.[15]

The rebels' record as soldiers also bore the imprint of peasant society. Capable of great enthusiasm, they were also poorly armed and even more poorly disciplined. In the first days of the war their chief advantages lay in overwhelming numbers and the mortal terror of Creoles caught unawares by the revolt. "Nothing withstands the fury of the Indians!" one wrote.[16] But after an initial shock the Yucatecan state reorganized itself and its army, obtained assistance from Mexico, the United States, and Cuba, and eventually pushed the rebels back into the eastern forests. The army used standard techniques of counterinsurgency in the rebel territories: it relocated peasants, stripped the land of its crops, and, in one of the most disgraceful episodes of all Latin American history, sold prisoners of war into Cuban slavery. By mid-1850 the Yucatecan government had recovered most of its lost territory.[17]

Only then did the rebels discover their true calling as guerrilla fighters. Retreating with their forces to the eastern rain forests, the leaders of this conflict rallied their soldiers by instituting the religious cult of the Speaking Cross [Chan Santa Cruz], a powerful and mysterious oracle that preached war without compromise. The rebels now came to be known as *cruzob*, or "people of the cross."[18] In retrospect, the recourse to the supernatural was perhaps inevitable. Peasant-officiated religious cults had surfaced from time to time in the early national period, offering wealth and prestige to their founders and places of spiritual and intellectual relief to their participants.[19] In the early phases of the war, the caudillos had "ordained" their own Maya priest and equipped him with a device for pressing out "the Host"; they also used captured Creole priests to provide religious services for their troops.[20] The Speaking Cross was the culmination of a process that used religion as an instrument for popular mobilization.

Supported by the unyielding commands of their oracle, the *cruzob* instituted a society of total mobilization: the men divided their time between farming and military service, while women did household work but also prepared the supplies for campaigns. In February 1858 the *cruzob* capture of Bacalar, an old Spanish fort near the Río Hondo, gave them control over most of the south.[21]

Chan Santa Cruz was a peasant-based society fighting in an industrial age. As such, it was unable to make the guns, lead shot, and gunpowder necessary to its own survival. To buy these things its leaders had to find revenues. Direct taxes were, of course, impossible. The generals therefore devised a variety of disguised taxes that included a percentage of the spoils of war, as well as monopolies on tobacco, pigs, cattle, and rum, products that they sold to their Belizean neighbors.[22] They levied a tax on the Belizean logging companies for the right to cut mahogany trees along the Río Hondo, and charged peasants for the right to cultivate in these same regions.[23] The *cruzob* generals also rented out labor gangs, drawn from their own soldiers, to entrepreneurs interested in logging on *cruzob* territory. Ironically, many of their best trading partners were Yucatecan Creoles now living as refugees in Belize.[24] Despite its reputation as a fanatical religious-military cult, then, Chan Santa Cruz was both rational and resourceful in economic affairs.

Refugees and Hidalgos

For all of its violence, the Caste War never mobilized more than a minority of the region's Maya peasantry, most of whom were either too closely under Creole hegemony, outside of the areas of politicization, or simply uninterested in an all-or-nothing rebellion. Theirs was quite a different story.

For many the best option was flight. The Yucatecan Mayas (and a good many non-Mayas as well) fled outward, for at the time Yucatán was ringed by a number of thinly populated frontiers. Many from the Campeche area migrated into Tabasco.[25] Others relocated to the largely uninhabited islands of Cozumel and Isla Mujeres.[26] In the Petén, the vast rain forest of northern Guatemala, many peasants found the world they had long dreamed of: low taxes, little scrutiny by church or state, and relatively abundant land.[27] Finally, northern Belize took on a sizeable Yucatecan refugee community, which included numerous Mayas but was in fact dominated by the remnants of the old Creole planter class.[28]

In the deep south still other unique societies took shape. The so-called *pacífico* settlements were ragtag collections of Mayas, deserted soldiers, and Central Americans who seized the opportunity to negotiate a separate peace with the Yucatecan government: in exchange for local autonomy (including total tax exemption), they promised support for the Yucatecan war against the *cruzob*. *Pacífico* communities were highly decentralized, almost anarchistic in their political structure. Leaders had little authority over the rank-and-file. They skirmished with Chan Santa Cruz over Belizean trade routes and mahogany rents, but had no taste for sustained warfare. Government plans to enlist the *pacíficos* in some glorious reconquest were mere pipe dreams.[29]

For those who remained behind, life in the Yucatecan countryside became decidedly harsher. The war itself was a searing event. Maya peasants lived in fear of starvation, epidemic, violent death, and forced service in either the rebel or government army. So while the war itself did not bring about Yucatán's later plantation society, it did contribute to a hardening of social relationships in the better-known Porfirian years.

Shortly after the outbreak of the war, the government began to mobilize the peasants in the area under its control as a sort of ancillary unit of the army. They called them hidalgos, borrowing on an old colonial term for Mayas who had received special status in return for cooperating with the Spanish conquest.[30] *Hidalguía* was a matter of carrot-and-stick. Like the peasant civil patrols of Guatemala's recent civil war, it was largely coercive, with army representatives rounding up likely candidates, just as colonial officials had once forced peasants into building roads and cleaning plazas. But, at least initially, it offered some advantages, since hidalgo service supposedly exempted the peasant from taxes. After the worst of the danger had passed, estate-owners quickly lost interest in fighting the war, and began to protect their workers from hidalgo obligation. Those most at risk for the service were Mayas living in small outlying hamlets.

But the *cruzob* were no less intimidating than the government. Far from sympathizing out of some ethnic solidarity, most Mayas of the north and west lived in mortal terror of the Speaking Cross and its outlaw minions.[31] *Cruzob* raids could result in death or enslavement for peasants in the pacified zones.

The aftermath of the war also saw a hardening of the relationship between estate-owner and peasant. Dislocated and starving, peasants now accepted long-term labor contracts akin to slavery.[32] And, after 1870, the dramatic growth of the world market for Yucatán's henequen fibers resulted in the formation of a thoroughgoing plantation society characterized by coerced labor, debt peonage, and sharp polarizations of wealth and culture. Autonomous village life did endure, but it remains relatively understudied. The power and status of the *repúblicas de indígenas* continued to decline, while the *batab* role underwent a transition from official to unofficial cacique, another subject meriting further investigation.[33] Overall, the exigencies of war cut away much of the earlier elasticity of rural society and replaced it with a culture of command and obedience.

Events in the South

Yucatán's rural upheavals received new impetus with the arrival of Maximilian's French-sponsored empire in 1863. Few events were as important in the Caste War as the imperial crusade against Chan Santa Cruz, and few are as unexplored.[34]

Like much during Maximilian's empire, this project was ill-advised but initially seemed useful. Yucatecans had questionable loyalties to the Mexican polity, and certainly there were enough voices calling for an end to the Maya upstarts. However, few Yucatecans were willing to pay the price necessary for this war, which ultimately proved to be almost as large and costly as the war against Benito Juárez's government-in-exile. Consequently, what began as yet another counterinsurgency quickly escalated into an all-encompassing mobilization that antagonized most sectors of the society. As much as they hated the *cruzob*, property-owners hated even more to see their workers, goods, and capital drawn away to fight the war. Those "recruited" as soldiers had no ideological motivation for another war against the Cross, and desertion was both chronic and widespread. Indeed, the population of the *pacífico* communities ballooned as escaped soldiers fled south. The crusade reached its nadir when *cruzob* forces trapped the government forces in Tihosuco; although new troops eventually arrived to relieve the siege, the empire was by now on the point of collapse, and the idea of further initiatives against Chan Santa Cruz were out of the question.[35]

The imperial episode also meant changes for Mayas in the pacified zones. Maximilian's commissars tried to restore the corporate balance of colonial Spain by special administrative devices such as public defenders for peasants, but these maneuvers merely served to antagonize Creole elites.[36] After Col. Manuel Cepeda Peraza routed the Yucatecan imperialists in 1867, the newly reinstated liberal government abolished indigenous self-government forever.

The collapse of the empire's crusade resulted in power struggles in the south. The imperial threat had mobilized and unified *cruzob* society just as it was about to fragment. An 1864 power struggle purged would-be peace factions, leaving hardliners in command of the Cross. Energized by their victorious resistance at Tihosuco, the *cruzob* quickly moved to crush their hated enemies, the *pacíficos*. Seeking out allies within those communities, they precipitated a series of raids and revolts which, if they failed to end the *pacíficos* entirely, nonetheless weakened them as potential rivals.[37] The last *pacífico* caudillo to seriously challenge *cruzob* claims to Río Hondo trade and mahogany rights—the celebrated Marcos Canul—perished during a raid on the Belizean town of Orange Walk on September 1, 1872.[38]

The Speaking Cross had won the war. But it could not resist the entropic tendencies of peasant society. As the threat of imminent warfare receded, the unity of Chan Santa Cruz also deteriorated. Outside forces gradually began to penetrate the *cruzob* domain in order to exploit rain forest resources such as lumber and chicle. Although slowed by the massive social revolution of 1910, the Mexican state gradually reestablished its control over eastern Yucatán between 1899 and 1930.[39] The *cruzob* continued to exercise considerable control over their internal affairs; but by now their society was hopelessly and permanently divided among rival villages. The great days of the One True Cross were gone forever.

Later Years

Few Mexican provinces witnessed a nineteenth century more violent and chaotic than Yucatán. While almost all regions of the country experienced some degree of insurgency and violence, the phenomenon of an independent rebel territory was unique. The keys to their success were the fragmentations of Yucatecan elites, the availability of Belizean arms and supplies, and the presence of a group of brokers and middlemen willing to act as leaders. In short, the Caste War prospered not because of some absolute polarization, but because various "middles" —social, economic, and geographical—permitted strategies and alliances favoring rural revolt.

Recent years have not been kind to Yucatán's rural inhabitants. The modern-day state of Quintana Roo depends on a coastal tourist industry the pleasures and benefits of which are out of the peasants' reach. Although this industry has not involved massive land dispossessions, the lure of construction work has tended to further fragment once-militant villages. At the same time, rising prices hit hard at a people only partially linked to the money economy.

Rural life in the rest of the peninsula is also difficult. The revolution liberated Maya peons from forced servitude, redistributed land, and nationalized the henequen industry. It helped bring about greater Maya participation in state and local politics and, harder to measure but nonetheless important, helped reestablish the dignity and legitimacy of indigenous culture. But the revolutionary solution contained its own problems. Members of the new henequen collectives, or ejidos, tended to become subservient to the agrarian bureaucracy. More important, after the 1930s henequen was a dying industry that provided fewer and fewer returns for its workers. Its final collapse in the 1990s, coupled with the nonappearance of a successor, has meant poverty, outmigration, and abandoned land throughout the northwest. The entire peninsula now finds itself in an uncertain process of reorganization involving tourism, low-skilled assembly plants (*maquiladoras*), urban service sectors, and the remains of rural agriculture.

Notes

1. Standard recent accounts of the war are Nelson Reed, *The Caste War of Yucatán* (Stanford: Stanford University Press, 1964); Ramón Berzunza Pinto,

Guerra social en Yucatán (Mexico: Costa Amic, 1965); Moisés Gonzalez Navarro, *Raza y tierra: La guerra de castas y el henequen* (Mexico: El Colegio de México, 1970).

2. On the colonial period in Yucatán, see Nancy M. Farriss, *Maya Society under Colonial Rule: The Collective Enterprise of Survival* (Princeton: Princeton University Press, 1984); Robert Patch, *Maya and Spaniard in Colonial Yucatán* (Stanford: Stanford University Press, 1993).

3. Terry Rugeley, *Maya Peasantry and the Origins of the Caste War* (Austin: University of Texas Press, 1996), chapter 1.

4. Ibid., chapter 2.

5. Ibid., chapters 3 and 4. Important information on the *repúblicas* also appears in Matthew Bennet Restall, "The World of the *Cah*: Postconquest Yucatec Maya Society" (Ph.D. diss., UCLA, 1992).

6. Archivo General del Estado de Yucatán (AGEY), Poder Ejecutivo (PE), Gobernación, legajo 11, expediente 23, January 7, 1840, "Información sumaria hecha en averiguación . . ."

7. Rugeley, *Maya Peasantry*, chapter 5.

8. Archivo Histórico de la Arquidiócesis de Yucatán (AHAY), Decretos y Ordenes (DO), February 6, 1847.

9. As examples of post-Imán tax resistance, see AGEY, PE, Gobernación, XI, 32, April 13, 1840; AGEY, PE, box 12, Gobernación, April 17, 1843; and AHAY, DO, August 28, 1842.

10. There was, for example, the assassination of the prominent Maya office-holders of Tiholop in January 1847. See AGEY, PE, box 26, J, 2-10-1847.

11. See Archives of Belize (AB), Records #29 (R29), December 4, 1848, 153–55.

12. The most significant of these was Bonifacio Novelo, a mestizo peddlar from Valladolid. See Rugeley, *Maya Peasantry*, chapter 6.

13. Before the peak of the rebel offensive, the principal chief, Jacinto Pat, was already negotiating for a separatist state in the southeast. See AB, R28, February 18, 1848, 220. The correspondence of the Caste War leaders consistently identifies taxes as their principal concern, with provincial autonomy emerging as the only possible solution.

14. AB, R28, April 23, 1849, 223.

15. Archivo de Defensa Nacional, "Informe de la muerte de Jacinto Pat," expediente XI/481.3/2914. Reproduced in Letitia Reina, *Las rebeliones campesinas en México (1819–1906)* (Mexico: Siglo Veintiuno, 1980), 400–401.

16. Centro de Apoyo a la Investigación Histórica de Yucatán (CAIHY), letter of Father Manuel Mezo Vales, April 19, 1848.

17. For the traditional narrative of these events, see Serapio Baqueiro, *Ensayo histórico de las revoluciones de Yucatán desde el año de 1840 hasta 1864* (Mérida: Manuel Heredia Argüelles, 1879), 2:1–385.

18. The allure of the Speaking Cross has attracted a great deal of attention, if not necessarily much information. For an analysis of the prophetic writings of the early Speaking Cross, see Victoria Bricker, *The Indian Christ, the Indian King: The Historic Substrate of Maya Myth and Ritual* (Austin: University of Texas Press, 1981). An extensive ethnography of *cruzob* society in the early twentieth century appears in Alfonso Villa Rojas, *The Mayas of East-Central Quintana Roo* (Washington, DC: Carnegie Institute, 1943).

19. See, for example, the cult of San Antonio de las Ciruelas (AHAY, DO, May 5, 1824; May 7, 1824).

20. Archivo General de la Nación de México, Ramo de Bienes Nacionales, legajo 19, expediente 9, July 15, 1851.

21. Bancroft Library (BAN), British Foreign Office records (FO) #39–5, March 13, 1858.

22. Tulane University, ms. collection #26 (Yucatecan Collection), box 2, folder 18, c. 1868.

23. AB, R26, September 2, 1956, 145–146; BAN, FO 39–3, October 1, 1857.

24. The *cruzob* generals had close associations with refugee Yucatecan merchants; see, for example, *La nueva época*, #88, June 24, 1864.

25. Mariano Barrera, *Apuntes sobre los ríos de Usumacinta* (Mérida: R. Pedrara, 1865), 43–44.

26. For example, see AGEY, PE, box 39, Población, "Censo de Cozumel," 1850.

27. The arrival of peasant refugees is amply documented in the papers of the Petén in the Archivo General de Centroamérica, located in Guatemala City.

28. Documentation on Caste War exile groups in Belize is massive. For an overall report on their effect on the northern districts, see AB, R36, December 30, 1850, 123–32.

29. Barbara Angel, "The Reconstruction of Rural Society in the Aftermath of the Mayan Rebellion of 1847," *Journal of the Canadian Historical Association* 4 (1993): 33–53.

30. Like the civil patrols of the recent Guatemalan civil war, *hidalguía* quickly became another peasant corveé, unpopular among peasants and landowners alike. See the litany of complaints against the practice in AGEY, PE, box 36, "Disposiciones y decretos en respuesta a exposiciones y solicitudes," 1849.

31. During the upheavals of 1868, popular rumor held that anyone taken prisoner by the *cruzob* would be used as slave labor on the massive church under construction at Chan Santa Cruz. See AGEY, PE, box 169, Gobernación, Correspondencia, March 4, 1868; and March 11, 1868.

32. A number of these contracts are to be found in the Archivo Notarial del Estado de Yucatán. See, for example, the contract of October 22, 1851, pp. 84–85.

33. See Terry Rugeley, "Maya Elites of Nineteenth-Century Yucatán," *Ethnohistory* 42, 3 (1995): 447–93.

34. The principal study of the French imperial period is still Fausto Sánchez Novelo, *Yucatán durante la intervención francés* (Mérida: Maldonado Editores, 1983).

35. One of the best accounts of the 1866 military campaign is found in CAIHY, "Libro copiador de cartas de la comandancia superior de la 7.a división militar en Yucatán de mayo 22 de 1866 a agosto 8 de 1866."

36. Terry Rugeley, "El abogado defensor de indios: Experiencias de un oficial imperialista en el campo yucateco," *El unicornio* (May 7, 1995): 3–8.

37. See, for example, AGEY, PE, box #169, Gobernación, Correspondencia, March 4, 1868.

38. AB, R111, September 11, 1972, 101–5.

39. Herman W. Konrad, "Capitalism on the Tropical-Forest Frontier: Quintana Roo, 1880s to 1930," in Jeffry T. Brannon and Gilbert M. Joseph, eds., *Land,*

Labor, and Capital in Modern Yucatán: Essays in Regional History and Political Economy (Tuscaloosa, AL: University of Alabama Press, 1991), 143–71; Paul Sullivan, *Unfinished Conversations: Mayas and Foreigners between Two Wars* (New York: Alfred A. Knopf, 1989).

3

The Struggle of the Zapatistas

Robert P. Millon

More than any of the other leaders of the Mexican Revolution, Emiliano Zapata captured the hearts and minds of the peasants and other rural workers of Mexico. In the aftermath of the military phase of the revolution, when so many of the leaders sought positions of prestige and wealth, Zapata continued his stubborn, principled struggle for "Land and Liberty," not for himself but for the peasants of Morelos who had placed their faith in him.

As Robert Millon indicates in this encapsulated description of the trajectory of Zapata and his followers, the chronic shortage of military equipment forced the peasants from Morelos to become experts in guerrilla warfare. Because, like many of his predecessors, he refused to betray his principles and side with the oligarchy formed after 1914, Zapata was drawn into an ambush and killed in 1919.

Mexico in 1910 was a land dominated by large landed estates called haciendas. Labor on the hacienda was provided by peasants bound by debt to the estate and by sharecroppers and renters. . . .

The political, economic and social life of the nation was controlled by an oligarchy composed of the *hacendados*, of members of the upper echelons of the military, political and religious structures, and of wealthy merchants and businessmen—all in tacit league with a small number of foreign capitalists. The vast majority of the population consisted of peasants bound by debt to the haciendas.

The economic and political life of the state of Morelos, the birthplace of Emiliano Zapata and the heartland of his movement, was controlled by a few wealthy men. According to one author,[1] 30 haciendas

From Robert P. Millon, *Zapata: The Ideology of a Peasant Revolutionary* (New York: International Publishers Company, 1969), 11–36, 143–45. Reprinted by permission of International Publishers Company.

owned 62 percent of the total surface area and almost all of the cultivated land in Morelos. Eyler Simpson noted that "of all states in the Republic, Morelos was the prize exhibit of a state in which the villages in their corporate capacity and the inhabitants thereof in their private capacity before 1910 had suffered the greatest losses of land and in which the concentration of landholding in the hands of a few *hacendados* had reached its apogee."[2]. . .

Large sugar mills with modern machinery dotted Morelos which, in spite of its reduced area, accounted for a third of Mexico's total sugar production. The haciendas constantly encroached upon village lands, not only enlarging their possessions but also depriving small holders of means of support and thereby forcing them to labor for the large estates.

Emiliano Zapata was a mestizo born in Anenecuilco, Morelos, on August 8, 1879.[3] His father owned a small piece of land or *rancho*; the son assisted in the farm chores and attended the local primary school. Emiliano was only 18 when his father died and left him to support his mother and three sisters. (Emiliano's older brother, Eufemio, was married and maintained a separate household.) Emiliano took charge of his father's *rancho* and rented additional land from a neighboring hacienda on which he planted watermelons. He prospered sufficiently to purchase several teams of mules to haul corn for additional income.

Zapata early came into conflict with the system, defending his fellow workers against the haciendas and the local police and *rurales* (rural constabulary). His activities several times forced him to leave the state for his safety and once caused him to be drafted into the army for a short term.

The residents of Anenecuilco elected Zapata president of the village's defense committee in September 1909. In assuming this office, Zapata became the successor of a series of men whom their fellow villagers had elected throughout the centuries to defend the interests of their community. As president, Zapata followed established legal procedures to defend his village's rights before President Porfirio Díaz and before the governor of Morelos, Pablo Escandón. When the village's demands were not met and the neighboring hacienda of *El Hospital* continued to encroach upon Anenecuilco's lands, Zapata led his village on two occasions in 1910 in peaceful occupations and divisions of hacienda lands. . . .

According to those who knew him personally, Zapata was quite frank, simple and accessible, and possessed great strength of character. Later on he was always considerate with his followers and especially with the peasants, who almost venerated him. He had a great natural talent, learned readily and displayed rapid, almost clairvoyant, insight into people and their problems; it was difficult to deceive him.

In 1910, Francisco Madero, son of a wealthy *hacendado* of the state of Coahuila, initiated the revolution against Porfirio Díaz, the strongman of Mexico since 1876 and the president since 1884. Although Madero's objectives, which were expressed in the formula "effective suffrage and no reelection," were largely political, his revolutionary pronouncement, the "Plan of San Luís" (Potosí), included a provision for the return to small proprietors of lands which had been taken from them illegally. Zapata, attracted especially by this provision of Madero's Plan, immediately enlisted followers and, after contacting Madero through an emissary, initiated the revolution in Morelos. The siege and capture of Cuautla by the *zapatistas* in May 1911 was the decisive victory in the South. Pascual Orozco and Pancho Villa captured Ciudad Juárez in the same month and the Díaz government conceded victory to the revolutionaries. The victories of the *zapatistas* and the possibility that the revolutionaries of the South might attack the poorly defended capital greatly influenced Díaz to take his decision to renounce the presidency. In accordance with the terms of an agreement reached by representatives of Madero and Díaz, known as the Treaties of Ciudad Juárez, Francisco León de la Barra, Mexican ambassador to the United States under Díaz, assumed the interim presidency of the Republic pending general elections.

The *zapatistas* were at first sympathetic toward Madero and tolerated the interim government; they trusted that Madero was sincere in his promises to undertake a program of agrarian reform in Morelos after previous study of the problem and in accordance with legal procedures. Zapata consequently ordered his troops to comply with Madero's request to disband and to disarm. Soon four-fifths of Zapata's forces were disbanded.

The old regime, however, had been defeated in name only. The Díaz bureaucracy and the federal army were intact, and the *hacendados* still dominated the countryside. These elements of the old order proceeded to undermine attempts at reform and to create antagonisms and rifts among the *maderistas*. The federal army provoked bloody conflicts with revolutionary elements in Puebla, León, Tlaxcala, Torreón, Zacatecas and other places but, nevertheless, Madero continued to insist that the revolutionary forces which had brought him victory disarm.

Federal troops, who had been completely driven from Morelos in May, reentered that state and made hostile movements toward the *zapatistas*; consequently, Zapata stopped disbanding his forces. Madero visited Zapata in Cuautla, Morelos, to discuss the problem. At the outset of the discussions, Zapata contemptuously rejected the president-elect's offer to give him a hacienda in the state of Vera Cruz and the right to maintain a small, armed personal escort as the price for his withdrawal from the revolutionary scene. Zapata heatedly explained that he was fighting for the restoration of lands to the peasant villages and was incapable of selling out his followers.

In spite of this bad start, Madero and Zapata finally greed that the latter would disarm his followers and that, in the measure the *zapatistas* disarmed, the federal troops would withdraw from Morelos. They also agreed upon installing a provisional governor and a military commander in Morelos acceptable to the men of the South. The governor would be authorized to form a commission which would resolve the agrarian problems of Morelos as quickly as possible. Upon hearing of this agreement, León de la Barra, the provisional president of Mexico, ordered General Victoriano Huerta to move against the Liberator Army of the South, as Zapata's forces were called. The *zapatistas*, who had begun to disarm in accordance with the agreement, saw themselves again obliged to retain their arms.

The hostile federal action was taken without the knowledge of Madero. Indeed, Madero's life was endangered because he was still in Cuautla when the threatening federal movements began. Zapata, however, ordered that Madero be allowed to return to Mexico City. Huerta forced an armed conflict upon Zapata's forces at the end of August, and in September the federals launched a general offensive against the *zapatistas*. A personal enemy of Zapata, Ambrosio Figueroa, was named governor of Morelos.

Madero stated publicly in the Capital that the renewal of combat in the South was due to the failure on the part of the government to name Eduardo Hay as governor of Morelos and to the advance of Huerta's forces upon the *zapatistas*. He promised that when he assumed the presidency he would rectify the government's errors and make peace in Morelos on the basis of the agreements of Cuautla. However, Madero did not formally break relations with León de la Barra or Huerta, nor did he insist that the government stop its offensive in Morelos.[4]

The men of the South, confronted with superior forces, resorted to the tactics of guerrilla warfare. Zapata made two attempts to negotiate with the government in spite of the armed conflict which prevailed. When these failed, he led a raid upon the outskirts of Mexico City on October 22–23, 1911, which alarmed the national congress.

Madero assumed the presidency on November 6, 1911. He immediately dispatched Gabriel Robles Domínguez to negotiate with Zapata. The federal troops advanced upon the *zapatistas* while the negotiations were in progress, repeating thereby the tactics they had employed to destroy the peace conferences the previous August.

This time, however, Madero did not even reprimand the federal commanders. Zapata's terms for peace included the withdrawal of federal troops; the formation of a constabulary of 500 *zapatistas* under the command of Raul Madero [Francisco's brother] or Eufemio Zapata or some other acceptable leader to preserve peace in Morelos; the replacement of the governor, and the promulgation of a law of agrarian reform. Although Zapata's conditions were similar to those to which Madero had agreed in Cuautla the previous August, Madero categorically rejected them. He ordered the *zapatistas* to surrender immediately and unconditionally, in which case he would pardon them.[5] He instructed Robles Domínguez to inform Zapata that "his attitude of rebellion is damaging my government a great deal and that I am not able to tolerate its continuation for any reason."[6]

Zapata's answer was to continue his struggle and to proclaim the Plan of Ayala [Zapata's denunciation of Madero] on November 28, 1911. It remained the banner of the men of the South throughout the revolution.

The federal general, Juvencio Robles, devastated Morelos in a cruel campaign. His excesses led Madero to replace him with General Felipe Ángeles (later a prominent follower of Francisco Villa) and the fighting subsided somewhat.

Stanley Ross, a student of Madero and his epoch, arrives at the conclusion in regard to the break between Madero and Zapata that "if Zapata's basic demands had been met, it is reasonably certain that the Morelos insurgents would have submitted to the government." Charles Cumberland, author of another major study on the Madero era, reaches a similar conclusion. Both authors place the responsibility for the conflict between the federal government and the *zapatistas* upon the maneuverings of reactionaries and counterrevolutionaries.[7]

The break between Madero and Zapata indeed was inevitable, considering that Madero conceived the revolution in almost purely political terms and retained intact the bureaucracy and army inherited from the Díaz regime. As we have seen, Madero had called for at least partial measures of land reform in his Plan of San Luís. He claimed, however, that the Treaties of Ciudad Juárez by which his victory over Díaz was confirmed prevented him from fulfilling this provision of his Plan because these treaties obliged him to accept the legality of the court judgments and administrative acts of the previous Díaz administration.[8] The latter had succeeded in tying Madero's hands before relinquishing power.

Madero stated he wished to promote the formation—at a moderate pace—of small private properties in rural Mexico and to return *ejidos* (communal lands) to villages. He formed two commissions to study the problem of agrarian reform, the National Agrarian Commission and the Executive Agrarian Commission. The latter commission issued a report in April 1912 which stated that the purchase by the government of lands from large estates and the division of national lands was an unsatisfactory and impractical way to carry out an agrarian reform, and recommended the return of *ejidos* to the villages. The government, however, did little to implement the recommendation of the commission, limiting itself to recovering *ejido* lands which could be proven to have been illegally alienated from the villages. In addition, the government bought some lands from large landowners and surveyed and recovered some national lands which, in turn, were divided among small holders. These activities, however, barely scratched the surface of the agrarian problem.[9] . . .

Madero's ideal of establishing a regime of political democracy in Mexico was impossible to realize while the economic and social organization of the nation remained semi-feudal in character. Likewise, it was impossible to carry out an agrarian reform "in accordance with the law and on the basis of previous study" while the Díaz bureaucracy and army remained intact and the *hacendados* retained control of their estates.

The conservatives succeeded in provoking an armed conflict between the federal government and the Liberator Army of the South before Madero assumed the presidency. Once president, Madero played into the hands of those who wished to conserve the old order when he failed to come to terms with the *zapatistas* and other revolutionary elements. That he failed to do so indicated Madero's essential conservatism in respect to economic and social reforms. His primary goal was political reform, but he failed to comprehend that political reforms could be implemented only if accompanied by profound changes in the nation's social structure. . . .

Huerta put an end to the inept Madero government by a military coup in February 1913, and instituted a dictatorship in support of the old order. While the coup was in process, Zapata offered Madero 1,000 men to combat the rebellious federal soldiers garrisoned in Mexico City; Madero did not accept the offer.[10] Also, when General Felipe Ángeles returned to Mexico City with some of his troops to assist Madero in putting down the revolt, Zapata agreed not to attack either Ángeles's troop train or the virtually undefended Cuernavaca. Rosa King, an observant British woman resident in Cuernavaca at the time of these events, has noted that "I know now that when Madero waited in prison only one military man in Mexico was preparing to lead his troops to the rescue—and that was, of all men, Zapata, whom he had treated badly."[11]

Shortly before he was assassinated on Huerta's orders, Madero told his fellow prisoner, General Ángeles, that Zapata had been right in distrusting the federal officers and in predicting their defection when the two had met in August 1911. At the same time, Madero told another fellow prisoner of Huerta, Federico González Garza: "As a politician I have committed two grave errors which have caused my downfall: to have tried to content everyone and not to have known to trust my true friends. Ah! If I had but listened to my true friends, our fate would have been different; but I paid more attention to those who had no sympathy for the revolution and today we are experiencing the consequences."[12]

Huerta at first attempted to negotiate with Zapata, but the lines were too clearly drawn between the *hacendado*-government elements and the peon revolutionary groups for him to be successful. And Zapata, personally, could not be bought off. Zapata's replies to Huerta's overtures were eloquent in their revolutionary spirit. For example, Zapata declared to Huerta: "We do not want the peace of slaves nor the peace of the grave. . . . We want peace based on liberty, on the political and agrarian reform promised by our political creed; we are incapable of trafficking with the blood of our brothers and we do not want the bones of our victims to serve us as a staircase to public offices, prebends or canonships."[13]

The intransigence of the *zapatistas* forced Huerta to commit a considerable number of troops to the campaign in the South, thereby frustrating his plans to crush the revolution in the North before it could get organized. Huerta returned to the old policy of devastation in Morelos, with Robles in charge again. The bulk of the *zapatista* forces were driven from Morelos in the latter part of 1913, but they continued to be active in neighboring states. Zapata himself operated in Guerrero where his forces occupied the major towns and laid siege to Chilpancingo, the state capital, which fell on March 24, 1914. In April 1914 the *zapatista* forces returned to Morelos and by the end of May had taken all the towns in that state except the capital, Cuernavaca. It was placed under siege in June and taken in August 1914.

Meanwhile, the Constitutionalists, nominally under the leadership of Venustiano Carranza, advanced on the capital from the North. Pancho Villa's Division of the North bore the brunt of the fighting; it broke the back of the federal army in the battles of Torreón, San Pedro de las Colonias, and Zacatecas. Threatened from the north and south, Huerta fled the country in July 1914.

The revolution was not immediately victorious, however, for a rift had opened between the Villa and Carranza factions of the Constitutionalists. The *zapatistas* represented a third force, although they tended to be friendly toward the *villistas*.

The men of the South mistrusted the *carrancistas* and especially Carranza himself. The sources of this mistrust were many. Carranza had never clearly defined his position on political, social and agrarian reforms and he had assumed the executive power of the nation without consulting the will of other revolutionary chieftains in the country. The Constitutionalist army under the command of General Álvaro Obregón occupied

Mexico City in August 1914 without first coming to an understanding with the Army of the South. Before entering the capital, Obregón negotiated with the federal commanders the Treaties of Teoloyucan, under the terms of which Constitutionalist troops substituted federal troops in outposts facing the Army of the South. The fourth clause of the second treaty of Teoloyucan reads: "Federal troops garrisoned in the towns of San Angel, Tlalpan, Xochimilco and others facing the *zapatistas* will be disarmed in the places which they occupy as soon as the Constitutionalist forces relieve them."[14]

When the Constitutionalists moved into the federal positions, clashes began with the *zapatista* forces. As shall be noted later, a more radical group within the Constitutionalist movement wished to implement social reforms, including land reform, similar in content to those advocated by the *zapatistas*. Nevertheless, it was the moderates under Carranza's leadership who dominated the Constitutionalists and gave that movement its political orientation.

Carranza apparently was willing to take some measures of agrarian reform; however he did not contemplate implementing such an immediate and thoroughgoing reform as the men of the South wished. In a speech delivered in Hermosillo, Sonora, on September 24, 1913,[15] Carranza made a brief reference to land reform without, however, entering into details on the reforms he proposed to implement. In the summer of 1914, the governor and military commander of Nuevo León, Antonio I. Villarreal, issued a decree, with Carranza's consent, which suppressed debt-peonage in his State.[16] . . .

On many occasions, however, Carranza had manifested hostility toward measures of immediate and thoroughgoing land reform. He had ordered Villa in 1913 (according to the account of Villa's chief of staff, Colonel Manuel Medina) not only to desist from dividing lands among the peasants, but also to return to their original owners those already partitioned in Chihuahua during the governorship of Abraham González. Carranza adopted a similar attitude in respect to the division of lands which General Lucio Blanco had initiated in the region of Matamoros, Tamaulipas.[17]

Villa's and Carranza's representatives, meeting in Torreón in the summer of 1914, had reached an agreement to end the dispute between the two leaders. Carranza, however, rejected the eighth clause of the agreement on the grounds that "the matters treated in it are alien to the incident which motivated the conferences." The clause which Carranza found unacceptable stated that the revolutionary conflict was "a struggle of the disinherited against the abuses of the powerful," noted that Mexico's misfortunes were due to praetorianism, plutocracy and clericalism, and promised to continue fighting until the federal army was destroyed and replaced by the Constitutionalist army. The clause went on to promise that the Constitutionalists would install a democratic regime in Mexico, "procure the well-being of the workers," "emancipate the peasants economically" by distributing lands equitably "or by other means which tend to resolve the agrarian problem," and "punish and demand responsible conduct from the members of the Catholic clergy who supported Victoriano Huerta either intellectually or materially."[18] . . .

As for the possibility of cooperating with the *zapatistas*, Carranza had expressed his intransigent attitude toward the revolutionaries of the South shortly after initiating his armed movement. In the spring of 1913, Dr. Francisco Vázquez Gómez tried to induce Carranza to unite his forces with those of other revolutionaries, including the *zapatistas*. Vázquez Gómez, a medical doctor, had served as Minister of Public Education during the interim presidency of León de la Barra. His brother Emilio had served in the same cabinet as Secretary of the Interior, but had resigned in protest over the rightist policies of that regime. Both brothers, sons of poor peasant parents from Tula, Tamaulipas, favored a thoroughgoing land reform in Mexico and sympathized with the *zapatistas*. . . .

After his interview with Vázquez Gómez, Carranza wrote again to his confidential agent in Washington on May 18, 1913. Carranza said he rejected Dr. Vázquez Gómez's suggestion that all revolutionaries unite under a single program and demanded as the price for cooperation between the Constitutionalists and the *vazquistas* the "unconditional adhesion" of the latter to the Plan of Guadalupe.* Carranza asserted he made it clear to Vázquez Gómez that the Constitutionalists would make no compromises in return for support from the *vazquistas*.[19]

General Alfredo Breceda, Carranza's private secretary at the time of the interview, has made his chief's attitude even clearer. In a work which he published later, Breceda declared that Vázquez Gómez's proposals, which he judged were intended to unite the *carrancistas* "in abominable union with the rabble of Zapata," were "absurd." He added that Carranza announced to the press at the time that he would never accept alliances with elements which were not "strictly clean and honest." . . .

Representatives of Zapata had six interviews with Carranza shortly after the Constitutionalists occupied the capital; the first two interviews were held in Tlalnepantla and the others in the National Palace. Carranza's

---

*Carranza's political plan issued in March 1913. It called for the overthrow of Huerta and the restoration of constitutional government in Mexico and it designated Carranza as "First Chief of the Constitutionalist Army in charge of the Executive Power."

attitude was hostile. He refused to accept the Plan of Ayala, claimed that it was illegal to partition lands and declared he had 60,000 rifles with which to subject the *zapatistas*. During the fourth interview, he denied the *zapatistas* permission to enter Mexico City because, he claimed, they were bandits and lacked a banner. Before they could enter the capital the men of the South must submit themselves unconditionally to his government and accept the Plan of Guadalupe. He went on to counsel Zapata's representatives to abandon their leader, to forget about land reform and to join the Constitutionalist army, receiving in return promotions to the next higher rank. In the last interview Carranza declared land reform illegal and demanded, as the condition for peace, the unconditional submission of the *zapatistas* to the Constitutionalists.

Respecting the Plan of Ayala, Carranza maintained, according to the account of one of the *zapatistas* present, that "he was not disposed to recognize anything enunciated in the Plan of Ayala for the Constitutionalist army had fought for another Plan, that of Guadalupe; . . . that he considered the land revolution illegal because it was unquestionable that if a landlord or another person was stripped of properties which he had acquired—no matter how, so long as legally—he would have to protest and with the protest would come another armed struggle." He went on to say that "I cannot recognize what you have offered because the *hacendados* have rights sanctioned in law and it is not possible to take their properties from them and give them to those who have no right to them." Finally, he exclaimed: "The notion of dividing lands is preposterous. Tell me what haciendas you have, as your property, which you can divide, because one divides one's own, not another's."[20]

In the latter part of August 1914, Carranza sent "unofficial" representatives to Cuernavaca to parley with representatives of the revolution in the South. The *zapatistas*, who by now thoroughly distrusted Carranza's motives, insisted adamantly, as conditions for coming to terms, that the *carrancistas* accept the social and political principles of the Plan of Ayala—land reform and the designation of an interim president by a convention of revolutionary chieftains. In a letter to his "unofficial" negotiators, Carranza offered to accept the agrarian demands of the Plan of Ayala on condition that the *zapatistas* join the Constitutionalist army and submit themselves to Carranza's authority. The *zapatistas*, of course, felt they could not surrender to a man who had been a governor and senator under Díaz, whose revolutionary plan claimed for him the right to exercise the executive authority of the nation, and who never had stated clearly the social reforms which he intended to put into practice. Zapata would have betrayed his followers if he had delivered into Carranza's hands the cause for which his people had fought for so long and with so much bloodshed merely on the promise of the latter to carry out agrarian reforms. Huerta had made similar promises. The parleys ended in deadlock.[21]

A convention of revolutionary chieftains and their representatives was held at Aguascalientes to resolve the impasse between the revolutionary factions. The principal business of the Aguascalientes convention was to settle the rift between the Villa and Carranza factions of the Constitutionalists, but the Convention nevertheless promptly voted to invite Zapata to send representatives. Zapata sent a delegation of 26 members headed by Paulino Martínez and Antonio Díaz Soto y Gama. Villa had a large representation but Carranza's delegates were in the majority at the frequently unruly meetings.

The *villistas* immediately announced their complete support for the Plan of Ayala, and the Convention voted to accept the Plan "in principle." In addition, the Convention assumed national sovereignty,[22] accepted an apparent offer by Carranza to resign his position as "First Chief of the Constitutionalist Army and in charge of the Executive Power," and elected Eulalio Gutiérrez interim president of the nation.

Carranza, however, refused to accept the dispositions of the Convention, claiming that he had merely stated that he was "disposed to resign," but that the Aguascalientes Convention lacked the authority to accept his resignation or to depose him. The *carrancista* delegates did an about-face and supported their chief. Then the Constitutionalists retreated from Mexico City to Vera Cruz, where they promptly issued decrees on land reform in order to reinforce their revolutionary following. Villa's and Zapata's forces jointly occupied the capital.[23]

Frictions soon developed between the *villistas* and *zapatistas*, although the formal relations between the two revolutionary forces remained good. Villa began to take arbitrary actions which did little to cement relationships between his followers and the men of the South. When the first elements of the Liberator Army of the South had entered the capital in November 1914, two *zapatista* intellectuals, Octavio Paz and Conrado Díaz Soto y Gama, began to publish a revolutionary newspaper entitled *El Nacional* on the press of the former newspaper, *El Imparcial*. Only five numbers were issued, however, because when Villa entered the capital early in December he ordered all presses closed for five or six days. Afterwards, according to Octavio Paz, Villa gave the press on which *El Nacional* was printed to certain private individuals, "who had intrigued greatly to obtain it." In addition, Villa initiated a series of reprisals against his personal enemies, which included revolutionaries who had criticized him as well as counterrevolutionaries. In this fashion, Villa ordered the assassination of Paulino Martínez, one of the most prominent intellectuals associated with the *zapatistas*, because Martínez had dared criticize him publicly in the past.[24] . . .

Neither the *villistas* nor the *zapatistas* submitted themselves completely to the authority of the Convention government. The Convention's authority was weakened by the conflicts of interests within it and, especially, by conflicts between Zapata's representatives and the *villistas* in charge of the executive authority of the Convention, General Eulalio Gutiérrez and later General Roque González Garza. Furthermore, in practice, the exigencies of constant warfare made for military dictatorships under Zapata on the one hand, and Villa on the other.[25]

Effective military cooperation between the Division of the North and the Liberator Army of the South, which had always been extremely limited, ceased shortly after it began, Villa remaining supreme in the North and Zapata dominating the South. The *zapatistas* took Puebla and Villa attempted to mop up *carrancista* elements which threatened his supply lines from their positions in Jalisco, Michoacán, Tamaulipas and Sonora. The Constitutionalist army in Vera Cruz, under the command of Obregón, armed and provisioned itself well, and early in January 1915 retook Puebla from the poorly equipped *zapatista* defenders and on January 28 entered Mexico City.[26] Obregón withdrew his forces from the strategically unimportant capital in March, and in April shattered Villa's forces in the famous two battles of Celaya. Subsequently, the *villistas* suffered one defeat after another until by the late summer of 1915 their area of effective operation was reduced to Chihuahua and Durango. The *villistas* never again possessed national military potential.

Much of southern Mexico was under the control of the Army of the South, and Mexico City changed hands several times between the *zapatistas* and *carrancistas*. When the men of the South evacuated the capital for the last time in August 1915, the Convention government withdrew with them, establishing itself first in Toluca and then in Cuernavaca. Later when the Convention withdrew from Toluca, many of the *villista* members tried to journey north to join Villa but were largely dispersed by *carrancista* forces. The Convention government in Cuernavaca, nevertheless, still included a few *villista* delegates from the northern and central states.

Carranza clearly indicated his attitude toward the *zapatistas* in a speech delivered in Querétaro on January 2, 1916. Carranza's words revealed the contempt of the bourgeois for the peasant and of the head of an organized army for the guerrilla. "The military struggle is now almost ended. The most important forces of the Reaction have been defeated and dispersed in the North, and there remains only that which is not Reaction, which is not anything: *zapatismo*, composed of hordes of bandits, of men without consciences who cannot defeat our forces because they are a nullity as soldiers and who know only how to blow up undefended trains. . . . but who will have to disappear when the Constitutionalist Army very soon begins to concern itself with them."[27]

In the spring of 1916, Carranza sent General Pablo González into Morelos with 40,000 soldiers organized into six columns. Although the rapacious general gained many initial victories and captured the principal towns in Morelos and neighboring states, his forces were discouraged by persistent *zapatista* attacks and by the scourges of malaria and dysentery. The *zapatistas* recaptured some of the major towns of Morelos from the *carrancistas* in December 1916 and January 1917, including Jojutla, Yautepec and Cuautla. González retreated to the federal district in February 1917, leaving Morelos, the greater part of Guerrero and parts of Puebla in the hands of the men of the South.

How were the *zapatistas*, standing alone, able to defeat a well-equipped army? A word of explanation is in order concerning the nature of Zapata's forces and the character of the struggle in which they engaged for so many years.

Zapata's army was unlike the other major armies of the revolution, which had access to financial resources and to international supplies of arms and munitions which the *zapatistas* lacked. Suffering a chronic shortage of military equipment, especially of the two essentials of contemporary warfare—artillery and machine guns—the *zapatistas* adopted the tactics of guerrilla warfare, at which they became expert. They organized themselves into bands, which in turn could be marshaled rapidly into larger forces for major engagements, varying in size from a few dozen to several hundred members, each with its own leader who in turn was subject to Zapata's authority. The peasant communities supplied both men and sustenance to these bands. In turn, the Army of the South established the procedure of alternating its soldiers between three-month periods of active service and of agricultural labors in their villages. The *zapatistas*, in short, were a people in arms.

Zapata attempted to organize his forces efficiently, as is evident from his decree of January 31, 1917, which provided for the reorganization of the army on the basis of infantry, cavalry and artillery units with supporting engineering, military sanitation, justice and administrative services. In spite of Zapata's efforts, his forces never attained the discipline and organization of a regular army nor, apparently, of a modern guerrilla force such as that which operate[d] in South Vietnam in the 1960's. Thus, for example, we have the testimony of *zapatista* veteran Octavio Paz who mentions an attack upon Puebla in May 1916, which not only failed but resulted also in the death of one of the attacking generals because various *zapatista* forces failed to arrive in time for the battle due to a "misinterpretation of the hour" of attack.[28]

In spite of their shortcomings in organization, Zapata's men nevertheless were quite effective fighters. They laid traps and ambushes, cut supply lines, took small towns by storm, destroyed the smaller enemy units and harassed his larger forces. They were expert at capturing the elements of war from the enemy and, in addition, fabricated explosives and cartridges on their own. True to the tenets of guerrilla warfare, they avoided formal battles with major enemy forces until they were fairly certain of victory, thereby denying the enemy the opportunity to destroy them as an effective military force at one blow (as Obregón did the *villistas*). As their strength grew, the men of the South besieged and took major towns, such as Cuautla, Cuernavaca and Puebla and, as we have seen, they occupied Mexico City on several occasions. After its final retreat from the capital in 1915, the Army of the South reverted to the guerrilla warfare tactics which it had employed so successfully in the past.[29]

Octavio Paz has given a vivid account of the effectiveness of Zapata's tactics in his struggle against Pablo González's army in 1916–17. According to Paz, Zapata maintained only a few small forces with him at general headquarters which could be sent speedily into action at any place, at any time. The individual guerrilla units, meanwhile, kept in constant movement, attacking the *carrancistas* not only within Morelos, but also in the states of Mexico, Puebla, Tlaxcala, Oaxaca and Hidalgo.

These tactics completely disconcerted the enemy who could never put his fire power into effective use. If the enemy advanced with a large force, he never found anyone to fight; if he divided his forces, he exposed them to destruction in ambushes and assaults. The *carrancistas* had against them "not only armed men who knew the terrain, but the terrain itself, which was suitable for ambushes, as well as the climate and the inhabitants in general." Guerrilla warfare and malaria soon decimated the "resplendent army" of Pablo González.[30] Baltasar Dromundo aptly summarized the results of the *carrancista* campaign. "More than 8,000 malarial soldiers, more than 5,000 dead and as many more wounded and mutilated, a return home of wretches and men undone; this is the result of the campaign in Morelos which weakened the *gonzalistas* in spite of the war material which Carranza received."[31]

The prominent *carrancista*, Luís Cabrera, speaking in the national congress in 1917, recognized the effectiveness of Zapata's methods of warfare when he claimed that, although it was easy to defeat the *zapatistas* politically and economically, it was indeed quite difficult to conquer them militarily.[32]

The various forces engaged in the Mexican Revolution, including the Army of the South, frequently committed excesses. However, the forces which combated the *zapatistas*, from those of Díaz to those of Madero (with the exception of General Ángeles's command), Huerta and Carranza were especially cruel and vicious in their campaigns. The torture, mutilation and assassination of unarmed peasants as well as of prisoners of war, the rape of peasant women, the sacking of towns, the burning of villages, the deporting of inhabitants of Morelos to other parts of the republic, and the destruction of crops, animals and implements of work were commonplace occurrences. We even have the case of the *maderista* general, Juvencio Robles, who, in imitation of General Weyler's procedure during Cuba's struggle for independence, attempted to "reconcentrate" the villagers of Morelos into the larger towns. Crimes of Nazi proportions were perpetrated against the *zapatistas*. For example, in June and August 1916, *carrancista* troops killed 466 men, women and children in Tlaltizapán, Morelos, where Zapata maintained his general headquarters. The Mexican writer, Alfonso Taracena, claims in his study of Zapata's movement that "the *carrancistas* burned, robbed and killed with more ferocity than that displayed by the *huertistas* in their work of desolation and extermination against the *zapatistas*." The *carrancistas* under Pablo González were guilty even of dismantling the sugar mills and selling the machinery, along with railroad rails and engines, as scrap-iron in the capital.[33]

In respect to the latter depredations, we again have the testimony of Alfonso Taracena, among others, who states that when the *carrancista* soldiers withdrew from Morelos in February 1917, they carried with them as booty to be sold in Mexico City such things as household furniture, doors and windows; machinery and other articles of iron and bronze from the sugar mills; church bells; and "even the lead piping of the sewers."[34]

Former *zapatista* general Gildardo Magaña enters into this matter in greater detail. He notes that sugar production—the principal economic activity of Morelos—diminished from 1911 onwards until it virtually ceased due to the vicissitudes of warfare. The *zapatistas*, continues Magaña, "carried off horses, arms and objects easy to transport" from the haciendas, but they did not harm the machinery of the sugar mills, "which could have been used with but few repairs" when the armed conflict ended. However, Magaña explains, the forces under the command of Pablo González completely plundered the haciendas of Morelos in 1918 and 1919, destroying the buildings and carrying the mill machinery to Mexico City to sell as scrap iron. In their campaign, the *carrancistas* "used the most reprehensible procedures, and not only on the haciendas but also in the cities and towns, carried out the most unbridled rapine in the memory of the state, to the point of overshadowing the nefarious labor of the *huertista* general, Juvencio Robles." The *zapatistas*, of course, were blamed for this destruction but, since it was impossible to charge them with carrying off the machinery, "silence was guarded on this fact." Many persons believed the *carrancista* tales, concludes Magaña, because they did not know the true state of affairs in Morelos and, furthermore, because the "mercenary press" had predisposed them against the men of the South.[35]

Although they did not match their adversaries, Zapata's followers nevertheless were at times guilty of murder and pillage. The division of the Army of the South into bands which frequently operated on a semi-independent basis increased the problem of discipline. Some of the *zapatista* chieftains had reputations for cruelty, and a few even fought among themselves. Zapata's associate, Antonio Díaz Soto y Gama, readily admits these facts, but claims that Zapata did all in his power to control excesses and punished leaders guilty of crimes.[36]

Octavio Paz, another of the intellectuals associated with the men of the South, has claimed that although Zapata had a kindly heart and generally pardoned mistakes, he was inflexible with traitors and with those who committed crimes against peaceful villagers. Zapata realized that the peasant villages were the principal support of the armed movement and that they might well turn against the revolution if it abused them. Zapata, says Paz, always brought the accused to trial before a special military tribune when he was at his general headquarters in Tlaltizapán.[37]

Zapata gave numerous evidences of his desire to prevent excesses by his followers. Thus, he told Otilio Montaño on April 30, 1911, that he wanted the support of intellectuals "so that they may put order into these people for whom, once the fight begins, there is no God who can hold them back."[38]

In several of his military circulars Zapata showed his concern to prevent abuses by his followers. In July 1913 he issued instructions to his officers which said, in part: "You will endeavor at all costs to maintain good order among the troops, especially when they enter the villages, giving every guarantee to the lives and interests of the inhabitants, improving the behavior of the soldiers as much as possible."

Zapata issued an extensive order on October 4, 1913, in which he commanded his armed followers to respect the lives and properties of others: "Under no pretext nor for any personal cause should crimes be committed against lives and properties." The order prohibited pillaging, robbery, or "any other kind of depredation" when a town or other center of population was taken, "no matter what its importance." Those in command were charged with the responsibility to prevent such abuses and to punish infractors "energetically" with the objective of "suppressing those acts which are contrary to our creed and to the cause which we defend."

The document went on to order the revolutionary chieftains to punish civilians who took advantage of disorders and combats to steal or commit other depredations and to warn these leaders that they would be held responsible for depredations which occurred in villages taken by revolutionary forces in the zones under their command. The order concluded with an exhortation to the revolutionary chiefs to preserve the greatest possible discipline and order among the troops because "the constant practice of order and justice will make us strong" and "the Revolution and the motherland will esteem their worthy sons who make our creed the verdict of equity and justice, our efforts the tomb of tyrants, and the triumph of our ideals the prosperity and well-being of the Republic."[39]

A circular May 31, 1916, authorized villagers to organize and to arm themselves in defense against "evildoers and bad revolutionaries."[40]

After the men of the South forced Pablo González's army to withdraw from Morelos, Zapata appointed General Prudencio Casals "Inspector General of the entire zone governed by revolutionary troops," with authority to judge summarily and execute all individuals caught committing robbery, armed assault, or rape by violence.[41] These and other measures were necessary in order to suppress the vagabondage and brigandage which had arisen as a consequence of the disorganization and misery which the *carrancista* terror had wrought in Morelos.

Fighting did not cease in the South with the retreat of Pablo González's army early in 1917; the *carrancistas* made a number of raids in Morelos in 1917 and 1918, killing peasants, burning crops and driving off cattle. Hunger and misery spread in Morelos as a consequence of these depredations. Many starved to death and others in their weakened condition were easy victims of an epidemic of "Spanish influenza" which assaulted the state in 1918. Demoralization spread among Zapata's followers and some desertions occurred. Four *carrancista* columns attacked Morelos in August 1918, and in December General Pablo González led some 40,000 men into that state; a number of *zapastistas* surrendered as the enemy advanced. According to Octavio Magaña, former general in the Army of the South, by 1919 only 10,000 *zapatista* soldiers remained of the some 70,000 who had withdrawn from Mexico City in 1915.[42] Nevertheless, the revolutionaries of the South were still able to give worthy combat to the federal forces.

Zapata's concern over the dwindling of his forces led him to fall into a trap which the *carrancista* colonel, Jesús M. Guajardo, carefully laid for him. The latter offered to join his forces with those of Zapata, and when Zapata rode into the hacienda of Chinameca to accept the transfer, he was shot down. Many Mexicans recall the date of Zapata's death, April 10, 1919.

Many of Zapata's followers either surrendered or retired from the struggle after their leader's death, but a nucleus led by Generals Genovevo de la O and Everardo González continued the struggle. These remaining *zapatistas* made their peace with Obregón after the latter overthrew Carranza in 1920.

Notes

1. Gildardo Magaña (continued by Carlos Pérez Guerrero), *Emiliano Zapata y el agrarismo en México,* 5 vols., 1:77 (México, 1951–1952). See also George McCutchen McBride, *The Land Systems of México* (New York, 1923).
2. Eyler N. Simpson, *The Ejido: Mexico's Way Out* (Chapel Hill, North Carolina, 1937), 36.
3. The following account of Zapata's life and of the vicissitudes of the *zapatistas* in the revolutionary conflict is based upon the work of Magaña; Antonio Díaz Soto y Gama, *La Revolución agraria del sur y Emiliano Zapata, su caudillo* (Mexico, 1960); José T. Meléndez, ed., *Historia de la Revolución Mexicana,* 2 vols. (Mexico, 1936), 1:315–78; Baltasar Dromundo, *Emiliano Zapata* (Mexico, 1934); Floyd Rittenhouse, *Emiliano Zapata and the Suriano Rebellion: A Phase of the Agrarian Revolution in Mexico, 1910–1920,* Ph.D. Dissertation (Ohio State University, 1947); Sergio Valverde, *Apuntes para la historia de la revolución y de la política en el estado de Morelos* (Mexico, 1933); Alfonso Taracena, *La tragedia zapatista* (Mexico, 1931). This latter work is an amplification of material presented by the same author in his *En el vértigo de la revolución mexicana* (Mexico, 1930), which the author in turn amplified and published as the well-known work, *Mi vida en el vértigo de la revolución mexicana* (Mexico, 1936). Jesus Sotelo Inclán, *Raíz y Razón de Zapata* (Mexico, 1943), gives an excellent account of the struggle of Anenecuilco to defend its lands and its autonomy from pre-Cortesian times to the outbreak of the Revolution in 1910, and also provides (169–200) a valuable account of Zapata's formation as a revolutionary leader. Rosa E. King, *Tempest over Mexico* (Boston, 1938), relates her experiences in Morelos during the revolution; Edgcumb Pinchon's book, *Zapata the Unconquerable* (New York, 1941), is a biography of Zapata in English. For an account of Zapata's amours and the fate of his descendants, see Mario Gill, "Zapata, su pueblo y sus hijos," *Historia Mexicana,* 2:294–312.
4. Meléndez, 1:335–40; Charles Curtis Cumberland, *Mexican Revolution: Genesis under Madero* (Austin, Texas, 1952), 172–84; Stanley R. Ross, *Francisco I. Madero, Apostle of Mexican Democracy* (New York, 1955), 188–202; Magaña, 1:197–261; Taracena, *La tragedia zapatista,* 17–20.
5. Ross, 250–51; Cumberland, 182–84; Magaña 2:63–79; Taracena, *La tragedia zapatista,* 20–24; Meléndez, 1:340–341.
6. Ross, 251; Cumberland, 183.
7. Ross, 202; Cumberland, 182–84.
8. Ross, 241; Díaz Soto y Gama, 122.
9. Ross, 242–46.
10. Isidro Fabela, *Historia diplomática de la Revolución Mexicana, 1912–1917,* 2 vols. (Mexico, 1958–1959), 1:63.
11. King, 140.

12. Díaz Soto y Gama, 141.

13. Magaña, 3:116.

14. Quoted in Alvaro Obregón. *Ocho mil kilometros en campaña* (Mexico, 1917), 251.

15. Alfredo Breceda, *México Revolucionario, 1913–1917*, 2 vols. (Madrid, 1920; Mexico, 1941), 2:197–201.

16. Juan Barragán Rodríguez, *Historia del ejército y de la revolución constitucionalista*, 2 vols. (Mexico, 1946), 2:44, 39–41.

17. Magaña, 4:242–43; 3:280–82.

18. Alfonso Taracena, *Venustiano Carranza* (México, 1963), 241–42.

19. *Documentos Históricos de la Revolución Mexicana: Revolución y Régimen Constitucionalista*, 1:497–98.

20. Magaña, 4:247–71; 5:12–14. Magaña presents the *zapatista* account of these interviews. I have not found a *carrancista* account.

21. *Ibid.*, 4:247–71; 5:72–102; Díaz Soto y Gama, 173–81.

22. For a discussion and justification of the assumption of sovereignty by the Aguascalientes Convention, see Confidential Agency of the Provisional Government of Mexico, *The Sovereign Revolutionary Convention of Mexico and the Attitude of General Francisco Villa* (Washington, D.C., 1915), esp. 1–22.

23. For a lucid eyewitness account of the entry of the *zapatistas* into the capital, see Francisco Ramírez Plancarte, *La ciudad de México durante la revolución constitucionalista*, 2nd ed. (Mexico, 1941), 241–55.

24. Meléndez, 1:366–67.

25. For information on the Aguascalientes Convention, see Magaña, 5:118–360; Carlos Basave del Castillo Negrete, *Notas para la convención Revolucionaria, 1914–1915*; Papeles Históricos Mexicanos, vol. 4 (Mexico, 1947); Ramírez Plancarte, 73–307, 375–513, *passim*; Taracena, *La Tragedia Zapatista*, 51–52, 54, *passim*, and Robert E. Quirk, *The Mexican Revolution, 1914–1915: The Convention of Aguascalientes* (Bloomington, Indiana, 1960), 153–58, 165–79, 228–52, *passim*.

26. Several authors attribute Obregón's victory to the fact that the president of the Convention Government, General Eulalio Gutiérrez, did not provide the defenders with adequate arms and ammunition. Taracena (*La tragedia zapatista*, 49) states that "the government of General Gutiérrez took elements [of war] away from the defending *zapatistas*." Valverde declares that "the *zapatista* generals realized that they could not undertake the defense of Puebla because the munitions that the president of the Convention sent were blanks" (159). See also Dromundo, 115.

27. Felix F. Palavicini, ed., *El Primer Jefe* (Mexico, 1916), 258.

28. Meléndez, 1:371.

29. Magaña, 3:257–59, 264, 267–70; Rittenhouse, 318–19; Díaz Soto y Gama, 226–27, 287; Meléndez, 1: 323, 325–33, 350, 371, 372–75, *passim*; François Chevalier, "Un factor decisivo de la revolución agraria de México: 'El levantamiento de Zapata' (1911–1919)," *Cuadernos Americanos*, CXIII (Noviembre–Diciembre, 1960), 169–72, 185. For comments on shortcomings in the organization and discipline of the *zapatista* forces, see Ramírez Plancarte, 401–06; Valverde, 158; and King, 222–23.

30. Meléndez, 1:373.

31. Dromundo, 160. For additional comments on the effectiveness of the *zapatistas'* guerrilla warfare, see King, 78, 88–89, 130–31.

32. *Méjico Revolucionario a los pueblos de Europa y de América, 1910–1918* (Havana, n.d.), 127.

33. Taracena, *La tragedia zapatista*, 29, 36, 39, 70, 71, 74; Valverde, 179, 180, 185, Dromundo, 81, 82, 84, 88, 108, 117–18, 122–23, 146–47, 159, 161–62, 171, 185; Díaz Soto y Gama, 110–13, 157, 226, 228, 233; Meléndez, 1:339–40, 347–48, 349, 350, 351, 354, 374; King, 89–94, 130–31, 298, 301–302; Alfonso H. Reyes, *Emiliano Zapata, su vida y su obra* (Mexico, 1963), 105.

34. Taracena, *La tragedia zapatista*, 12.

35. Magaña, 1:39–40.

36. Díaz Soto y Gama, 116–18, 274–79. See also Chevalier, 171; and Meléndez, 1:351, 352.

37. Meléndez, 1:321.

38. Taracena, *La tragedia zapatista*, 12.

39. Magaña, 3:267, 269–70.

40. Reyes, 109.

41. *Ibid.,* 105.

42. Chevalier, 186.

4

The Kid from Niquinohomo

Sergio Ramírez

One of the main contributions made by the Mexican Revolution to the rest of Latin America was the fact that it demonstrated that the status quo could be transformed through revolutionary violence. One of the first Latin Americans to put the lesson into practice was Augusto César Sandino, a Nicaraguan of modest birth. Young Sandino resented Nicaragua's loss of sovereignty, and, beginning in 1926, he fought a successful guerrilla war against occupying American troops until he succeeded in having them removed from Nicaragua. After the withdrawal of the foreign forces, at a time of relative peace, Sandino was assassinated by Anastasio Somoza García's National Guard. Twenty-seven years later, a group of young Nicaraguan rebels named their revolutionary organization after him: the Sandinista National Liberation Front (FSLN). They began a war to overthrow the Somoza dynasty. The FSLN, imbued with the spirit of Sandino, finally defeated Anastasio Somoza Debayle in July of 1979.

Sergio Ramírez, a well-known Latin American writer and a vice president of Nicaragua after the triumph of the revolution, has written one of the most widely circulated biographies of Sandino. Although Ramírez makes no secret of his affiliation, his biography presents Sandino as a human being committed to a revolutionary cause. Ramírez avoids the dogmatic overtones that characterize many of the hagiographies of revolutionaries written by their peers.

The [Nicaraguan] caudillos defended nothing more than the interests of the supremacy of their class, and in the civil wars squabbled over merely personal advantages—access to the power to cut business deals, buy land, traffic in taxes, and the like. They submitted unconditionally to the dictates of foreign domination and the voracious will of the consortia

From *Latin American Perspectives* 16, no. 3 (1989): 59–82. Translated by Lyman Baker. © 1989 Sage Publications. Reprinted by permission of Sage Publications.

and the bankers. They were wrapped up in nothing more than the rhetoric of their patriotic demands for vindication of the nation and the constitution. Through the caudillos were compromised the lives of thousands of peasants who never managed to learn why they fought and died. Those were the Central American figures who fill the dreadful murals of what for a long time were known as the banana wars—Adolfo Díaz, Emiliano Chamorro, and José María Moncada. Thanks to them, Nicaragua for a quarter of a century appeared to the eyes of the world as a North American protectorate, as it continued in fact to be, even in the absence of occupation troops.

But there would come forth a young man, a teetotaler, shy, short of stature, who had emerged from a tiny Nicaraguan town situated on a plateau covered with coffee bushes and nestled in the foothills dropping from the Adean cordillera down to the Pacific littoral, who had wandered through banana plantations and sugar mills of the northern coasts of Guatemala and Honduras and through the petroleum centers of Mexico, who, making himself into a military caudillo in this war, would contradict those "deliverers" of their country. Working as a peon, as a lathe-turner, as a foreman of city street-cleaning crews, as an artisan, and as an agricultural laborer, he arrived finally in Mexico, along with many other young Latin American men who went in search of better fortune. In 1926, just when the marines were landing once more in his country to intervene in the civil war on behalf of the Conservatives, he was sitting in some public place in the bustling city of Tampico, the focal point of the petroleum boom, of anarcho-syndicalist ideas, of the full-rein socialism of the Bolshevik Revolution, of Zapata's Mexican agrarianism, chatting with friends among the stevedores and oil workers; and, the day's newspaper spread out over the table, this Nicaraguan kid happened to let fall the remark that he was seriously considering returning to his country to take up arms against the intervention.

"Why bother, man?" one of them answered. "All you Nicaraguans are nothing but a bunch of *vendepatrias*."

Those words were to play a great role in deciding his destiny, because, as he was to tell it later, they made him think deeply that night and many to come, reflecting that if *vendepatrias*—country-sellers—were what the politicians of his country were, those who kept silent before that ignominy were effectively the same. In the course of his years as a worker he had set aside a sum of money. Now he withdrew part of his savings to finance the beginning of an armed resistance against the occupation of Nicaragua, where he returned on the first of June, 1926.

Augusto César Sandino was born on May 18, 1895, in the little hamlet of Niquinohomo, built of straw and mud huts, populated by peasants who worked as peons on the coffee plantations in a region full, too, of cornfields, tobacco stands, and banana tracts, situated in the Department of Masaya, the most densely populated of the country. Next to the colonial church that fronted on a humble plaza, there were a few tile houses that belonged to the well-off *ladinos* [culturally Hispanicized mestizos] who had lands of some extent and who traded in grain which they bought from small producers before the harvest. (An irony of destiny would be that within a small radius of territory of not quite ten kilometers Sandino would be born in Niquinohomo and, in other small villages a bit to the south, José María Moncada in Masatepe and Anastasio Somoza in San Marcos.)

To that group of propertied ladinos in Niquinohomo belonged his father, Don Gregorio Sandino, whose relation with a peasant woman named Margarita Calderón who picked coffee on his farm would result in this son (the only one between them), born the same year [1895] that José Martí fell in Cuba fighting for the independence of his country.

The distresses and privations that shaped the childhood of Sandino would be the same that generally, in Nicaraguan society of a feudal and patriarchal cast, had to be suffered by peasants who were the natural offspring of well-off fathers, especially when, as in the case of Don Gregorio, the father married another woman of the same condition. In such a case the children born out of wedlock, in order finally to be received into the paternal house—and this was the case with Sandino—stood under the obligation to work hard in various tasks in order to pay for their own upkeep. When it came time to sit down to eat, these natural children were obliged to do so in the kitchen, set apart from the legitimate children, whose cast-off clothing it was also their lot to wear. From Don Gregorio's marriage there resulted three children, two girls and a boy named Sócrates, who would later join his brother's army of liberation.

In accordance with the same feudal system then existing in Central America even in the twentieth century, a heritage from the preceding ones, the peasants could receive from their employers advances secured against their future labor, redeeming the debt with a number of hours of work set by the *padrón*. Should they be unable to make good on the agreement, by reason for example of illness, they went to jail. When Sandino was nine years old, before he went to live in his father's house, his mother was imprisoned for a debt of this sort; and it was the custom as well that the children had to go to jail with their parents if there were no one to look after them. There he watched his mother, who had entered pregnant, hemorrhage when the child miscarried. Thus would he emerge from childhood with a host of questions about the reality of justice.

He would be twenty when he left the house of his father to seek a living on his own. He passed through haciendas and plantations, working as a mechanic's helper. He would return once more to Niquinohomo to apply himself to the grain trade and in 1920, on the verge of marrying his cousin Mercedes, he appears to have been involved in a bloody affair that would have a great deal to do with his future life: in connection with some point of honor or some business matter, he badly wounded a man named Dagoberto Rivas during the Sunday mass in the parish church and had to leave town, fleeing toward Honduras. As banana fever was raging in the kingdoms of "the fruit company," many Central Americans were emigrating toward these hot lands of the north coast, which were a kind of tropical Wild West: the streets of Tela and La Ceiba boiled with strangers, and gambling dens and cantinas multiplied, along with crimes and gun duels.

Sandino hired on in La Ceiba as a warehouse watchman with the Montecristo Mill, property of the Honduras Sugar and Distilling Co. In 1923 he would have to leave Honduras, arriving in Guatemala where he worked as a banana peon on the plantations of the United Fruit Co. in Quiriguá. That same year he would continue his journey toward Mexico where he would begin working in Tampico for the South Pennsylvania Oil Co. In 1925 he transferred to the workcamp run by the Huasteca Petroleum Co. in Cerro Azul, Veracruz, where he was made head of the department of wholesale gasoline sales and where he remained until his return to Nicaragua in 1926.

As soon as he entered the country he set out for the San Albino mine, another North American holding situated in northern Nicaragua, the environs of which later on would constitute the theater of the Sandinista war. There he secured employment and began to carry out a proselytizing campaign among the miners on behalf of the nationalist cause. By November he had formed a small column of soldiers recruited from among the workers and with his savings bought a few old rifles from gun traffickers operating around the Honduran border.

The Liberal Party, in arms against the government of the Atlantic coast, was fighting a war which to Sandino's thinking ought to be one against foreign intervention as well, and for this reason he sought to make his own fight from within those ranks. With his men he opened his first battle on the second of November, 1926, attacking the village of El Jícaro, which was in the hands of the government forces. The poor preparation of his column and the scarcity and low quality of his weapons and munitions caused him to suffer a defeat, inasmuch as he was unable to occupy the central square. But that loss would serve only to confirm his vocation for fighting. He regrouped his people and, having left them in safety in a place that afterward would come to be the legendary redoubt of the

Sandinista guerrillas—the hill of El Chipote in the heart of the Segovia Mountains—he headed with a few men toward the Atlantic coast where the main body of the Liberal troops was quartered, traveling by dugout down the Río Coco in the middle of the jungle, a voyage of many days and much hardship which could never have been accomplished without the help of the indigenous zambos and Miskitos who inhabited the area. To Sandinista soldiers during the war later on, these indigenous peoples would constitute an efficient if primitive navy, carrying with their dugouts guerrillas, munitions, and food.

Several weeks later Sandino reached General Moncada in Río Grande and held a discussion with him to ask for weapons and munitions for his men, who according to his plans would form a Segovian unit that would operate in the northern region of the country when the army began its drive to the Pacific. Moncada refused, and Sandino continued on to Puerto Cabezas, where Sacasa was with his government, arriving there by Christmas 1926, just when the Navy declared it a neutral zone and disarmed Sacasa, throwing the weaponry into the river. At night, lighting their way with torches of resinous candlewood pine branches, he and his men, aided by the people of the port, worked until dawn gathering rifles and munitions from the estuary. With these arms he returned to where his soldiers were awaiting him.

In the civil wars of that era the armies were made up of peons from the haciendas, and the hacendados acted as generals; the government forcibly recruited peasants to send them to the front of battle with no prior military training and armed with old Krag rifles that had been used in the war between the United States and Spain at the end of the previous century. The result was a terrible death toll, all the more so since they fought with crude tactics—open infantry advances, hand-to-hand clashes, besiegings of villages—while the generals stayed in the rear guard, always conveniently distant. Civil war meant hunger and widowhood, abandoned fields and families, and streets full of orphan beggar children.

In addition to an old rifle, soldiers received a pair of crude leather *caites*, a kind of open sandal, a *salbeque* with ten shots, and a palm hat with an emblem of red or green, according to which party, Liberal or Conservative, had done the recruiting. This forced military service was part of the tribute that, along with his labor for almost nothing, the Nicaraguan peasant had to pay to the owner of the land under the servile system of agriculture.

In the midst of a traditional civil war, Sandino stood forth as a general of the people who, far from shunning the battle, took part in it shoulder-to-shoulder with the soldiers of his column, who in a great multitude but in disciplined fashion came behind him and behind the flag hoisted from that time forward in his ranks—red and black with the motto "Freedom or Death."

Put out with the military successes of this column of ragged peasants, a popular column of a lower-class general, which again and again fiercely whipped the Conservative army at the last moment, saving the makeshift Liberal generals from defeat, the chief of the insurgent army, [José María] Moncada, one day sarcastically asked Sandino, "And you, who made you a general?" "My men, sir," he replied, humbly but firmly.

After having trounced the government forces in San Juan de Segovia and Yucapuca after a twelve-hour battle, Sandino's Segovian column in March 1927 took the city of Jinotega, advancing on the right flank of Moncada. On May 2, while Moncada was getting ready to surrender in his encounter with [U.S. peace negotiator Henry L.] Stimson, Sandino occupied the hill of El Común facing the city of Boaco, representing the most advanced position in the drive toward the capital. It was there that Moncada would summon him in order to announce the conditions of the armistice, but when Sandino arrived at general headquarters, the disarmament had already been accepted in the council of generals.

He returned to Cerro del Común and withdrew from his men in order that they not see him weep, while he reflected bitterly on the eternal destiny of the nation: the sale, the handing over. Just as Moncada had in the face of Stimson's demand, Sandino examined through this long night of meditation two alternatives: either to deliver his arms and dismiss his men or to stand up to the death to the powerful army of the United States with its warships, airplanes, cannons, and limitless resources. The interests that traditionally had come to play in the country's civil wars suggested that it would be madness to resist. To Sandino himself they were offering mules, horses, money, and a public office as political boss of the Department of Jinotega, with its attendant stipends, rents, and profits. But that night he recalled the mocking voice of his worker friend in Tampico who had called him a *vendepatria*. He remembered that he had not come from such a distance to fight for a party but for a country, that what was important was not who would be the candidate for the presidency in some upcoming elections that the Marines were bent on holding in their own way but the fact that the United States did not have the right to invade and humiliate a small country.

Sandino decided that night to hold out, more with the intent of sacrificing himself as a future example than with the expectation of any military victory. That decision would transform a civil war between oligarchic factions into a long war of national liberation; it would convert a war of soldiers recruited by force and of opportunistic generals into a war in which generals and soldiers would alike be poor and sons of the people, who would go about in tatters, who would call each other brothers, and whose slogan, written at the bottom of all official documents together with a stamp depicting a peasant decapitating a yankee soldier, would be "Patria y Libertad." The conventional war of mounted bands of marauding rebels would turn into the first guerrilla war joined on the American continent.

"How did it come to occur to you to die for the people?" Moncada would ask Sandino in their last meeting. "The people won't thank you. The important thing is to live well."

And, leaving him there with the gratifying prospect, already in his pocket, of becoming the president of an occupied and humiliated country, Sandino on the twelfth of May withdrew with his army to the city of Jinotega, where, through a letter telegraphed to all the departmental authorities of the country, he announced his decision not to accept the capitulation and to resist, whatever the final consequences. He demobilized all his men who were married or had other family obligations so that they might return to their homes. Thirty men remained with him, and with them he went into the already familiar lonely reaches in the cold heights of Yucapuca, three days after having married Blanca Aráuz, the telegraph girl in San Rafael del Norte who throughout the recent campaign had transmitted all his messages from the town's little communications office. The wedding took place in the early morning of May 18; he would recall later that when he entered the plain little church which was like that of his own small town, the smell of wax candles and forest flowers took him back in his memory to his childhood.

On the first day of July he published his first manifesto: "The man who demands of his country nothing more than a span of earth for his grave deserves to be heard, and not merely heard but believed." From then on his proclamations, his letters, even his telegrams would be cast in that sort of language—never rhetorical or gratuitous, charged with passion but charged as well with truth. It was the voice of an artisan, of a peasant, explaining his war in plain yet lyric speech, the tone simple as that of a country teacher in which he addressed his generals who, far off with their columns in the forests and the mountains, received those letters from the general-in-chief, letters that were like lessons, like poems—illiterate generals who learned to read in the course of battle, and to write their own letters on the fancy machines of the enemy. It was all like one big school.

On July 16, 1927, Sandino attacked the city of Ocotal in the Department of Nueva Segovia, which was then under the protection of a Marine garrison. With that battle, which lasted from dawn into the afternoon, the world would know that the war of liberation had begun.

On September 2, 1927, Sandino gathered his soldiers on the slope of El Chipote, and in that secret and impregnable place the peasants in arms who had converged from all around swore their commitment to the constituting document of the Army for the Defense of the National Sovereignty, at the conclusion of which there were hundreds of signatures of those able to write and the thumbprints of those who were illiterate.

The attack upon Ocotal two months before had been a conventional battle, an attempt to besiege the marine garrison; the yankee airplanes arrived promptly and bombed the city, causing many casualties not only among the Sandinistas, who fought in the open field and could be easily spotted from the air, but also among the inhabitants of the town. In that same month of July, yankee troop reinforcements, sent from Managua with strict orders to finish off the "bandits" as the rebels came to be called, pursued the Sandinistas without letup and engaged them in two battles. One was in the city of San Fernando on July 25, where they surprised the Sandinistas as they were camped in a hamlet, and the other in Santa Clara two days later, where once again the rebels got the worst part. The Marines' superiority in numbers, war matériel, and tactical support would have left the Sandinistas no chance of lasting if they had not radically changed their tactics after their defeats. Guerrilla warfare was being born, and Sandino and his men disappeared into the mountains to reorganize. The North American intelligence service jubilantly reported in the month of August that "the bandits no longer stand in any capacity to cause any further problems."

A week after presenting its constitution the Army for the Defense gave its first sample of combat in the style the Marines would later be unable to recall without terror: that of the ambush, the surprise attack, the rapid retreat, an enemy unit waiting for them no one knew where—up any unfamiliar creekbed or path, in the midst of underbrush, firing from the crowns of trees, holding back to let them cross a river and shooting them when they were stranded in the water. The first guerrilla battle took place on September 9, 1927, at Las Flores, where a column of Marines on march from one garrison to another was surprised and suffered many casualties; then on September 19, the garrison at Telpaneca, near the Río Coco, was the victim of a lightning attack.

These would come to be the two types of Sandinista guerrilla tactics: ambushes of columns on the move through mountain areas and assaults on garrisons in small villages. The objectives were simple and clear: to cause the greatest number of casualties with the least ammunition; to capture weapons, bullets, and other war matériel; not to expose one's forces to prolonged combat but to withdraw in an orderly way along secret paths in order later to regroup in an agreed upon place; not to leave tracks; and to recover one's casualties. After an attack, while the Marines were still expecting the fire to continue, the Sandinistas were already far away, and nothing was to be heard but the noises of the mountains.

The well-trained and elegantly uniformed yankee soldiers found only one phrase to adequately describe that nightmare: "damned country!" The soldiers faced rains, mosquitoes, swamps, high rivers, wild animals, the dread of falling in a sudden ambush, and fevers, but never a visible enemy.

A branch stripped from a tree, a stone placed in the road, an animal cry, or a bird call could be a message in Sandinista code telling that the yankees were approaching or giving an order to fire. All the noises of the mountains were enemies of the invader. Any peasant whose house they approached to ask for water or orientation could be a Sandinista who tended his little parcel of corn by day and served as a courier by night or as a soldier every other day.

On February 8, 1927, the Army for the Defense first accomplished one of those deeds that would be so frequently repeated afterward: with machine-gun fire it brought down a Marine aircraft, captured its pilots, and executed them after summary judgment. The same day in El Zapotillo they surprised a patrol sent to rescue the crew, scattering them in defeat. This was the kind of news the North American press would begin to move to the front pages, and the press in Latin America to discuss with jubilation. The Chilean poet Gabriela Mistral—later declared an honorary member of the Army for the Defense long before she won the Nobel Prize for Literature—would dub these barefoot, ragged men "the crazy little army." And where was this General Sandino, where were the chiefs of his mobile columns, and where were these soldiers?

When the tacticians of the U.S. Navy began to try to locate a mountain called El Chipote, no such place appeared on their maps under that name or any other. Chipote, it was said, did not exist. It was a name created in the fantasy of the peasants who, when interrogated by the Marines concerning its whereabouts, would answer merely, "I wonder, sir, maybe somewhere over that way."

"That way" were the Segovias, the mountainous region of Nicaragua which ran from the border with the Republic of Honduras in the north eastward, dropping toward the forests and swamps of the Atlantic littoral and southwestward in gentle undulations toward the plains along the

Pacific. Their tall crowns overlaid with dense pine stands, with towering hundred-year-old trees that formed gigantic natural caverns of vegetation, their stretches of bare rock through which their rivers plunged, their ravines and cramped passageways, covered several departments of the country: Nueva Segovia, Estelí, Madriz, Matagalpa, and Jinotega. This was the region of rich coffee fields, of lumber operations, and of mines in the hands of European planters or North American companies.

Somewhere in this region, and near the Honduran border, was that mythical place El Chipote, a tall prominence defended by narrow passages, accessible by no known road, covered always by clouds. On its heights were rustic palm huts, bunk houses, storehouses for keeping food, corrals for horses and cattle, and workshops for repairing weapons and fashioning munitions and for making clothing and shoes, all within the barrenness of the surrounding area. Across the border with Honduras a courier could with dispatch run a message to the city of Danlí. From there the Sandinistas' manifestoes and war communiqués went out to the world.

The number of soldiers active in the Army for the Defense varied from time to time from 2,000 to the 6,000 it came to have in the period of greatest expansion of its operations, in 1931–1932. Its eight columns were each under the command of a general, and each was in charge, for a given territorial area, of military operations, civil and paramilitary organization, collection of taxes, and agricultural production, which was accomplished through cooperatives. In these areas, too, classes in basic literacy began to be held for soldiers and peasants.

The Sandinista generals were peasants and artisans, most of them Segovians, though there were some from the interior of the country and from other places in Central America. . . .

In addition to their regular allotment of troops, these mobile columns were able to count on the contribution of paramilitary units, civilian volunteers who served as couriers and spies. There was also an active network of urban agents who kept them posted when troops left for the mountains or when aircraft arrived.

But there was also in the mountain quarters a host of children orphaned by the war who played their own important role in the army: they were known as the "choir of angels." They were present at ambushes and assaults, where their job consisted in giving loud cries, shouting *"vivas!"* and making all sorts of noises—a children's chorus with voices raised deafeningly in the forest—with tin plates and firecrackers, giving the impression sometimes that the number of Sandinistas was larger than it was and other times that reinforcements were arriving. When they grew up, these children became regular soldiers once they had won their own rifles, as in the case of Comandante Santos López [who, in 1961, would join Carlos Fonseca Amador and Tomás Borge in founding the Sandinista Front for the National Liberation]. . . .

There was also an international brigade—made up principally of intellectuals and students who came to the Segovias from various points in Latin America to offer military service—men from Mexico, Argentina, El Salvador, Guatemala, Costa Rica, the Dominican Republic, Venezuela, Colombia, and Honduras. Some fought as frontline soldiers, others served on the General Staff, and still others as secretaries to Sandino. Several died in the course of the campaign.

At the end of December 1927, the yankee reconnaissance aircraft were finally able to find El Chipote and began an intense bombardment that went on day after day in preparation for a land assault for which they amassed hundreds of soldiers. The Marine march toward El Chipote, methodically planned by General Lejeune, a veteran of the First World War, began in January 1928.

Once its location was discovered, the redoubt lost its importance and could no longer serve as a general headquarters; Sandino decided to abandon it. He ordered dummies to be made of hay and placed in the trenches and other strategic points, in the tops of trees and in the brush, while the Army for the Defense withdrew its columns in orderly fashion along secret pathways. On February 3, while Sandino was in San Rafael del Norte receiving the North American journalist Carlton Beals of *The Nation*, the Marines finally conquered the summit of El Chipote, deserted and abandoned except for the grass soldiers looking out impassively from their firing positions.

A short time after, on February 27, the youngest of the Sandinista generals, Miguel Angel Ortez, almost an adolescent, caught a yankee column by surprise and inflicted upon the invaders one of their most grievous defeats; it was known as the Battle of El Bramadero.

From that time on the official navy documents ceased to call Sandino a "bandit" and began to refer to him as a "guerrilla." It was a promotion won by bullets.

"We call him a 'bandit,' " said Secretary of State Cordell Hull, "in a purely technical sense."

In January 1928 there took place in Havana the Sixth Panamerican Conference, personally attended by the President of the United States Calvin Coolidge. The central theme in the debates of the assembly would be the armed intervention in Nicaragua. By now the name of Sandino was a rallying point throughout Latin America, except among the representatives of his Conservative government who tried everything at the conference to justify the presence of the United States and to delegitimize Sandino's resistance. Nor was it all that strange that the Bishop of Granada should, in a public ceremony, bless the weapons of the Marines who left in February for the Segovias. These gestures made it clearer than ever that this was indeed a war of the people.

The war would soon extend to the regions near where the Río Coco empties into the Atlantic; there the Sandinista attacks would have a precise objective: to ravage the installations of the North American mining companies. Sandino moved his headquarters from San Rafael del Norte toward Pis Pis in March 1928, and in April his troops occupied the mines of La Luz and Los Angeles, which, as will be recalled, were properties of the Buchanan family who had contributed to the defeat of [José Santos] Zelaya a decade earlier. Yankee aircraft carried out extensive bombardments in search of the Sandinistas and in so doing managed to destroy a number of small peasant villages: Murra, Ojoche, Naranjo, and Quiboto. Aerial terror had begun.

But the mines were put to the torch by the Sandinistas, their tunnels dynamited, and the items for sale in the commissaries confiscated. The Marines continued to die in the Nicaraguan forests; and as the lists began to appear daily in North American newspapers, public opinion started to get restless. Senators starred in passionate debates in which it was asked why, if the Marines wanted to apply themselves to combating "bandits," they didn't do so in Chicago against Al Capone and his thugs. In April 1928 the Senate Foreign Relations Committee summoned the Secretary of the Navy to explain what was going on in Nicaragua, and a resolution adopted that same month questioned the authority of the President of the United States to maintain troops there. In New York, Los Angeles, Chicago, and Detroit committees began to emerge dedicated to the fight against imperialism and in support of Sandino's cause; meetings were held to raise funds. The government prosecuted these committees as illegal. Meanwhile they appeared elsewhere, in Venezuela, Mexico, Argentina, and Costa Rica.

From France the writer Henri Barbusse publicly hailed Sandino as "the general of free men." The First Anti-Imperialist conference, which convened in Frankfurt in 1928, threw full support behind the Nicaraguan struggle in the mountains.

In the Battle of La Flor, next to the Rio Cuas, Captain Hunter of the U.S. Marine Corps fell along with many of his soldiers; in the Battle of Illiwas on August 7, the Marines were defeated once again. The resistance of the Army for the Defense seemed invincible, and confronted with internal pressure back home and the international outcry which continued to grow louder, the Navy took its first step backward: it would no longer commit its men to direct actions of war but would use them only as "technical advisers." From then on, the brunt of the responsibility for battle would fall to a local army created and trained by the Marines. The National Guard of Nicaragua, founded in December 1927 through a contract between the governments of the United States and Nicaragua, went into operation a year later. The Battle of Cuje on December 6, 1928, would be the last "official battle" of the occupation forces in Nicaragua, even though the number of deaths to follow in their ranks would show that the withdrawal was not altogether real.

The electoral victory which two years earlier Stimson had foreseen for General Moncada came to pass toward the end of 1928. The Liberal Party, with Moncada at its head, won the presidential elections that took place in November. The election boards were presided over by the yankee officials and consisted of Marines. General Charles McCoy, appointed by President Coolidge as Director of the Council of Elections of Nicaragua, counted the votes. Moncada took possession of that so-long-awaited post on January 1, 1929, and in no way sought the withdrawal of the Marines from the national territory, in spite of the fact that Sandino continued to declare every day that as soon as the last interventionist soldier left the country the war would be over. On the contrary, he went out of his way to maintain the presence of the occupying forces and redoubled the fight against Sandino, for which he created a kind of private army at the margins of the National Guard, which he called the "Force of Volunteers," and which under the command of a Mexican adventurer, Juan Luis Escamilla, committed every sort of atrocity in the Segovias region.

At the beginning of January 1929, faced with the Marines' decision to stay in the country and Moncada's to keep them there, Sandino foresaw a more prolonged struggle. Now it was a matter of a war of national resistance from which had vanished any vestige of partisanship; it would be against Liberals and Conservatives alike—the oligarchy bolstered by the intervention.

Sandino knew that to confront the prospect of a long war he would need many more resources, for up to then his weapons had been the few antiquated rifles from the last civil war or those wrested from the Marines in ambushes and battles; international solidarity had yielded very little in the way of effective aid in munitions, weapons, food, and medicines. Hence he decided in January 1929 to write to the provisional president of Mexico, Emilio Portes Gil, to ask permission to travel there, his intention being to seek personally the aid that he needed. The most enthusiastic committees of support for his struggle were to be found in Mexico.

Meanwhile the repression against the peasants who lived in the areas where the war was unfolding became ever more cruel: their huts were burned, their crops destroyed, and they themselves were forced to abandon their homes to be taken to distant places which served as concentration camps. All were suspected of being members of or collaborators with the Army for the Defense. According to a report of the Foreign Policy Association, in 1929 alone more than two hundred persons, women and children together, died in these concentration camps from hunger and cold. The terror redoubled a few months later under the operations of the column of the infamous Lieutenant Lee—renowned for his cruelties, tortures, and mutilations. (The photograph of a North American soldier holding in his hand the head of a murdered Nicaraguan would be published throughout the world.)

When the world economic crisis struck in this same year of 1929, the impoverished Nicaraguan economy, which depended on its coffee exports, suffered a grave collapse, along with those of the other Central American countries. Total unemployment befell the countryside, and with it came starvation. The repression hardened even more, and hundreds of peasants swelled the Sandinista ranks. For all these new people it was necessary to get more rifles.

Sandino left for Honduras on his way to Mexico in May 1929, and toward the end of the month arrived secretly at the port of La Unión in El Salvador from which he continued to Guatemala; on June 28 he arrived at the port of Veracruz, where he was greeted by a huge crowd. He was accompanied by lieutenants belonging to the international brigades: Farabundo Martí, the Salvadoran communist leader, murdered in his country in 1932 when the peasant rebellion was crushed, leaving more than ten thousand dead; José Pavletich of Peru; José de Paredes of Mexico; and Gregorio Gilbert of the Dominican Republic. There, too, his brother Sócrates would arrive from the United States, where he had been active in Sandinista political events in New York.

In Veracruz he received instructions from the government to go to Mérida, in Yucatán, to await permission to proceed to Mexico City; there he was obliged to remain stationed a good while since the word to proceed was a long time coming. In the capital the U.S. Ambassador was bringing to bear great pressure on the administration not to receive him, and Sandino began to realize that the intentions of the Mexican government to provide him with truly effective aid had never really been all that clear.

Desperate, Sandino wrote once again to President Portes Gil in 1930. Finally he was authorized to go to Mexico City, where he arrived on January 27 aboard a plane that had been christened with his name. In the airport union delegations, young people's organizations, journalists, and members of the Sandinista Committee were awaiting him. He met with Portes Gil on January 29, but after so long a wait, nothing concrete came of the encounter. He went back to Mérida and embarked secretly for Nicaragua, which he entered across the Honduran border. On May 16, 1930, he was once again in his mountain quarters.

In his absence General Pedro Altamirano had been in command of the forces, and to be sure the level of military activity had somewhat declined; nevertheless, a great part of the army that remained on inactive status was ready and waiting for a new call to arms, for this kind of peasant soldier did not think in terms of limited stints of enlistment.

Sandino having returned, the struggle broke out again without delay: new fronts opened up, the columns moving into new territory, nearer and nearer the more populated areas of the country toward the Pacific. In June 1930, there were important battles at El Bálsamo, El Tamarindo, and San Juan de Telpaneca. Sandino's wife, Blanca, was forced to move from San Juan del Norte to the city of León, where she remained under military surveillance.

The insurrections and mutinies by Nicaraguan soldiers in the garrisons of the National Guard would begin to repeat themselves; putting to death their yankee commanding officers, they went over with all their weaponry to the Sandinista ranks. There were even cases of desertions by North American soldiers who showed up at Sandino's camps to deliver their arms.

At the end of 1930 for lack of resources the Moncada government ordered the closing of all the schools in the country. And as the government languished, the power of the interveners imposed itself more harshly.

The fearsome column of General Miguel Angel Ortez, that young officer barely out of adolescence, whose pale hair streaming in the wind was the very symbol of resistance, succeeded in attacking the city of Telica in the Department of León, close to the capital. This was in November 1930, and in December the same column inflicted on the Marines one of the most decisive defeats of the war. On New Year's Eve a column consisting entirely of North Americans was surprised on the road from Achuapa, with the result that all but two who managed to flee were killed.

The news had an extraordinary impact in the United States, and the debates redoubled in the newspapers and in the Senate. In February 1931 Henry L. Stimson, the former peace negotiator in Nicaragua and current Secretary of State (appointed by President Herbert Hoover, who had assumed office in 1929), found himself obliged to announce that the occupation forces would remain in Nicaragua only through the presidential elections set for November 1932: that was one more step backward.

In April 1931 the Army for the Defense unleashed a broad offensive against the plantation of the United Fruit Co. in the Puerto Cabezas region along the Atlantic. Pitched battles were fought at Logtown and on the Río Wawa; the Army for the Defense, after devastating the installations of the United Fruit Company, advanced upon Puerto Cabezas, provoking the hasty arrival of North American warships and a landing of soldiers. The Sandinistas in turn took Cabo Gracias a Dios, toward the north, and after they had withdrawn, aircraft bombarded the town.

The day after these events, Stimson made known in Washington that the U.S. government would extend no protection to the life or property of North Americans in Nicaragua. United Fruit had gone running to the State Department to beg for such protection because the Sandinista attacks had left them with millions of dollars in losses. The decision of the United States to pull its army out of Nicaragua was now irreversible.

The shadow of Moncada's government finally disappeared altogether on March 31, 1931, when an earthquake destroyed the capital city of Managua, and the Navy commander became the actual governor of the country.

Between 1931 and 1932 the Sandinista campaign reached the proportions of a national war. Except for the part of the Pacific region closest to the capital, every place in the country—not to mention the Segovias, which were altogether under Sandino's control—would soon be reached by the rebel columns, which extended all the way to Santo Domingo de Chontales, the cattle and mining region in the plains lying east of the Gran Lago de Nicaragua, and to Rama City at the confluence of the tributaries which fed into the Río Escondido to form a river port communicating with the Atlantic to the southeast. They took the city of Chichigalpa on the western coast and took over the railroad to the capital in November 1931, causing a great shock in the city, according to a dispatch by the U.S. Ambassador in Managua. And on October 2, 1932, they occupied San Francisco del Carnicero on the north coast of Lake Nicaragua.

Meanwhile the pressing issues of criollo politics were hastily getting worked out with the Department of State. The Liberal Party put forward as presidential candidate an old and familiar figure who had been put off for so long but who was finally getting his turn—Dr. Juan Bautista Sacasa, who returned duly anointed from Washington, where he had been Ambassador. The U.S. Congress, however, refused to appropriate funds to finance these new elections.

As the elections approached, the U.S. Ambassador imposed a set of conditions upon the traditional parties, one of which was that upon the withdrawal in the coming January of the occupation forces, they would have to designate by mutual agreement a Director-in-Chief of the National Guard who would for the first time be a Nicaraguan.

With Sacasa's election in November 1932, as expected the North American Ambassador's candidate to lead the National Guard was selected—a nephew of Sacasa by marriage, Anastasio Somoza García.

Somoza had studied mechanical drawing and business at a school in Philadelphia. He had learned to speak English with the slang turns of phrase of the taxi drivers, an accomplishment that much amused the yankee ambassador, an old fellow named Hanna, whose somewhat younger wife found Somoza captivating. Somoza, who was a regular at the Embassy, had conferred his generalship upon himself at the beginning of the Constitutionalist War after having assaulted the barracks at his native village San Marcos and having been repelled by the Conservative forces.

Within the power structure which the Marines bequeathed when they pulled out, the directorship of the National Guard was the crucial post. For the first time the nation would have a professional army which, owing to its institutionalization and the political conditions existing in a country torn and confused by twenty years of foreign intervention, would unavoidably play a role that would be crushingly decisive. It was an army equipped, trained, and indoctrinated to act as an occupation force in its own country.

On New Year's Day 1933 the last Navy contingent of the United States of America embarked at the Port of Corinto and left Nicaragua. Six long years of lonely heroism on the part of a handful of workers and peasants, suffering privations, living in the harshness of the mountains, fighting tooth and nail for their nationhood, had achieved that victory. Having given his word to end his fight as soon as the last invader left, Sandino was immediately ready to negotiate. His letter announcing his conditions for peace was in the hands of his agents from December 1932 and was delivered to Sacasa the very day the Marines left.

The government organized a peace mission led by the Minister of Labor, Sofonias Salvatierra, an intellectual and union leader. The mission went to Las Segovias to meet with Sandino, and on January 23 a truce was declared; on February 2, 1933, General Sandino arrived by plane in Managua to discuss the conditions for peace with President Sacasa. The people acclaimed him tumultuously at the airport and in the streets: everyone wanted to meet that man who, so small of stature and so simple of bearing, had accomplished such an incredible feat. For many, this general of the humble, in whose boyish face were etched traces of the hardships of the long struggle, had earned a right that the politicians given over to the interests of the yankee companies had never taken into account: *that of nationality, that of a people's power to call themselves Nicaraguans, Central Americans, or Latin Americans, the right not to be colonials of an empire.*

At midnight on February 2, 1933, the peace agreement was signed in the presidential palace. Sandino was asked to remain a while in the city in order to receive homage, but he refused all requests. He was, he said, not a man for receptions, and would rather go back to the mountains where, as so many times before, his men were awaiting his return.

On February 22, 1933, the Army for the Defense of the National Sovereignty of Nicaragua was officially disarmed in San Rafael del Norte. From distant and hidden places came the columns of those men, many of them aged, others still children, covered with mud, with sweat, with dust, shoeless, on foot with old rifles, a few others mounted, their red and black standard flying from some mountain stick, entering the town in hundreds, under the strictest discipline, to deposit their weapons in the places designated, in order to go back again with no recompense, without ever having expected any, to their towns and villages, to their families, thousands of men whose toils were paid for by nothing more than that victory.

Sandino picked a group of a hundred of his soldiers to form the personal guard provided for under the terms of the peace agreement. With them he withdrew to the wilderness regions of Wiwilí on the banks of the Río Coco, where he intended to organize a farming and mining cooperative among the peasants.

There was, however, in spite of the hugs and handshakes and celebrations of peace, a point that remained unclear for Sandino: the National Guard was beginning to act as an occupying army, and that fact did not pass him by unnoticed. Its hostility would persist toward Sandino's men, who had inflicted upon it such great defeats. Throughout the year 1933 this hostility continued to pursue the Sandinistas in the hamlets and villages to which they had returned: jailings and harassment in places where cooperatives were emerging sometimes degenerated into real battles.

Sacasa was a weak and indecisive man, who had not the slightest control over the army. Sandino made several trips to Managua to discuss these troubles with Sacasa and each time he put it on record through the newspaper that he regarded the National Guard as an army contrived in the margins of the country's constitution and laws, as the product of an illegal enactment on the part of the departed intervening power.

The last of these journeys would take place in February 1934.

The night of February 21, 1934, when Sandino left the president's house after having attended a dinner with President Sacasa, the automobile in which he was traveling with his father, with General Salvatierra, and with generals [Francisco] Estrada and Umanzor was stopped across from the Campo de Marte barracks by a National Guard patrol, which ordered them to get out. Salvatierra and Sandino's father were taken aside under guard and the three generals were led off in a different direction.

The previous afternoon, Sacasa had signed a decree appointing a Sandinista general, Horacio Portocarrero, as Presidential Military Delegate with jurisdiction in the northern Segovian departments. This measure made it clear that Sacasa was seeking to recover, through redress of balance, some of the authority Somoza had undermined as head of the National Guard and at the same time to guarantee to Sandino the safety of his cooperatives.

But Somoza, who saw in the move a mortal blow to his ambitions for power, hastily called a meeting for the next afternoon of officers in his confidence, and explained to them the necessity of liquidating Sandino without delay, an act for which he was relying on the approval of the U.S. Ambassador, Arthur Bliss Lane. The word of the yankee proconsul transmitted by Somoza amounted to a death sentence, and all of them hurried to approve it.

When from his cell Sandino's father Don Gregorio heard distant shots in the silence of that hot Managua night, he said to Salvatierra, "Now they are killing them: he who becomes a savior dies crucified. . . ."

But the shots he heard were probably those of the assault by the National Guard on Salvatierra's house where Sandino was staying with his people. A brief fight took place in which Sandino's younger brother Sócrates was killed. General Santos López, although wounded, managed to flee. Meanwhile Sandino and his two lieutenant generals were taken to their place of execution—some vacant lots on the outskirts of the city near the airfield.

They were lined up before a trench that had been dug earlier and, under the light of the headlamps of a truck, were murdered with machine-gun and rifle fire. Their bodies were dumped in a ditch, once stripped of clothing and such personal effects as watches and rings, to be sold the next day in Managua. The location of the grave would thenceforth be kept as a state secret, and is unknown to this day.

The next day National Guard patrols fell suddenly upon the peasants of the farming cooperatives along the Río Coco, massacring more than three hundred peasants. The last resistance to be overcome was that of General Pedro Altamirano, killed through betrayal a year later, decapitated, and his head brought to Managua.

Scarcely two months later Somoza took public credit for the murder in a speech he delivered in Granada in which he declared he had done it "for the good of Nicaragua," with the backing of the North American ambassador. A short while afterward, in 1936, again with the support of the United States, he toppled his uncle-in-law Sacasa from the presidency. Later he had himself elected—with better luck than his counterpart,

General [Emiliano] Chamorro, [who, abandoned by his old backer, the United States, could only stand and watch in frustration Anastasio Somoza's rise to power] inasmuch as he continued reelecting himself for some twenty years, amassing during that time a huge personal fortune, until in 1956 a young poet and artisan from the city of León, Rigoberto López Pérez, shot him down during a party at which he was celebrating the announcement of his intention to serve another presidential term. He bequeathed to his family the power he had derived from the foreign intervention, and the name of Sandino was forbidden for half a century until the triumph of the Sandinista Revolution on July 19, 1979.

General Sandino's six-year fight in the Nicaraguan mountains at the head of a handful of peasants and workers must be seen as the historical result of centuries of foreign domination in his country and of the repeated handing over of the nation by its own ruling elites to these same foreign powers. Those men, fighting desperately with their work machetes and their old rifles, contriving bombs by filling old tin cans with rock chips and scraps of metal, downing enemy airplanes practically with stones, keeping through it all a high fighting morale before an army a hundred times more powerful, proved something that until the appearance of this army of the people had remained hidden in the hard paths of Latin American history: the beautiful possibility that some common country people, with their own leaders, their tactics forged in the clash of their forward march, their doctrine emerging from the same process of the struggle, might organize a successful resistance on behalf of the national sovereignty.

The political thought of Sandino, expressed in his letters and other documents, is not the result of a formal intellectual preparation, for an artisan who set aside his tools in order to go directly into combat could achieve such an education only with the greatest difficulty. But precisely because what he thinks is nothing else than the result of his daily experience as leader in that war of resistance, and because it is the circumstances of the struggle that continue to mold that thought, everything he says and declares carries the weight of truth.

Stripped of the old Latin American rhetoric of the nineteenth-century politicians, still the reigning idiom in the twentieth century itself, Sandino's thinking develops into something that stands out in authentic relief, a product of praxis. His words are loaded with telling political insight, and at the same time are expressive of a spirit of truth which will have nothing to do with holding back one's real understandings, with casual approximations, deceptions and disguises, or with taking back one's words: it expresses, in a word, a war without quarter against imperialism.

Every single soldier of that army, from the smallest child of the "choir of angels," understood both in heart and mind that all the sacrifices had no other object than the expulsion of the invader and that the invader represented the cause of oppression in Nicaragua. Again and again Sandino's anti-imperialism speaks to moral sensibility and the cry for justice so long buried in the heart of Latin American man, through centuries of oppression, simply because that oppression is nothing else than the result of foreign domination. It was not for nothing that those who took up arms against the powerful U.S. Navy were landless peasants, slaves of United Fruit and of the criollo landowners, day laborers, tenant farmers, and braceros, as their ancestors had been from colonial times.

Throughout the years of struggle, Sandino stood alone, showered with a dazzling chorus of praise and lyrical exaltations of rhetorical gestures of support which sufficed to buy not so much as a single rifle cartridge; outside the country he was besieged by opportunists, by sectarians; many of those who supported him from the civilian front inside Nicaragua were old politicians, some of them well-intentioned but cut acccording to the Liberal measure of the Latin American nineteenth century. It was quite something to see how there emerged from among them the future candidates for the presidency of the Republic.

When the time came to cease the struggle and to give up his arms, understanding full well that to do so would be to set himself on a path that could lead even to his death, Sandino performed his sacrifice without wavering. The North Americans were leaving Nicaragua, and the era of their physical presence in the national territory was coming to an end; the United States was entering upon a new tactic in its imperialist relations with Latin America, and the "Big Stick" of the first Roosevelt was turning into "the Good Neighbor" of the second. In the context of world politics, the democratic struggles were beginning to train their aim upon fascism in Italy, Nazism in Germany, and militarism in Japan. Soon there would be the Spanish Civil War. Thus, to ask why Sandino did not continue his battle until the conquest of power is nothing more than a piece of romanticism. He accomplished his task, even to the final sacrifice, to the end that his life and his actions and those of his men could be remembered as an example in the Latin American future.

5

General Principles of Guerrilla Warfare

Ernesto "Che" Guevara

In the early morning of January 1, 1959, Cuban dictator Fulgencio Batista, facing impending disaster, fled the island in his private airplane to seek refuge in the United States. A little more than two years earlier, a group of eighty-two young, would-be revolutionaries belonging to the July 26 Movement (M-26), under the leadership of Fidel Castro, landed on the coast of Oriente province. Within a matter of hours, most of its members had been either killed or arrested. The few survivors made their way into the mountains of the Sierra Maestra, where they set up camp. With the support of the local peasants, they began an unparalleled guerrilla war that culminated in the overthrow of one of the most repressive of Latin American dictators.

One of the survivors of the original group of irregulars was the then-unknown Argentine physician Ernesto "Che" Guevara. During the Sierra Maestra period, Guevara distinguished himself as an outstanding military and ideological leader, was promoted to commander, and proved instrumental in the victory of the rebels. After the barbudos *("the bearded ones," as the rebels were called by the Cuban people) took power, Guevara was appointed minister of industry and later became one of the most outstanding exponents of the virtues of guerrilla warfare as an instrument of liberation for Latin America. At the height of the Cold War, Che Guevara, thanks in part to the publication of his experiences in the Cuban revolutionary war and of his primer,* Guerrilla Warfare, *became one of the most widely read revolutionaries in the Americas. A faithful practitioner of his own philosophy, the paradigmatic guerrilla leader was captured and assassinated in Bolivia on October 9, 1967, while pursuing his*

From Che Guevara, *Guerrilla Warfare* (New York: Monthly Review Press, 1961), 161–71. © 1961 by Monthly Review Press. Reprinted by permission of the Monthly Review Press Foundation.

dream of liberating Latin America. The following selection, taken from his Guerrilla Warfare, *sketches out the basic conditions for a successful guerrilla campaign.*

1. Essence of Guerrilla Warfare

The armed victory of the Cuban people over the Batista dictatorship was not only the triumph of heroism as reported by the newspapers of the world; it also forced a change in the old dogmas concerning the conduct of the popular masses of Latin America. It showed plainly the capacity of the people to free themselves by means of guerrilla warfare from a government that oppresses them.

We consider that the Cuban Revolution contributed three fundamental lessons to the conduct of revolutionary movements in America. They are:

1. Popular forces can win a war against the army.
2. It is not necessary to wait until all conditions for making revolution exist; the insurrection can create them.
3. In underdeveloped America the countryside is the basic area for armed fighting.

Of these three propositions the first two contradict the defeatist attitude of revolutionaries or pseudo-revolutionaries who remain inactive and take refuge in the pretext that against a professional army nothing can be done, who sit down to wait until in some mechanical way all necessary objective and subjective conditions are given without working to accelerate them. As these problems were formerly a subject of discussion in Cuba, until facts settled the question, they are probably still much discussed in America.

Naturally, it is not to be thought that all conditions for revolution are going to be created through the impulse given to them by guerrilla activity. It must always be kept in mind that there is a necessary minimum without which the establishment and consolidation of the first center is not practicable. People must see clearly the futility of maintaining the fight for social goals within the framework of civil debate. When the forces of oppression come to maintain themselves in power against established law, peace is considered already broken.

In these conditions popular discontent expresses itself in more active forms. An attitude of resistance finally crystallizes in an outbreak of fighting, provoked initially by the conduct of the authorities.

Where a government has come into power through some form of popular vote, fraudulent or not, and maintains at least an appearance of constitutional legality, the guerrilla outbreak cannot be promoted, since the possibilities of peaceful struggle have not yet been exhausted.

The third proposition is a fundamental of strategy. It ought to be noted by those who maintain dogmatically that the struggle of the masses is centered in city movements, entirely forgetting the immense participation of the country people in the life of all the underdeveloped parts of America. Of course, the struggles of the city masses of organized workers should not be underrated; but their real possibilities of engaging in armed struggle must be carefully analyzed where the guarantees which customarily adorn our constitutions are suspended or ignored. In these conditions the illegal workers' movements face enormous dangers. They must function secretly without arms. The situation in the open country is not so difficult. There, in places beyond the reach of the repressive forces, the inhabitants can be supported by the armed guerrillas.

We will later make a careful analysis of these three conclusions that stand out in the Cuban revolutionary experience. We emphasize them now at the beginning of this work as our fundamental contribution.

Guerrilla warfare, the basis of the struggle of a people to redeem itself, has diverse characteristics, different facets, even though the essential will for liberation remains the same. It is obvious—and writers on the theme have said it many times—that war responds to a certain series of scientific laws; whoever ignores them will go down to defeat. Guerrilla warfare as a phase of war must be ruled by all of these; but besides, because of its special aspects, a series of corollary laws must also be recognized in order to carry it forward. Though geographical and social conditions in each country determine the mode and particular forms that guerrilla warfare will take, there are general laws that hold for all fighting of this type.

Our task at the moment is to find the basic principles of this kind of fighting and the rules to be followed by peoples seeking liberation; to develop theory from facts; to generalize and give structure to our experience for the profit of others.

Let us first consider the question: Who are the combatants in guerrilla warfare? On one side we have a group composed of the oppressor and his agents, the professional army, well armed and disciplined, in many cases receiving foreign help as well as the help of the bureaucracy in the employ of the oppressor. On the other side are the people of the nation or region involved. It is important to emphasize that guerrilla warfare is a war of the masses, a war of the people. The guerrilla band is an armed nucleus, the fighting vanguard of the people. It draws its great force from the mass of the people themselves. The guerrilla band is not to be considered inferior to the army against which it fights simply because it is inferior in firepower. Guerrilla warfare is used by the side which is supported by a majority but which possesses a much smaller number of arms for use in defense against oppression.

The guerrilla fighter needs full help from the people of the area. This is an indispensable condition. This is clearly seen by considering the case of bandit gangs that operate in a region. They have all the characteristics of a guerrilla army: homogeneity, respect for the leader, valor, knowledge of the ground, and, often, even good understanding of the tactics to be employed. The only thing missing is support of the people; and, inevitably, these gangs are captured and exterminated by the public force.

Analyzing the mode of operation of the guerrilla band, seeing its form of struggle, and understanding its base in the masses, we can answer the question: Why does the guerrilla fighter fight? We must come to the inevitable conclusion that the guerrilla fighter is a social reformer, that he takes up arms responding to the angry protest of the people against their oppressors, and that he fights in order to change the social system that keeps all his unarmed brothers in ignominy and misery. He launches himself against the conditions of the reigning institutions at a particular moment and dedicates himself with all the vigor that circumstances permit to breaking the mold of these institutions.

When we analyze more fully the tactic of guerrilla warfare, we will see that the guerrilla fighter needs to have a good knowledge of the surrounding countryside, the paths of entry and escape, the possibilities of speedy maneuver, good hiding places; naturally, also, he must count on the support of the people. All this indicates that the guerrilla fighter will carry out his action in wild places of small population. Since in these places the struggle of the people for reforms is aimed primarily and almost exclusively at changing the social form of land ownership, the guerrilla fighter is above all an agrarian revolutionary. He interprets the desires of the great peasant mass to be owners of land, owners of their means of production, of their animals, of all that which they have long yearned to call their own, of that which constitutes their life and will also serve as their cemetery.

It should be noted that in current interpretations there are two different types of guerrilla warfare, one of which—a struggle complementing great regular armies such as was the case of the Ukrainian fighters in the Soviet Union—does not enter into this analysis. We are interested in the other type, the case of an armed group engaged in struggle against the constituted power, whether colonial or not, which establishes itself as the only base and which builds itself up in rural areas. In all such cases, whatever the ideological aims that may inspire the fight, the economic aim is determined by the aspiration toward ownership of land.

The China of Mao begins as an outbreak of worker groups in the South, which is defeated and almost annihilated. It succeeds in establishing itself and begins its advance only when, after the long march from Yenan, it takes up its base in rural territories and makes agrarian reform its fundamental goal. The struggle of Ho Chi Minh is based in the rice-growing peasants, who are oppressed by the French colonial yoke; with this force it is going forward to the defeat of the colonialists. In both cases there is a framework of patriotic war against the Japanese invader, but the economic basis of a fight for the land has not disappeared. In the case of Algeria, the grand idea of Arab nationalism has its economic counterpart in the fact that nearly all of the arable land of Algeria is utilized by a million French settlers. In some countries, such as Puerto Rico, where the special conditions of the island have not permitted a guerrilla outbreak, the nationalist spirit, deeply wounded by the discrimination that is daily practiced, has as its basis the aspiration of the peasants (even though many of them are already a proletariat) to recover the land that the Yankee invader seized from them. This same central idea, though in different forms, inspired the small farmers, peasants, and slaves of the eastern estates of Cuba to close ranks and defend together the right to possess land during the thirty-year war of liberation.*

Taking account of the possibilities of development of guerrilla warfare, which is transformed with the increase in the operating potential of the guerrilla band into a war of positions, this type of warfare, despite its special character, is to be considered as an embryo, a prelude, of the other. The possibilities of growth of the guerrilla band and of changes in the mode of fight, until conventional warfare is reached, are as great as the possibilities of defeating the enemy in each of the different battles, combats, or skirmishes that take place. Therefore, the fundamental principle is that no battle, combat, or skirmish is to be fought unless it will be won. There is a malevolent definition that says: "The guerrilla fighter is the Jesuit of warfare." By this is indicated a quality of secretiveness, of treachery, of surprise that is obviously an essential element of guerrilla warfare. It is a special kind of Jesuitism, naturally prompted by circumstances, which necessitates acting at certain moments in ways different from the romantic and sporting conceptions with which we are taught to believe war is fought.

War is always a struggle in which each contender tries to annihilate the other. Besides using force, they will have recourse to all possible tricks and stratagems in order to achieve the goal. Military strategy and tactics

---

*The war fought by Cubans for independence from Spain began in 1868 and ended in 1898, with a period of peace from 1878 to 1895.

are a representation by analysis of the objectives of the groups and of the means of achieving these objectives. These means contemplate taking advantage of all the weak points of the enemy. The fighting action of each individual platoon in a large army in a war of positions will present the same characteristics as those of the guerrilla band. It uses secretiveness, treachery, and surprise; and when these are not present, it is because vigilance on the other side prevents surprise. But since the guerrilla band is a division unto itself, and since there are large zones of territory not controlled by the enemy, it is always possible to carry out guerrilla attacks in such a way as to assure surprise; and it is the duty of the guerrilla fighter to do so.

"Hit and run," some call this scornfully, and this is accurate. Hit and run, wait, lie in ambush, again hit and run, and thus repeatedly, without giving any rest to the enemy. There is in all this, it would appear, a negative quality, an attitude of retreat, of avoiding frontal fights. However, this is consequent upon the general strategy of guerrilla warfare, which is the same in its ultimate end as is any warfare: to win, to annihilate the enemy.

Thus, it is clear that guerrilla warfare is a phase that does not afford in itself opportunities to arrive at complete victory. It is one of the initial phases of warfare and will develop continuously until the guerrilla army in its steady growth acquires the characteristics of a regular army. At that moment it will be ready to deal final blows to the enemy and to achieve victory. Triumph will always be the product of a regular army, even though its origins are in a guerrilla army.

Just as the general of a division in a modern war does not have to die in front of his soldiers, the guerrilla fighter, who is general of himself, need not die in every battle. He is ready to give his life, but the positive quality of this guerrilla warfare is precisely that each one of the guerrilla fighters is ready to die, not to defend an ideal, but rather to convert it into reality. This is the basis, the essence of guerrilla fighting. Miraculously, a small band of men, the armed vanguard of the great popular force that supports them, goes beyond the immediate tactical objective, goes on decisively to achieve an ideal, to establish a new society, to break the old molds of the outdated, and to achieve, finally, the social justice for which they fight.

Considered thus, all these disparaged qualities acquire a true nobility, the nobility of the end at which they aim; and it becomes clear that we are not speaking of distorted means of reaching an end. This fighting attitude, this attitude of not being dismayed at any time, this inflexibility when confronting the great problems in the final objective is also the nobility of the guerrilla fighter.

2. Guerrilla Strategy

In guerrilla terminology, strategy is understood as the analysis of the objectives to be achieved in light of the total military situation and the overall ways of reaching these objectives.

To have a correct strategic appreciation from the point of view of the guerrilla band, it is necessary to analyze fundamentally what will be the enemy's mode of action. If the final objective is always the complete destruction of the opposite force, the enemy is confronted in the case of a civil war of this kind with the standard task: he will have to achieve the total destruction of each one of the components of the guerrilla band. The guerrilla fighter, on the other hand, must analyze the resources which the enemy has for trying to achieve that outcome: the means in men, in mobility, in popular support, in armaments, in capacity of leadership on which he can count. We must make our own strategy adequate on the basis of these studies, keeping in mind always the final objective of defeating the enemy army.

There are fundamental aspects to be studied: the armament, for example, and the manner of using this armament. The value of a tank, of an airplane, in a fight of this type must be weighed. The arms of the enemy, his ammunition, his habits must be considered; because the principal source of provision for the guerrilla force is precisely in enemy armaments. If there is a possibility of choice, we should prefer the same type as that used by the enemy, since the greatest problem of the guerrilla band is the lack of ammunition, which the opponent must provide.

After the objectives have been fixed and analyzed, it is necessary to study the order of the steps leading to the achievement of the final objective. This should be planned in advance, even though it will be modified and adjusted as the fighting develops and unforeseen circumstances arise.

At the outset, the essential task of the guerrilla fighter is to keep himself from being destroyed. Little by little it will be easier for the members of the guerrilla band or bands to adapt themselves to their form of life and to make flight and escape from the forces that are on the offensive an easy task, because it is performed daily. When this condition is reached, the guerrilla, having taken up inaccessible positions out of reach of the enemy, or having assembled forces that deter the enemy from attacking, ought to proceed to the gradual weakening of the enemy. This will be carried out at first at those points nearest to the points of active warfare against the guerrilla band and later will be taken deeper into enemy territory, attacking his communications, later attacking or harassing his bases of operations and his central bases, tormenting him on all sides to the full extent of the capabilities of the guerrilla forces.

The blows should be continuous. The enemy soldier in a zone of operations ought not to be allowed to sleep; his outposts ought to be attacked and liquidated systematically. At every moment the impression ought to be created that he is surrounded by a complete circle. In wooded and broken areas this effort should be maintained both day and night; in open zones that are easily penetrated by enemy patrols, at night only. In order to do all this the absolute cooperation of the people and a perfect knowledge of the ground are necessary. These two necessities affect every minute of the life of the guerrilla fighter. Therefore, along with centers for study of present and future zones of operations, intensive popular work must be undertaken to explain the motives of the revolution, its ends, and to spread the incontrovertible truth that victory of the enemy against the people is finally impossible. *Whoever does not feel this undoubted truth cannot be a guerrilla fighter.*

This popular work should at first be aimed at securing secrecy; that is, each peasant, each member of the society in which action is taking place, will be asked not to mention what he sees and hears; later, help will be sought from inhabitants whose loyalty to the revolution offers greater guarantees; still later, use will be made of these persons in missions of contact, for transporting goods or arms, as guides in the zones familiar to them; still later, it is possible to arrive at organized mass action in the centers of work, of which the final result will be the general strike.

The strike is a most important factor in civil war, but in order to reach it a series of complementary conditions are necessary which do not always exist and which very rarely come to exist spontaneously. It is necessary to create these essential conditions, basically by explaining the purposes of the revolution and by demonstrating the forces of the people and their possibilities.

It is also possible to have recourse to certain very homogeneous groups, which must have shown their efficacy previously in less dangerous tasks, in order to make use of another of the terrible arms of the guerrilla band, sabotage. It is possible to paralyze entire armies, to suspend the industrial life of a zone, leaving the inhabitants of a city without factories, without light, without water, without communications of any kind, without being able to risk travel by highway except at certain hours. If all this is achieved, the morale of the enemy falls, the morale of his combatant units weakens, and the fruit ripens for plucking at a precise moment.

All this presupposes an increase in the territory included within the guerrilla action, but an excessive increase of this territory is to be avoided. It is essential always to preserve a strong base of operations and to continue strengthening it during the course of the war. Within this territory, measures of indoctrination of the inhabitants of the zone should be utilized; measures of quarantine should be taken against the irreconcilable enemies of the revolution; all the purely defensive measures, such as trenches, mines, and communications, should be perfected.

When the guerrilla band has reached a respectable power in arms and in number of combatants, it ought to proceed to the formation of new columns. This is an act similar to that of the beehive when at a given moment it releases a new queen, who goes to another region with a part of the swarm. The mother hive with the most notable guerrilla chief will stay in the less dangerous places, while the new columns will penetrate other enemy territories following the cycle already described.

A moment will arrive in which the territory occupied by the columns is too small for them; and in the advance toward regions solidly defended by the enemy, it will be necessary to confront powerful forces. At that instant the columns join, they offer a compact fighting front, and a war of positions is reached, a war carried on by regular armies. However, the former guerrilla army cannot cut itself off from its base, and it should create new guerrilla bands behind the enemy acting in the same way as the original bands operated earlier, proceeding thus to penetrate enemy territory until it is dominated.

It is thus that guerrillas reach the stage of attack, of the encirclement of fortified bases, of the defeat of reinforcements, of mass action, ever more ardent, in the whole national territory, arriving finally at the objective of the war: victory.

3. Guerrilla Tactics

In military language, tactics are the practical methods of achieving the grand strategic objectives.

In one sense they complement strategy and in another they are more specific rules within it. As means, tactics are much more variable, much more flexible than the final objectives, and they should be adjusted continually during the struggle. There are tactical objectives that remain constant throughout a war and others that vary. The first thing to be considered is the adjusting of guerrilla action to the action of the enemy.

The fundamental characteristic of a guerrilla band is mobility. This permits it in a few minutes to move far from a specific theatre and in a few hours far even from the region, if that becomes necessary; permits it constantly to change front and avoid any type of encirclement. As the circumstances of the war require, the guerrilla band can dedicate itself exclusively to fleeing from an encirclement which is the enemy's only way of forcing the band into a decisive fight that could be unfavorable; it can also change the battle into a counter-encirclement (small bands of men are presumably surrounded by the enemy when suddenly the enemy is surrounded by stronger contingents; or men located in a safe place serve as a lure, leading to the encirclement and annihilation of the entire troops and supply of an attacking force). Characteristic of this war of mobility is the so-called minuet, named from the analogy with the dance: the guerrilla bands encircle an enemy position, an advancing column, for example; they encircle it completely from the four points of the compass, with five or six men in each place, far enough away to avoid being encircled themselves; the fight is started at any one of the points, and the army moves toward it; the guerrilla band then retreats, always maintaining visual contact, and initiates its attack from another point. The army will repeat its action and the guerrilla band, the same. Thus, successively, it is possible to keep an enemy column immobilized, forcing it to expend large quantities of ammunition and weakening the morale of its troops without incurring great dangers.

This same tactic can be applied at nighttime, closing in more and showing greater aggressiveness, because in these conditions counterencirclement is much more difficult. Movement by night is another important characteristic of the guerrilla band, enabling it to advance into position for an attack and, where the danger of betrayal exists, to mobilize in new territory. The numerical inferiority of the guerrilla makes it necessary that attacks always be carried out by surprise; this great advantage is what permits the guerrilla fighter to inflict losses on the enemy without suffering losses. In a fight between a hundred men on one side and ten on the other, losses are not equal where there is one casualty on each side. The enemy loss is always reparable; it amounts to only one percent of his effectives. The loss of the guerrilla band requires more time to be repaired because it involves a soldier of high specialization and is ten percent of the operating forces.

A dead soldier of the guerrillas ought never to be left with his arms and his ammunition. The duty of every guerrilla soldier whenever a companion falls is to recover immediately these extremely precious elements of the fight. In fact, the care which must be taken of ammunition and the method of using it are further characteristics of guerrilla warfare. In any combat between a regular force and a guerrilla band it is always possible to know one from the other by their different manner of fire: a great amount of firing on the part of the regular army, sporadic and accurate shots on the part of the guerrillas.

Once one of our heroes, now dead, had to employ his machine guns for nearly five minutes, burst after burst, in order to slow up the advance of enemy soldiers. This fact caused considerable confusion in our forces, because they assumed from the rhythm of fire that that key position must have been taken by the enemy, since this was one of the rare occasions where departure from the rule of saving fire had been called for because of the importance of the point being defended.

Another fundamental characteristic of the guerrilla soldier is his flexibility, his ability to adapt himself to all circumstances, and to convert to his service all of the accidents of the action. Against the rigidity of classical methods of fighting, the guerrilla fighter invents his own tactics at every minute of the fight and constantly surprises the enemy.

In the first place, there are only elastic positions, specific places that the enemy cannot pass, and places of diverting him. Frequently, the enemy, after easily overcoming difficulties in a gradual advance, is surprised to find himself suddenly and solidly detained without possibilities of moving forward. This is due to the fact that the guerrilla-defended positions, when they have been selected on the basis of a careful study of the ground, are invulnerable. It is not the number of attacking soldiers that counts, but the number of defending soldiers. Once that number has been placed there, it can nearly always hold off a battalion with success. It is a major task of the chiefs to choose well the moment and the place for defending a position without retreat.

The form of attack of a guerrilla army is also different; starting with surprise and fury, irresistible, it suddenly converts itself into total passivity.

The surviving enemy, resting, believes that the attacker has departed; he begins to relax, to return to the routine life of the camp or of the fortress, when suddenly a new attack bursts forth in another place, with the same characteristics, while the main body of the guerrilla band lies in wait to intercept reinforcements. At other times an outpost defending the camp will be suddenly attacked by the guerrilla, dominated, and captured. The fundamental thing is surprise and rapidity of attack.

Acts of sabotage are very important. It is necessary to distinguish clearly between sabotage, a revolutionary and highly effective method of warfare, and terrorism, a measure that is generally ineffective and indiscriminate in its results, since it often makes victims of innocent people and destroys a large number of lives that would be valuable to the revolution. Terrorism should be considered a valuable tactic when it is used to put to death some noted leader of the oppressing forces well known for his cruelty, his efficiency in repression, or other quality that makes his elimination useful. But the killing of persons of small importance is never advisable, since it brings on an increase of reprisals, including deaths.

There is one point very much in controversy in opinions about terrorism. Many consider that its use, by provoking police oppression, hinders all more or less legal or semiclandestine contact with the masses and makes impossible unification for actions that will be necessary at a critical moment. This is correct; but it also happens that in a civil war the repression by the governmental power in certain towns is already so great that, in fact, every type of legal action is suppressed already, and any action of the masses that is not supported by arms is impossible. It is therefore necessary to be circumspect in adopting methods of this type and to consider the consequences that they may bring for the revolution. At any rate, well-managed sabotage is always a very effective arm, though it should not be employed to put means of production out of action, leaving a sector of the population paralyzed (and thus without work) unless this paralysis affects the normal life of the society. It is ridiculous to carry out sabotage against a soft-drink factory, but it is absolutely correct and advisable to carry out sabotage against a power plant. In the first case, a certain number of workers are put out of a job but nothing is done to modify the rhythm of industrial life; in the second case, there will again be displaced workers, but this is entirely justified by the paralysis of the life of the region. We will return to the technique of sabotage later.

One of the favorite arms of the enemy army, supposed to be decisive in modern times, is aviation. Nevertheless, this has no use whatsoever during the period that guerrilla warfare is in its first stages, with small concentrations of men in rugged places. The utility of aviation lies in the systematic destruction of visible and organized defenses; and for this there must be large concentrations of men who construct these defenses, something that does not exist in this type of warfare. Planes are also potent against marches by columns through level places or places without cover; however, this latter danger is easily avoided by carrying out the marches at night.

One of the weakest points of the enemy is transportation by road and railroad. It is virtually impossible to maintain a vigil yard by yard over a transport line, a road, or a railroad. At any point a considerable amount of explosive charge can be planted that will make the road impassable; or by exploding it at the moment that a vehicle passes, a considerable loss in lives and materiel to the enemy is caused at the same time that the road is cut.

The sources of explosives are varied. They can be brought from other zones; or use can be made of bombs seized from the dictatorship, though these do not always work; or they can be manufactured in secret laboratories within the guerrilla zone. The technique of setting them off is quite varied; their manufacture also depends upon the conditions of the guerrilla band.

In our laboratory we made powder which we used as a cap, and we invented various devices for exploding the mines at the desired moment.

The ones that gave the best results were electric. The first mine that we exploded was a bomb dropped from an aircraft of the dictatorship. We adapted it by inserting various caps and adding a gun with the trigger pulled by a cord. At the moment that an enemy truck passed, the weapon was fired to set off the explosion.

These techniques can be developed to a high degree. We have information that in Algeria, for example, tele-explosive mines, that is, mines exploded by radio at great distances from the point where they are located, are being used today against the French colonial power.

The technique of lying in ambush along roads in order to explode mines and annihilate survivors is one of the most remunerative in point of ammunition and arms. The surprised enemy does not use his ammunition and has no time to flee, so with a small expenditure of ammunition large results are achieved.

As blows are dealt the enemy, he also changes his tactics, and in place of isolated trucks, veritable motorized columns move. However, by choosing the ground well, the same result can be produced by breaking the column and concentrating forces on one vehicle. In these cases the essential elements of guerrilla tactics must always be kept in mind. These are: perfect knowledge of the ground; surveillance and foresight as to the lines of escape; vigilance over all the secondary roads that can bring support to the point of attack; intimacy with people in the zone so as to have sure help from them in respect to supplies, transport, and temporary or permanent hiding places if it becomes necessary to leave wounded companions behind; numerical superiority at a chosen point of action; total mobility; and the possibility of counting on reserves.

If all these tactical requisites are fulfilled, surprise attack along the lines of communication of the enemy yields notable dividends.

A fundamental part of guerrilla tactics is the treatment accorded the people of the zone. Even the treatment accorded the enemy is important; the norm to be followed should be an absolute inflexibility at the time of attack, an absolute inflexibility toward all the despicable elements that resort to informing and assassination, and clemency as absolute as possible toward the enemy soldiers who go into the fight performing or believing that they perform a military duty. It is a good policy, so long as there are no considerable bases of operations and invulnerable places, to take no prisoners. Survivors ought to be set free. The wounded should be cared for with all possible resources at the time of the action. Conduct toward the civil population ought to be regulated by a large respect for all the rules and traditions of the people of the zone, in order to demonstrate effectively, with deeds, the moral superiority of the guerrilla fighter over the oppressing soldier. Except in special situations, there ought to be no execution of justice without giving the criminal an opportunity to clear himself.

4. Warfare on Favorable Ground

As we have already said, guerrilla fighting will not always take place in country most favorable to the employment of its tactics; but when it does, that is, when the guerrilla band is located in zones difficult to reach, either because of dense forests, steep mountains, impassable deserts or marshes, the general tactics, based on the fundamental postulates of guerrilla warfare, must always be the same.

An important point to consider is the moment for making contact with the enemy. If the zone is so thick, so difficult that an organized army can never reach it, the guerrilla band should advance to the regions where the army can arrive and where there will be a possibility of combat.

As soon as the survival of the guerrilla band has been assured, it should fight; it must constantly go out from its refuge to fight. Its mobility does not have to be as great as in those cases where the ground is unfavorable; it must adjust itself to the capabilities of the enemy, but it is not necessary to be able to move as quickly as in places where the enemy can concentrate a large number of men in a few minutes. Neither is the nocturnal character of this warfare so important; it will be possible in many cases to carry out daytime operations, especially mobilizations by day, though subjected to enemy observation by land and air. It is also possible to persist in a military action for a much longer time, above all in the mountains; it is possible to undertake battles of long duration with very few men, and it is very probable that the arrival of enemy reinforcements at the scene of the fight can be prevented.

A close watch over the points of access is, however, an axiom never to be forgotten by the guerrilla fighter. His aggressiveness (on account of the difficulties that the enemy faces in bringing up reinforcements) can be greater, he can approach the enemy more closely, fight much more directly, more frontally, and for a longer time, though these rules may be qualified by various circumstances, such, for example, as the amount of ammunition.

Fighting on favorable ground and particularly in the mountains presents many advantages but also the inconvenience that it is difficult to capture in a single operation a considerable quantity of arms and ammunition, owing to the precautions that the enemy takes in these regions. (The guerrilla soldier must never forget the fact that it is the enemy that must serve as his source of supply of ammunition and arms.) But much more rapidly than in unfavorable ground the guerrilla band will here be able to "dig in," that is, to form a base capable of engaging in a war of positions, where small industries may be installed as they are needed, as well as hospitals, centers for education and training, storage facilities, organs of propaganda, etc., adequately protected from aviation or from long-range artillery.

The guerrilla band in these conditions can number many more personnel; there will be noncombatants and perhaps even a system of training in the use of the arms that eventually are to fall into the power of the guerrilla army.

The number of men that a guerrilla band can have is a matter of extremely flexible calculation adapted to the territory, to the means available of acquiring supplies, to the mass flights of oppressed people from other zones, to the arms available, to the necessities of organization. But, in any case, it is much more practicable to establish a base and expand with the support of new combatant elements.

The radius of action of a guerrilla band of this type can be as wide as conditions or the operations of other bands in adjacent territory permit. The range will be limited by the time that it takes to arrive at a zone of security from the zone of operation; assuming that marches must be made at night, it will not be possible to operate more than five or six hours away from a point of maximum security. Small guerrilla bands that work constantly at weakening a territory can go farther away from the zone of security.

The arms preferable for this type of warfare are long-range weapons requiring a small expenditure of bullets, supported by a group of automatic or semiautomatic arms. Of the rifles and machine guns that exist in the markets of the United States, one of the best is the M-1 rifle, called the Garand. However, this should be used only by people with some experience, since it has the disadvantage of expending too much ammunition. Medium-heavy arms, such as tripod machine guns, can be used on favorable ground, affording a greater margin of security for the weapon and its personnel, but they ought always to be a means of repelling an enemy and not for attack.

An ideal composition for a guerrilla band of 25 men would be: 10 to 15 single-shot rifles and about 10 automatic arms between Garands and hand machine guns, including light and easily portable automatic arms, such as the Browning or the more modern Belgian FAL and M-14 automatic rifles. Among the hand machine guns the best are those of nine millimeters, which permit a larger transport of ammunition. The simpler its construction the better, because this increases the ease of switching parts. All this must be adjusted to the armament that the enemy uses, since the ammunition that he employs is what we are going to use when his arms fall into our hands. It is practically impossible for heavy arms to be used. Aircraft cannot see anything and cease to operate; tanks and cannons cannot do much owing to the difficulties of advancing in these zones.

A very important consideration is supply. In general, the zones of difficult access for this very reason present special problems, since there are few peasants, and therefore animal and food supplies are scarce. It is necessary to maintain stable lines of communication in order to be able always to count on a minimum of food, stockpiled, in the event of any disagreeable development.

In this kind of zone of operations the possibilities of sabotage on a large scale are generally not present; with the inaccessibility goes a lack of constructions, telephone lines, aqueducts, etc., that could be damaged by direct action.

For supply purposes it is important to have animals, among which the mule is the best in rough country. Adequate pasturage permitting good nutrition is essential. The mule can pass through extremely hilly country impossible for other animals. In the most difficult situations it is necessary to resort to transport by men. Each individual can carry twenty-five kilograms for many hours daily and for many days.

The lines of communication with the exterior should include a series of intermediate points manned by people of complete reliability, where products can be stored and where contacts can go to hide themselves at critical times. Internal lines of communication can also be created. Their extension will be determined by the stage of development reached by the guerrilla band. In some zones of operations in the recent Cuban war, telephone lines of many kilometers of length were established, roads were built, and a messenger service maintained sufficient to cover all zones in a minimum of time.

There are also other possible means of communication, not used in the Cuban war but perfectly applicable, such as smoke signals, signals with sunshine reflected by mirrors, and carrier pigeons.

The vital necessities of the guerrillas are to maintain their arms in good condition, to capture ammunition, and, above everything else, to have adequate shoes. The first manufacturing efforts should therefore be directed toward these objectives. Shoe factories can initially be cobbler installations that replace half soles on old shoes, expanding afterwards into a series of organized factories with a good average daily production of shoes. The manufacture of powder is fairly simple; and much can be accomplished by having a small laboratory and bringing in the necessary materials from outside. Mined areas constitute a grave danger for the enemy; large areas can be mined for simultaneous explosion, destroying up to hundreds of men.

5. Warfare on Unfavorable Ground

In order to carry on warfare in country that is not very hilly, lacks forests, and has many roads, all the fundamental requisites of guerrilla warfare must be observed; only the forms will be altered. The quantity, not the quality, of guerrilla warfare will change. For example, following the same order as before, the mobility of this type of guerrilla should be extraordinary; strikes should be made preferably at night; they should be extremely rapid, but the guerrilla should move to places different from the starting point, the farthest possible from the scene of action, assuming that there is no place secure from the repressive forces that the guerrilla can use as its garrison.

A man can walk between 30 and 50 kilometers during the night hours; it is possible also to march during the first hours of daylight, unless the zones of operation are closely watched or there is danger that people in the vicinity, seeing the passing troops, will notify the pursuing army of the location of the guerrilla band and its route. It is always preferable in these cases to operate at night with the greatest possible silence both before and after the action; the first hours of night are best. Here, too, there are exceptions to the general rule, since at times the dawn hours will be preferable. It is never wise to habituate the enemy to a certain form of warfare; it is necessary to vary constantly the places, the hours, and the forms of operation.

We have already said that the action cannot endure for long, but must be rapid; it must be of a high degree of effectiveness, last a few minutes, and be followed by an immediate withdrawal. The arms employed here will not be the same as in the case of actions on favorable ground; a large quantity of automatic weapons is to be preferred. In night attacks, marksmanship is not the determining factor, but rather concentration of fire; the more automatic arms firing at short distance, the more possibilities there are of annihilating the enemy.

Also, the use of mines in roads and the destruction of bridges are tactics of great importance. Attacks by the guerrilla will be less aggressive so far as the persistence and continuation are concerned, but they can be very violent, and they can utilize different arms, such as mines and the shotgun. Against open vehicles heavily loaded with men, which is the usual method of transporting troops, and even against closed vehicles that do not have special defenses—against buses, for example—the shotgun is a tremendous weapon. A shotgun loaded with large shot is the most effective. This is not a secret of guerrilla fighters; it is used also in big wars. The Americans used shotgun platoons armed with high-quality weapons and bayonets for assaulting machine-gun nests.

There is an important problem to explain, that of ammunition; this will almost always be taken from the enemy. It is therefore necessary to strike blows where there will be the absolute assurance of restoring the ammunition expended, unless there are large reserves in secure places. In other words, an annihilating attack against a group of men is not to be undertaken at the risk of expending all the ammunition without being able to replace it. Always in guerrilla tactics it is necessary to keep in mind the grave problem of procuring the war materiel necessary for continuing the fight. For this reason, guerrilla arms ought to be the same as those used by the enemy, except for weapons such as revolvers and shotguns, for which the ammunition can be obtained in the zone itself or in the cities.

The number of men that a guerrilla band of this type should include does not exceed ten to fifteen. In forming a single combat unit it is of great importance always to consider the limitations on numbers: ten, twelve, fifteen men can hide anywhere and at the same time can help each other in putting up a powerful resistance to the enemy. Four or five would perhaps be too small a number, but when the number exceeds ten, the possibility that the enemy will discover them in their camp or on the march is much greater.

Remember that the velocity of the guerrilla band on the march is equal to the velocity of its slowest man. It is more difficult to find uniformity of marching speed with twenty, thirty, or forty men than with ten. And the guerrilla fighter on the plain must be fundamentally a runner. Here the practice of hitting and running acquires its maximum use. The guerrilla bands on the plain suffer the enormous inconvenience of being subject to a rapid encirclement and of not having sure places where they can set up a firm resistance; therefore, they must live in conditions of absolute secrecy for a long time, since it would be dangerous to trust any neighbor whose fidelity is not perfectly established. The reprisals of the enemy are so violent, usually so brutal, inflicted not only on the head of the family but frequently on the women and children as well, that pressure on individuals lacking firmness may result at any moment in their giving way and revealing information as to where the guerrilla band is located and how it is operating. This would immediately produce an encirclement with consequences always disagreeable, although not necessarily fatal. When conditions, the quantity of arms, and the state of insurrection of the people call for an increase in the number of men, the guerrilla band should be divided. If it is necessary, all can rejoin at a given moment to deal a blow, but in such a way that immediately afterwards they can disperse toward separate zones, again divided into small groups of ten, twelve, or fifteen men.

It is entirely feasible to organize whole armies under a single command and to assure respect and obedience to this command without the necessity of being in a single group. Therefore, the election of the guerrilla chiefs and the certainty that they coordinate ideologically and personally with the overall chief of the zone are very important.

The bazooka is a heavy weapon that can be used by the guerrilla band because of its easy portability and operation. Today the rifle-fired anti-tank grenade can replace it. Naturally, it will be a weapon taken from the enemy. The bazooka is ideal for firing on armored vehicles, and even on unarmored vehicles that are loaded with troops, and for taking small military bases of few men in a short time; but it is important to point out that not more than three shells per man can be carried, and this only with considerable exertion.

As for the utilization of heavy arms taken from the enemy, naturally, nothing is to be scorned. But there are weapons such as the tripod machine gun, the heavy fifty-millimeter machine gun, etc., that, when captured, can be utilized with a willingness to lose them again. In other words, in the unfavorable conditions that we are now analyzing, a battle to defend a heavy machine gun or other weapon of this type cannot be allowed; they are simply to be used until the tactical moment when they must be abandoned. In our Cuban war of liberation, to abandon a weapon constituted a grave offense, and there was never any case where the necessity arose. Nevertheless, we mention this case in order to explain clearly the only situation in which abandonment would not constitute an occasion for reproaches. On unfavorable ground, the guerrilla weapon is the personal weapon of rapid fire.

Easy access to the zone usually means that it will be habitable and that there will be a peasant population in these places. This facilitates supply enormously. Having trustworthy people and making contact with establishments that provide supplies to the population, it is possible to maintain a guerrilla band perfectly well without having to devote time or money to long and dangerous lines of communication. Also, it is well to reiterate that the smaller the number of men, the easier it will be to procure food for them. Essential supplies such as bedding, waterproof material, mosquito netting, shoes, medicines, and food will be found directly in the zone, since they are things of daily use by its inhabitants.

Communications will be much easier in the sense of being able to count on a larger number of men and more roads; but they will be more difficult as a problem of security for messages between distant points, since it will be necessary to rely on a series of contacts that have to be trusted. There will be the danger of an eventual capture of one of the messengers, who are constantly crossing enemy zones. If the messages are of small importance, they should be oral; if of great importance, code writing should be used. Experience shows that transmission by word of mouth greatly distorts any communication.

For these same reasons, manufacture will have much less importance, at the same time that it would be much more difficult to carry it out. It will not be possible to have factories making shoes or arms. Practically speaking, manufacture will have to be limited to small shops, carefully hidden, where shotgun shells can be recharged and mines, simple grenades, and other minimum necessities of the moment manufactured. On the other hand, it is possible to make use of all the friendly shops of the zone for such work as is necessary.

This brings us to two consequences that flow logically from what has been said. One of them is that the favorable conditions for establishing a permanent camp in guerrilla warfare are inverse to the degree of productive development of a place. All favorable conditions, all facilities of life normally induce men to settle; but for the guerrilla band the opposite is the case. The more facilities there are for social life, the more nomadic, the more uncertain the life of the guerrilla fighter. These really are the results of one and the same principle. The title of this section is "Warfare on Unfavorable Ground," because everything that is favorable to human life, communications, urban and semiurban concentrations of large numbers of people, land easily worked by machine: all these place the guerrilla fighter in a disadvantageous situation.

The second conclusion is that if guerrilla fighting must include the extremely important factor of work on the masses, this work is even more important in the unfavorable zones, where a single enemy attack can produce a catastrophe. Indoctrination should be continuous, and so should be the struggle for unity of the workers, of the peasants, and of other social classes that live in the zone, in order to achieve toward the guerrilla fighters a maximum homogeneity of attitude. This task with the masses, this constant work at the huge problem of relations of the guerrilla band with the inhabitants of the zone, must also govern the attitude to be taken toward the case of an individual recalcitrant enemy soldier: he should be eliminated without hesitation when he is dangerous. In this respect the guerrilla band must be drastic. Enemies cannot be permitted to exist within the zone of operations in places that offer no security.

6. Suburban Warfare

If during the war the guerrilla bands close in on cities and penetrate the surrounding country in such a way as to be able to establish themselves in conditions of some security, it will be necessary to give these suburban bands a special education, or rather, a special organization.

It is fundamental to recognize that a suburban guerrilla band can never spring up of its own accord. It will be born only after certain conditions necessary for its survival have been created. Therefore, the suburban guerrilla will always be under the direct orders of chiefs located in another zone. The function of this guerrilla band will not be to carry out independent actions but to coordinate its activities with overall strategic plans in such a way as to support the action of larger groups situated in another area, contributing specifically to the success of a fixed tactical objective, without the operational freedom of guerrilla bands of the other types. For example, a suburban band will not be able to choose among the operations of destroying telephone lines, moving to make attacks in another locality, and surprising a patrol of soldiers on a distant road; it will do exactly what it is told. If its function is to cut down telephone poles or electric wires, to destroy sewers, railroads, or water mains, it will limit itself to carrying out these tasks efficiently.

It ought not to number more than four or five men. The limitation on numbers is important, because the suburban guerrilla must be considered as situated in exceptionally unfavorable ground, where the vigilance of the enemy will be much greater and the possibilities of reprisals as well as of betrayal are increased enormously. Another aggravating circumstance is that the suburban guerrilla band cannot depart far from the places where it is going to operate. To speed of action and withdrawal there must be added a limitation on the distance of withdrawal from the scene of action and the need to remain totally hidden during the daytime. This is a nocturnal guerrilla band in the extreme, without possibilities of changing its manner of operating until the insurrection is so far advanced that it can take part as an active combatant in the siege of the city.

The essential qualities of the guerrilla fighter in this situation are discipline (perhaps in the highest degree of all) and discretion. He cannot count on more than two or three friendly houses that will provide food; it is almost certain that an encirclement in these conditions will be equivalent to death. Weapons, furthermore, will not be of the same kind as those of the other groups. They will be for personal defense, of the type that do not hinder a rapid flight or betray a secure hiding place. As their armament the band ought to have not more than one carbine or one sawed-off shotgun, or perhaps two, with pistols for the other members.

They will concentrate their action on prescribed sabotage and never carry out armed attacks, except by surprising one or two members or agents of the enemy troops.

For sabotage they need a full set of instruments. The guerrilla fighter must have good saws, large quantities of dynamite, picks and shovels, apparatus for lifting rails, and, in general, adequate mechanical equipment for the work to be carried out. This should be hidden in places that are secure but easily accessible to the hands that will need to use it.

If there is more than one guerrilla band, they will all be under a single chief who will give orders as to the necessary tasks through contacts of proven trustworthiness who live openly as ordinary citizens. In certain cases the guerrilla fighter will be able to maintain his peacetime work, but this is very difficult. Practically speaking, the suburban guerrilla band is a group of men who are already outside the law, in a condition of war, situated as unfavorably as we have described.

The importance of a suburban struggle has usually been underestimated; it is really very great. A good operation of this type extended over a wide area paralyzes almost completely the commercial and industrial life of the sector and places the entire population in a situation of unrest, of anguish, almost of impatience for the development of violent events that will relieve the period of suspense. If, from the first moment of the war, thought is taken for the future possibility of this type of fight and an organization of specialists started, a much more rapid action will be assured, and with it a saving of lives and of the priceless time of the nation.

6

To Free the Present from the Past

Régis Debray

One of the cornerstones of Guevara's revolutionary philosophy was the foco ("focus," or "nucleus") theory, which posited that since objective conditions for revolution already existed in most Latin American countries, it was possible for a small foco *of armed individuals to begin a guerrilla war and, acting as a core, build a popular revolutionary struggle that would culminate in victory for the rebels. This idea challenged the traditional Marxist-Leninist conception about the necessity to organize around a vanguard party in order to begin a revolutionary process. Guevara first suggested the* foco *theory in his book on guerrilla warfare in 1960, and he reiterated it in 1963. It was the French philosopher and journalist Régis Debray, an ardent admirer of the Cuban Revolution, who popularized the theory in two of his books published in the sixties,* Revolution in the Revolution? Armed Struggle and Political Struggle in Latin America *and* Strategy for Revolution.*

Thanks to the support of intellectuals like Debray, innumerable focos *erupted throughout Latin America. In this selection from* Revolution in the Revolution?, *Debray espouses the desirability and viability of the* foco *theory. He considers the defeats of guerrilla movements as temporary setbacks similar to those suffered by the Cuban Revolution in its early stages. On April 21, 1967, Régis Debray was captured in Bolivia, where he had gone to fight alongside Che Guevara. It was largely due to the guerrillas' attempts to return Debray to safety that the columns split and, unable to reunite, became easy prey for the army. A few months after his capture, he was sentenced to thirty years in prison. Freed after a massive campaign organized across the world, he is now living in France.*

From *Revolution in the Revolution? Armed Struggle and Political Struggle in Latin America*, trans. Bobbye Ortiz (New York: Monthly Review Press, 1967), 19–25. © 1967 by Monthly Review Press. Reprinted by permission of the Monthly Review Press Foundation.

W e are never completely contemporaneous with our present. History advances in disguise; it appears on stage wearing the mask of the preceding scene, and we tend to lose the meaning of the play. Each time the curtain rises, continuity has to be re-established. The blame, of course, is not history's, but lies in our vision, encumbered with memory and images learned in the past. We see the past superimposed on the present, even when the present is a revolution.

The impact of the Cuban Revolution has been experienced and pondered, principally in Latin America, by methods and schemas already catalogued, enthroned, and consecrated by history. This is why, in spite of all the commotion it has provoked, the shock has been softened. Today the tumult has died down; Cuba's real significance and the scope of its lessons, which had been overlooked before, are being discovered. A new conception of guerrilla warfare is coming to light.

Among other things, Cuba remembered from the beginning that the socialist revolution is the result of an armed struggle against the armed power of the bourgeois state. This old historic law, of a strategic nature if you like, was at first given a known tactical content. One began by identifying the guerrilla struggle with insurrection because the archetype—1917—had taken this form, and because Lenin and later Stalin had developed several theoretical formulas based on it—formulas which have nothing to do with the present situation and which are periodically debated in vain, such as those which refer to conditions for the outbreak of an insurrection, meaning an immediate assault on the central power. But this disparity soon became evident. American guerrilla warfare was next virtually identified with Asian guerrilla warfare, since both are "irregular" wars of encirclement of cities from the countryside. This confusion is even more dangerous than the first.

The armed revolutionary struggle encounters specific conditions on each continent, in each country, but these are neither "natural" nor obvious. So true is this that in each case years of sacrifice are necessary in order to discover and acquire an awareness of them. The Russian Social Democrats instinctively thought in terms of repeating the Paris Commune in Petrograd; the Chinese Communists in terms of repeating the Russian October in the Canton of the twenties; and the Vietnamese comrades, a year after the foundation of their party, in terms of organizing insurrections of peasant soviets in the northern part of their country. It is now clear to us today that soviet-type insurrections could not triumph in prewar colonial Asia, but it was precisely here that the most genuine Communist activists had to begin their apprenticeship for victory.

One may well consider it a stroke of good luck that Fidel had not read the military writings of Mao Tse-tung before disembarking on the coast of Oriente: he could thus invent, on the spot and out of his own experience, principles of a military doctrine in conformity with the terrain. It was only at the end of the war, when their tactics were already defined, that the rebels discovered the writings of Mao.* But once again in Latin America, militants are reading Fidel's speeches and Che Guevara's writings with eyes that have already read Mao on the anti-Japanese war, Giap, and certain texts of Lenin—and they think they recognize the latter in the former. Classical visual superimposition, but dangerous, since the Latin American revolutionary war possesses highly special and profoundly distinct conditions of development, which can only be discovered through a particular experience. In that sense, all the theoretical works on people's war do as much harm as good. They have been called the grammar books of the war. But a foreign language is learned faster in a country where it must be spoken than at home studying a language manual. In time of war questions of speed are vital, especially in the early stages when an unarmed and inexperienced guerrilla band must confront a well-armed and knowledgeable enemy.

Fidel once blamed certain failures of the guerrillas on a purely intellectual attitude toward war. The reason is understandable: aside from his physical weakness and lack of adjustment to rural life, the intellectual will try to grasp the present through preconceived ideological constructs and live it through books. He will be less able than others to invent, improvise, make do with available resources, decide instantly on bold moves when he is in a tight spot. Thinking that he already knows, he will learn more slowly, display less flexibility. And the irony of history has willed,

---

*It is well known that Fidel drew his fundamental political inspiration from Martí, an inspiration reinforced and rectified, even before Moncada, by the ideas of Marx and Lenin. In regard to Lenin, Fidel was especially interested in the ideas expressed in *State and Revolution*, in which the destruction of the old state apparatus and its repressive instruments becomes a revolutionary axiom. But the sources of his military inspiration were to be found elsewhere: *Realengo 18*, by Pablo de la Torriente Brau; accounts of the campaigns of Máximo Gomez; Engels' texts explaining the difficult conditions of street fighting imposed on the Parisian proletariat by the Chassepot [breech-loading rifle used by the French Army in the 1870s] and by the opening up of broad avenues; Hemingway's *For Whom the Bell Tolls* (in which Pablo and his quasi-guerrilla band lived in the Sierra in the very rearguard of the fascists, between Madrid and Segovia). These books were not so much sources as they were coincidences: Fidel found in them only what he was looking for. Mao Tse-tung's *Problems of Strategy in Guerrilla War Against Japan* came into Fidel's and Che's hands after the 1958 summer offensive; to their surprise, they found in this book what they had been practicing under pressure of necessity.

by virtue of the social situation of many Latin American countries, the assignment of precisely this vanguard role to students and revolutionary intellectuals, who have had to unleash, or rather initiate, the highest forms of class struggle.

Subsequently these errors, these misunderstandings have been paid for. At not too high a price if we compare with the disasters, repeated over so many years, in the first war of liberation from Spain. A reading of Bolívar's biography reveals an enormous amount about war and about America—including valid lessons for today's American revolutionary wars. The most valuable of these: tenacity. Five times expelled from American soil within four years, defeated, ridiculed, alone, and with an obstinacy characterized as insanity, five times he returned, and won his first victory, at Boyacá. Each time he learned a little more: the need for mobility and for cavalry, so as to compensate for the lack of troops and arms; the need to wage an aggressive and fast, not a defensive and static, war; the need to burn ships and to cut off any possible retreat by declaring a "war to the death" against the Spaniard, in order to hasten the formation of what we call today "subjective conditions" among his own followers and among the *criollos* [American-born descendents of Spaniards]; the trap that Caracas constituted as long as the Spaniards controlled the countryside; the need to encircle the cities by attacking from the plains and from solidly defended bases; the importance, lastly, of certain places ("Coro is to Caracas what Caracas is to America").

We have recently been given the same lesson in tenacity by Fidel, more than once on the brink of disaster. Moncada (1953), the *Granma* landing (1956), and to a lesser extent the failure of the April 1958 strike are other reverses which would have led most men to go home and wait for better days. How many guerrilla *focos* foundered in Guatemala prior to the consolidation of the Zacapa and Izabal guerrilla bands? Quite a few, annihilated or dismantled. How many defeats in Venezuela, how many betrayals and splits? Nonetheless, the guerrilla forces have survived and are beginning again, more vigorously than ever; perhaps the war itself is really beginning in earnest.

The reverses suffered by the Latin American revolutionary movement are truly minor if one measures them in terms of the short period of time which is the prologue to the great struggles of tomorrow, if we take into account the fact that the few years which have passed correspond to that period of "take-off" and readjustment through which all revolutions must go in their early stages. Indeed, what seems surprising is that guerrilla movements have been able to survive so many false starts and so many errors, some inevitable and others not. According to Fidel, that is the astonishing thing, and it proves the extent to which the movement is impelled by history. In fact, we must speak not so much of defeat as of a certain explicable stagnation and lack of rapid development, the consequences of, among other things, the inevitable blunders and errors at this stage of exploration of revolutionary conceptions and methods which are *new*, in spite of their deceptive kinship with other international experiences.

All decisive revolutionary processes must begin and have begun with certain missteps for the reason that we have mentioned: because the existing points of departure are those left by the preceding historical period, and they are used, even if unconsciously. Of all these false starts, the Latin American is the most innocuous. In each case it has been a matter of adjusting the pace without changing the direction of movement, of correcting tactics without renouncing correct strategies or principles. At such a time profound differences between two camps come to the surface.

In each country that has experienced a revolution a confrontation has taken place between revolutionaries on one side and reformists and future renegades on the other. After 1905, pacifism and the defeatist spirit gained strength in the Russian Social Democratic Party. Lenin, in exile in Geneva, and others had to raise their voices, not to oppose the representative democracy of the Dumas to a Workers' insurrection, but to oppose an undirected insurrección to a well-directed one. In China, after the 1927 defeats, it was necessary to oppose, as Mao and others did, a rapid uprising in the big cities under the domination of the Kuomintang enemy, not to a renewed commitment to worker's insurrection, but to a retreat to the countryside and the Long March—a form of struggle appropriate to Chinese conditions. After the Moncada disaster of 1953, Fidel and his surviving comrades did not consider abandoning the principle of armed struggle against Batista, but they gave it a different, more correct content. For a revolutionary, failure is a springboard. As a source of theory it is richer than victory: it accumulates experience and knowledge.

In Latin America a few years of experience in armed struggle of all kinds have done more to reveal the particularity of objective conditions than the preceding decades of borrowed political theory. Historically, Cuba has established the point of departure of the armed revolution in Latin America. It is this point of departure, assiduously preserved and based on a correct line, which is essential.

> Has the armed struggle really broken out? Are these its first fruits in Venezuela, Guatemala, Colombia, Peru, Ecuador? Or are they merely skirmishes, manifestations of a restlessness that has not yet borne fruit? The outcome of today's struggles is not important. As far as the final result is concerned it does not matter whether one movement or another is temporarily defeated.

What is decisive is the determination to struggle which is maturing daily, the awareness of the need for revolutionary change and the certainty of its possibility.*

In Latin America today a political line which, in terms of its consequences, is not susceptible to expression as a precise and consistent military line, cannot be considered revolutionary. Any line that claims to be revolutionary must give a concrete answer to the question: How to overthrow the power of the capitalist state? In other words, how to break its backbone, the army, continuously reinforced by North American military missions? The Cuban Revolution offers an answer to fraternal Latin American countries which has still to be studied in its historical details: by means of the more or less slow building up, through guerrilla warfare carried out in suitably chosen rural zones, of a *mobile strategic force*, nucleus of a people's army and of a future socialist state.

Any military line depends on a political line which it expresses. It so happens that during the past few years other military lines have been tested within the armed struggle itself, giving an entirely different meaning to guerrilla warfare. More than poor interpretations of the Cuban answer, they are *imported* political conceptions, disguised as military lines and applied to historic conditions very different from those in which they had their roots. We have in mind: the concept of armed self-defense; a particular way of interpreting armed propaganda and the guerrilla base; and finally, the subjection of the guerrilla force to the party as just one more component added to its peacetime organization.

To judge by results, these conceptions, which in many places have acquired the status of guiding policy lines, have emptied the popular armed struggle of much of its content. It is worthwhile investigating the political ideas which inspire them and the manner in which some have borrowed from revolutionary experiences alien to Latin America and its present-day conditions.

These negative experiences may help us to discover the essential lessons to be drawn both from the insurrectional phase of the Cuban Revolution and from today's armed struggles.

*Che Guevara, "La guerre de guérilla, une méthode," in *Souvenirs de la guerre révolutionnaire*, Maspero, Paris, 1967.

7

The Fall of Arbenz and the Origins of the Guerrillas

Richard Gott

The overthrow of progressive president Jacobo Arbenz Guzmán in 1954 is one of the most significant milestones in Guatemalan history. The coup, staged by a coalition of forces, including the CIA, the United Fruit Company, and conservative sectors in the country, claimed to be rescuing Guatemala from the clutches of international communism. The fall of Arbenz's reformist government marked the end of a democratic spring that had lasted less than ten years. After 1954, foreign companies and the United States felt free to dictate conditions to the various caretaker governments that ran Guatemala. As British journalist Richard Gott points out, it was the caretaker government of General Miguel Ydígoras Fuentes that allowed the CIA-inspired Cuban expatriates to train on Guatemalan soil in preparation for the invasion of Cuba planned for April 1960. In this selection, Gott, author of two seminal books on Latin American guerrillas, Rural Guerrillas in Latin America *and* Guerrilla Movements in Latin America, *examines the political conditions in Guatemala six years after Arbenz's overthrow and a year after the victory of the Cuban Revolution. He also traces the transformation of guerrilla leaders from disgruntled nationalistic junior army officers into revolutionaries convinced that the only way out for Guatemala was armed struggle.*

In June 1954, the constitutionally elected government of Jacobo Arbenz Guzmán, President of Guatemala, was overthrown by the United States Central Intelligence Agency. The history of the guerrilla movements in Latin America, indeed the contemporary history of Latin America itself,

From *Guerrilla Movements in Latin America* (London: Thomas Nelson and Sons, 1970), 31–40. © 1970 by Richard Gott. Reprinted by permission of Richard Gott.

cannot be understood without reference to this cardinal event. For the overthrow of Arbenz seemed to show—at least to a later generation of revolutionaries—that no government in Latin America which attempted to put through even the mildest economic and social reforms could survive the hostility of the United States. A powerful myth was created to the effect that no revolutionary movement could hope to succeed while the United States chose to topple governments at will.[1]

The myth was broken four and half years later when the Cuban Revolution triumphantly proved it wrong. This was perhaps one of the most important results of Castro's victory for the rest of Latin America. The dangerous belief was created that the United States was not invincible and could be challenged successfully. But in 1965, eleven years after Colonel Arbenz was deposed, the United States' invasion of Santo Domingo once again seemed to indicate that, in spite of the rhetoric of the Alliance for Progress, the United States was not prepared to tolerate even the most modest moves toward radical change. Perhaps the myth was not a myth after all.

The revolutionaries in the continent were to draw important lessons from the experience of Guatemala in 1954. They concluded that a revolution which did not go "all the way" in terms of dispossessing the wealthy and giving the peasants and poorer classes a solid stake in the revolution could be expected to fail.[2] Colonel Arbenz himself was the inheritor of the Guatemalan revolution of 1944 that had overthrown the dictator Jorge Ubico. Although this revolution had made important reforms, they were too small to appeal to the dispossessed and too large to be tolerated by the rich and powerful. In a polarized society where the power retained by the rich was threatened, counterrevolution was inevitable. And counterrevolution with United States support, in a situation where those who had benefited from the revolution had nothing to defend themselves with, could not fail to be effective.

The causes of United States anger with Arbenz were explained in a statement made on 25 May 1954 by the Secretary of State, John Foster Dulles. First, said Dulles, Guatemala was the only Latin American country that had voted against a resolution passed by the Organization of American States in March 1954 which declared that the "domination or control of the political institutions of any American state by the international Communist movement . . . would constitute a threat to the American states, endangering the peace of America." Second, Guatemala had failed to ratify the Río Defense Pact of 1947—an agreement which effectively ensured that all Latin American armies came under United States control. And thirdly, President Arbenz had been buying arms from Eastern Europe.

This latter charge was hardly the fault of Arbenz, since his government had been the victim of a United States blockade which the American government had successfully persuaded many of its allies to join. The British Foreign Office, for example, issued a statement on 18 July 1954 which said that "Her Majesty's Government strongly disapproves of the sale of arms to Guatemala, and for several years has been refusing licenses for the export of any arms to that country."[3]

At the time, many critics of the United States' involvement in the internal affairs of Guatemala believed that the American government was motivated chiefly by anger at the expropriation of the uncultivated lands of the United Fruit Company, a United States enterprise that played a key role in the Guatemalan economy.[4] With the advantage of hindsight, however, it seems reasonable to conclude that the blind ideological hatred and distrust of Communism which characterized United States foreign policy throughout the Cold War years was a more important factor in the State Department's decision to act than the minor misfortunes of a small United States firm. John Foster Dulles thought that Arbenz was "soft on Communism": no further argument for intervention was necessary.

In fact, neither Colonel Arbenz nor his predecessor, Juan José Arévalo, had Communist or even Socialist sympathies. The Arbenz land reform, for example, which so annoyed the United Fruit Company, had been specifically designed to improve conditions for capitalist farming.[5] But both Arbenz and Arévalo did attempt to secure a minor degree of political independence from the United States. For this their "revolution" had to be stopped.

The CIA candidate to take over the presidency of Guatemala was Colonel Carlos Castillo Armas, himself an unsuccessful contender in the elections of 1950 from which Arbenz had emerged victorious. He was also the organizer of a previous unsuccessful coup. Invading from Honduras in the middle of June 1954, Castillo Armas had little difficulty in overthrowing the Arbenz régime.[6] One of Arbenz's supporters, an Argentinian named Ernesto Guevara, hoped that the régime would arm the workers and peasants in order to repel the invading forces.[7] But Arbenz did not have sufficient fire in his belly to perform such a revolutionary act. At the end of June he resigned meekly, leaving the road open to a government of military colonels.

With the overthrow of Arbenz, Guatemala began a long period of counterrevolutionary government. Castillo Armas, wrote a correspondent some years later, "proved to be something less than a democratic crusader. Instead of pushing land reforms, he earned the indignation of many peasants by returning to the big landowners virtually all of the estimated 1.5 million acres expropriated by the Arbenz régime."[8] It was this reversal of the admittedly limited land reform of Arbenz that seems to have created conditions in which guerrillas were later able to flourish.

Castillo Armas, however, did not live to see the full results of his coup. On 22 July 1957 he was shot dead by one of his palace guards, who was immediately accused by the government of having Communist affiliations. President Eisenhower, true to form, declared that the death of Castillo Armas was "a great loss to our nation and for the whole free world."

Elections to find a presidential replacement were held on 20 October, and although the winner appeared to be Ortíz Pasareli, a former justice of the supreme court, the man who ran second, General Miguel Ydígoras Fuentes, immediately declared the election to be invalid. A further election on 19 January 1958 showed General Ydígoras Fuentes as the winner. The first election had not been a particularly fair one, since neither the Communists nor even the vaguely left-wing Revolutionary party had been allowed to participate. But in the second election the Revolutionary party was allowed to stand, putting up as their candidate a lawyer called Mario Méndez Montenegro, who made a reasonable showing at the polls.[9] Ydígoras won largely because Méndez split the vote.

In 1960 the United States once again involved itself in the affairs of Guatemala. President Eisenhower, who had been informed by Vice-President Nixon in April 1959 that Fidel Castro was "either incredibly naïve about Communism or under Communist discipline,"[10] had become increasingly concerned about the potential threat posed by the Cuban régime. Consequently, on 17 March 1960, after a trip through Latin America, he set in motion the machinery to destroy it. The following passage appears in his autobiography:

> I ordered the Central Intelligence Agency to begin to organize the training of Cuban exiles, mainly in Guatemala, against a possible future day when they might return to their homeland. More specific planning was not possible because the Cubans living in exile had made no move to select from among their number a leader whom we could recognize as the head of a government in exile.[11]

The Guatemalan ambassador in Washington, Carlos Alejos, had a brother, Roberto, who owned large coffee plantations in remote areas of Guatemala, and who was also one of President Ydígoras' most prominent backers. Roberto Alejos became the chief intermediary between the CIA and the President, and conveniently he was able to offer one of his own coffee ranches, at Helvetia de Retalhuleu, as a base for the CIA operations. Here Cuban exiles were trained as pilots and communications experts, and given general training to prepare them for an invasion of Cuba, scheduled for the following year.[12] Arthur Schlesinger, Jr., describes the scene:

> It was the rainy season, and they had to build their own camp in sticky volcanic mud five thousand feet above the sea. In their spare time, they received training from a Filipino colonel who had organized guerrillas against the Japanese during the Second World War.[13]

But such activities, which of course soon became widely known in Guatemala—but not outside—were by no means unanimously approved of by the Guatemalan army.[14] A number of nationalist officers who had no hostile feelings toward Fidel Castro (who had not at that stage declared himself to be a Marxist-Leninist) saw no reason why Guatemala should be used as a springboard for a United States-sponsored invasion of Cuba.[15] In particular, they disliked having to pretend that the Retalhuleu base was being used for nothing more sinister than the training of Guatemalan recruits.

Consequently a coup was planned. On the night of 13 November 1960 a military uprising led by colonel Rafael Sessan Pereira took place at the barracks of Fort Matamoros, outside Guatemala City. Among those who supported him were two young lieutenants, Marco Antonio Yon Sosa and Luís Augusto Turcios Lima. Turcios was in Petén Department at the time, but he returned to the city to help the uprising. The revolt was designed essentially to prevent the Cuban exiles and the CIA from using Guatemala as a base for their operations against Cuba. But the nationalist officers also hoped to end corruption and inefficiency in the army and the government.

The presence of Cuban exiles training in Guatemala, Turcios later declared "was a shameful violation of our national sovereignty. And why was it permitted? Because our government is a puppet." But he emphasized that his reasons for joining the revolt were essentially "the traditional ones of younger officers; fed up with corruption, desiring structural changes in the army; nothing really different."[16]

It was in fact a typical nationalist officers' revolt, though according to the government it also had the support of Mario Méndez Montenegro. It marked the culmination of several months of political and military unrest. Bombings in Guatemala City had been going on for more than a year, and there had been rumors for a long time that left-wing groups in the country were in touch with Colonel Carlos Paz Tejada who had been President Arévalo's defense minister and who was in open opposition to the post-Arbenz governments.[17]

Inevitably, President Ydígoras accused the opposition of being financed and organized from Cuba, and he was able to give more substance to this argument when, on 2 August, ex-President Arbenz announced on Havana television that in the future he intended to make his home in Cuba. (Hitherto he had lived in exile in Uruguay.)[18]

At Fort Matamoros, Colonel Pereira's rebel group, consisting of about a hundred men, killed a colonel and a captain and escaped, according to a government statement, "taking with them troops and armament."[19]

Another group managed to take over the military base at Zacapa, and also the banana port of Puerto Barrios on the Atlantic coast 150 miles north-east of the capital. On their arrival at Zacapa barracks, according to an account by Adolfo Gilly, 800 peasants presented themselves "and asked for arms with which to fight against the government. This was not in the program, nor was it even anticipated by the rebels, who could not make up their minds to arm the peasants."[20]

Puerto Barrios was in the very part of the country where the Cuban exiles were training, and in view of the delicacy of the situation the Guatemalan government immediately cabled Washington.[21]

Having received word from his Secretary of State, Christian Herter, that the situation was "not good," President Eisenhower decided (as he later recalled) that "if we received a request from Guatemala for assistance, we would move in without delay. At that moment, Cuban exiles were training in Guatemala, and we had to consider the possibility of Castro's sending forces of his own to attempt an overthrow of the Guatemalan government."[22] Consequently, five United States naval vessels were immediately sent down to the Guatemalan coast. At the same time freshly trained Cuban exile pilots from the Retalhuleu base were called in to help suppress the Guatemalan officers' revolt. One of them tried to land with a planeload of troops at the airport of Puerto Barrios, but he was repelled by hostile fire.[23] Another bombed the town and the airfield from the air. The runway was bombed, a Guatemalan army communiqué announced, to prevent the landing of Cuban planes that might have attempted to supply the rebels.

In these circumstances, the revolt could not last long. On 17 November President Ydígoras declared a victory, announcing from the balcony of the presidential palace in Guatemala City that:

> we shall be merciful to the soldiers who have been deceived, but we shall apply the full force of the law to the traitorous officers. We shall not pardon these leaders of treason who have been paid with Castro's money. We shall not pardon them here, nor in Honduras, nor wherever they have hidden themselves.[24]

But it had been a near thing. The correspondent of the *Christian Science Monitor*, writing from Guatemala City in December, pointed out that:

the fact that the rebels could take over two garrisons before the government learned of the revolt and that it took four days for huge government forces to put down ill-equipped men, is cause for much comment here. This indicates a greater degree of discontent than most people imagine. It is believed by many here that the presence of the United States Navy on the coast did discourage any intentions that local Communists might have had of taking advantage of the rebellion and potential help from Cuba.[25]

But the rebels had themselves to blame as well. According to Adolfo Gilly, of the 150 leaders and officers who were sworn members of the secret group that had begun plotting earlier in the year, only forty-five revolted on 13 November. Four years later, when some of them were more politically motivated, they produced a document giving a further reason for failure:

> It was the very limited scope of the movement's political orientation that caused its military downfall; having a huge arsenal and a military zone under its control signified nothing, so long as the military leaders did not understand clearly why they were fighting and toward what goal they were moving.[26]

Faced with military defeat and the prospect of execution if captured, the rebel officers retired to the mountains and then into exile. Colonel Pereira managed to escape to Mexico, while Yon Sosa crossed the border into Honduras. Turcios Lima made his way to El Salvador.

After four months of exile the last two, together with another officer, Alejandro de León, returned to Guatemala, where, inevitably separated from the army, they began looking for ways of continuing the struggle against the régime. Adolfo Gilly, in his account of the origins of the guerrilla movement in Guatemala, describes in some detail how during their flight the rebel officers were welcomed by the peasants. Alejandro de León, for example, was hidden and protected by a peasant who, "seeing him on the run, realized that he was a rebel officer and offered him refuge. It was raining that night and there was no food in the house. At one point the peasant began hacking away at some of the wooden wall-boards of his hut. 'It's to make a fire with. I don't have any dry wood and you're soaking wet. I can fix the wall tomorrow.' "[27] Yon Sosa in Honduras and Turcios Lima in El Salvador had similar experiences in their encounters with the peasantry. Although Gilly's stories are obviously more in the nature of propaganda than strict history, they go some way to providing an explanation of how rebel officers from the Guatemalan army gradually turned into left-wing guerrillas.

> In Guatemala, as in Honduras, and El Salvador [writes Gilly], all the peasants helped and protected the rebels, tried to influence them and

win them to their side. The peasants' motive was not only to offer their
solidarity but also to win allies and leaders in their struggle for the
land. The peasantry has done this with many rebel fighters, over and
over again; they have been doing it for years, for centuries. Many of the
rebels did not respond, but the effort was not in vain; the influence was
felt by some, although not immediately. Yon Sosa and Alejandro de León
and their *compañeros* did not jump to conclusions; but, little by little,
the peasants won them over.[28]

At the time, Second-Lieutenant Turcios Lima was barely nineteen.
He had been born on 23 November 1941, and came from what he himself
described as a lower middle class family. His father was a watch repair-
man and his mother worked in an office. His father died when he was
young. In an interview in 1966, Turcios described his mother as a "reactionary." She had approved of the United States-supported rebellion of
Castillo Armas in 1954.[29] He was educated at a private Catholic school
and later at a government vocational college.

His mother had wanted him to be an army officer, and so at the age of
fifteen he was sent to the Polytechnic School, Guatemala's military academy. He graduated in 1959 with the rank of second-lieutenant. Subsequently he spent six months at the Ranger training school at Fort Benning,
Georgia, in the United States, in late 1959 and early 1960.

Asked on one occasion to describe his experience in the United States,
he replied that "from the military point of view it was very good." And to
another interviewer he explained why he had liked it: "We had the officers' club, 15-ounce Texas steaks, good clothes, the best equipment. Plenty
of money, too: every month I sent $150 to my mother. What worries did I
have?"[30]

It is difficult, in fact, to understand the Guatemalan guerrillas without taking their military origins into account. Alan Howard, an American
journalist who talked to Turcios early in 1966, underlines his nationalist
outlook:

> Though he suddenly found himself in a position of political leadership,
> Turcios is essentially a soldier fighting for a new code of honor. If he
> has an *alter ego*, it would not be Lenin or Mao or even Castro, whose
> works he has read and admires, but Augusto Sandino, the Nicaraguan
> general who fought the U.S. Marines sent to Nicaragua during the
> Coolidge and Hoover administrations.[31]

Lieutenant Yon Sosa was three years older than Turcios and of Chinese extraction. He too had had the benefit of United States military training—at Fort Gulick in the Canal Zone—but he had not been impressed.
Later, he told an interviewer, "I was able to put to good use the little I had

learned in Panama—little, because the courses were poor, to tell the truth, and I learned a lot more here in the sierra, fighting against imperialism."[32]

During the course of 1961, Turcios Lima spent some time negotiating with the leaders of a number of political parties "to find out what they stood for." He seems to have been unimpressed by them all until finally, in July, he met the leaders of the banned Partido Guatemalteco del Trabajo (PGT), the Guatemalan Communist party. "They were different from the others," he told an interviewer some years afterward, "they really cared about the people." From these first meetings, there began what Turcios was later to describe as "close collaboration" between his group of military rebels and the PGT. But the Communists by no means dominated the group of Turcios' supporters. One guerrilla leader, Camilo Sánchez, recalls that when he joined up with the rebels at this stage, he found "not only Communists, but also sincere revolutionaries, Catholics, Communists, and people whose only aspiration was to overthrow the régime in order to replace it by something more equitable."[33]

Even at this early stage in the struggle, the lives of the members of the movement of Turcios and Yon Sosa were constantly in danger. At the same time as political discussions with the PGT were going on, in July 1961, Alejandro de León was captured by the chief of the political police, Ranulfo González Ovalle, and murdered. According to Adolfo Gilly's account, "the shock produced by the death of Alejandro de León . . . acted as a powerful stimulus in leading the movement to put an end to its negotiations with the opposition parties and to decide to launch guerrilla warfare." In addition, they appear to have been impressed by the initiative of a group of peasants who, in December 1961, offered them their support provided that they began an armed struggle for the land.

The fact is that, given their character as outlaws, the officers who had survived the revolt of the previous year had very few alternatives open to them. It was easier to survive capture in the country than in the town, and the peasants they had encountered—notably in their flight after 13 November—seemed friendlier than the politicians in the town. Given the Cuban example, guerrilla action seemed a logical choice. Consequently Yon Sosa and Turcios Lima abandoned their negotiations with the bourgeois politicians and took to the hills.

Notes

1. It was not always even necessary to overthrow a revolutionary government. The Bolivian revolution of 1952, led by Paz Estenssoro, and later by Siles Zuaso, was subverted by the United States from within.

2. At a Latin American Youth Congress held in Havana in August 1960, Che Guevara explained the importance of Arbenz's failure: "We should also like to

extend a special greeting to Jacobo Arbenz, president of the first Latin American country which fearlessly raised its voice against colonialism; a country which, in a far-reaching and courageous agrarian reform, gave expression to the hopes of the peasant masses. We should also like to express our gratitude to him, and to the democracy which gave way, for the example they gave us and for the accurate estimate they enabled us to make of the weaknesses which that government was unable to overcome. This allows us to go to the root of the matter and to behead those who hold power and their lackeys at a single stroke"—Ernesto Che Guevara, *Obra Revolucionaria*, Ediciones Era, Mexico City, 1967, p. 309. The essential lesson of Guatemala was that in any revolutionary process the old army had to be destroyed. Only the Bolivian Revolution of 1952 and the Cuban Revolution actually got rid of the army. In a document of the Central Committee of the Guatemalan Communist party of June 1955, which analyzed the failure of Arbenz, it stated clearly that "it is an error to try to secure revolutionary changes while leaving the old army intact"—quoted in Alain Joxe, *El conflicto chino-soviético en América Latina*, Editorial Arca, Montevideo, 1967, p. 35.

3. *Keesings Contemporary Archives*, p. 13677. Britain did not technically support the blockade.

4. Color was given to this argument by the fact that Secretary of State John Foster Dulles had been a member of the law firm that drew up the pre-war agreement between United Fruit and the Guatemalan government, and his brother Allen Dulles, then head of the CIA, had formerly been president of the company.

5. The preamble to the reform law stated that "the agrarian reform of the Revolution aims to liquidate feudal rural property and the relations of production arising from it, in order to develop capitalist methods and forms of production in agriculture and to prepare the way for the industrialization of Guatemala." See the study, *Tenencia de la Tierra y desarrollo socio económico del sector agrícola en Guatemala*, produced by the Comité Interamericano de Desarrollo Agrícola (CIDA), Panamerican Union, 1965.

6. One writer on guerrilla warfare considers that Castillo Armas' invading army should be classified as a guerrilla band, and he chalks up its success as a success for guerrilla warfare in general. See Andrés Cassinello Pérez, *Operaciones de guerrillas y contra-guerrillas*, Madrid, 1966, p. 154.

7. Guevara had in fact only been in Guatemala since February 1954—though apparently this was long enough for him to become known as "agitator" to the anti-Arbenz forces. After Arbenz's fall, he was forced to spend a month's asylum in the Argentine embassy in Guatemala City. See Ricardo Rojo, "Mon ami Guevara," *L'Express*, 29 April 1968: and *Mi amigo el Che*, Editorial Jorge Alvarez, Buenos Aires, 1968, pp. 59–71.

8. Dan Kurzman, *Washington Post*, 13 March 1966.

9. Although in the post-1954 period Méndez Montenegro had a reputation for being left of center, he had in fact been one of the leaders of the attempted coup against Arévalo in 1949.

10. Dwight D. Eisenhower, *Waging Peace*, Doubleday, New York, 1965, p. 523.

11. Ibid., p. 533.

12. David Wise and Thomas B. Ross, *The Invisible Government*, Random House, New York, 1964.

13. Arthur Schlesinger, Jr., *A Thousand Days*, p. 228; and see also Haynes Johnson and others, *The Bay of Pigs*, Norton, New York, 1964.

14. In October a student group in Quezeltenango issued a statement denouncing the fact that anti-Castro Cubans and North Americans were preparing an invasion of Cuba in Guatemalan territory—*New York Times*, 26 October 1960. In spite of articles by Professor Ronald Hilton in *The Nation* and the *Hispanic American Report* in November, the use of Guatemala as a springboard for a Cuban invasion did not become widely known until the following year. See the *New York Times*, 8 April 1961, where the paper finally screwed up its courage to mention the existence of a secret base.

15. President Ydígoras announced on 14 May that the Guatemalan armed forces would conduct continuous guerrilla warfare training maneuvers until further notice. Diplomatic relations with Cuba were suspended in April—*New York Times*, 15 May 1960.

16. Interview with Alan Howard, *New York Times*, 26 June 1966.

17. *New York Times*, 23 July 1960.

18. *New York Herald Tribune*, 4 August 1960.

19. *New York Times*, 14 November 1960.

20. Adolfo Gilly, "The Guerrilla Movement in Guatemala," *Monthly Review*, May 1965, p. 14. (This is an important source for a study of the Guatemalan guerrilla movement. A second article was published in the *Monthly Review* for June 1965. Adolfo Gilly is a Uruguayan Trotskyite who tends rather to romanticize the role of the peasantry.)

21. See John Gerassi, *The Great Fear in Latin America*, Collier Books, New York, 1965, pp. 184–85, for an account of how these cables became public.

22. Eisenhower, *Waging Peace*, p. 613.

23. Wise and Ross, *The Invisible Government*.

24. *Le Monde*, 19 November 1960.

25. *Christian Science Monitor*, 12 December 1960. The revolt did have the effect of giving President Ydígoras second thoughts about the political wisdom of allowing the Cuban exiles to continue training in Guatemala. In March 1961, Robert Alejos was dispatched to President Kennedy with a letter requesting that the exiles should be removed by the end of April. They were. They left for Cuba in the middle of the month and were resoundingly defeated at the Bay of Pigs.

26. Document produced by MR13 on the fourth anniversary of the revolt.

27. Gilly, "The Guerrilla Movement in Guatemala" (1), p. 15.

28. Ibid., p. 16.

29. Interview with Henry Giniger, *New York Times*, 18 March 1966.

30. Interview with Alan Howard, *New York Times Magazine*, 26 June 1966.

31. Gilly, "The Guerrilla Movement in Guatemala" (1), p. 16.

32. Gilly (2), p. 31.

33. Camilo Castaño, "Avec les Guérrilles de Guatemala," *Partisans*, No. 38, July–September 1967, p. 150.

8

Guerrilla Priest

Camilo Torres

Priest, sociologist, and eloquent defender of the oppressed, Camilo Torres, at different points of his life, brought the Catholic Church of Colombia to task for not doing everything within its power to change the conditions of inequality existing in the country. Frustrated by the complicity of the church with the oligarchy, Torres abandoned the peaceful ways of the clergy and joined the guerrillas of the National Liberation Army (ELN). He saw the act of taking up arms as the only alternative open to him as a Colombian and a priest. Prior to joining the guerrillas, he had published numerous documents inciting the Colombian people to revolt. Camilo was killed in a confrontation with the army on February 15, 1966. After his death, Camilo became part of a select pantheon of revolutionary martyrs and acquired a revolutionary stature second only to that of Che Guevara.

Platform of the United Front of the Colombian People

To all Colombians; to the popular sectors of our society; to the organizations of communal action; to the unions, cooperatives, fraternal organizations, peasant leagues, Indian communities, and workers' organizations; to all those who are dissatisfied; to all those not registered in traditional political parties—to all of you we present the following platform to unite the Colombian people in the pursuit of concrete objectives.

From *Revolutionary Priest*, ed. John Gerassi (New York: Random House, 1971), 306–10, 400–402, 425–27. © 1971 by Random House. Reprinted by permission of Random House.

Motives

1. The decisions that are indispensable for Colombian politics to be oriented for the benefit of the majorities, not the minorities, must be made by those who hold power.
2. Those now in power constitute an economic minority which makes all the fundamental decisions of national policy.
3. This minority will never be able to make a decision adversely affecting its own interests or the foreign interests to which it is bound.
4. The decisions required for the socioeconomic development of the country beneficial to the majorities and to national independence necessarily affect the interests of the economic minority.
5. These circumstances make it indispensable that the political power structure is changed so that the majorities can make the decisions.
6. At present the majorities reject the political parties and reject the present system but do not have a political apparatus suitable to take over the government.
7. The political apparatus to be organized should seek the greatest possible support of the masses, should have a technical orientation toward technology, and should be organized around principles of action rather than around a leader to avoid the danger of cliques, demagoguery, and personality cult.

Objectives

Agrarian Reform

The land will belong to the one who directly farms it. The government will designate agrarian inspectors to deliver land deeds to those peasants who are eligible to receive them but will require that the development of the land is carried out by the cooperative and community systems, in accordance with a national agrarian plan which will grant loans and give technical assistance.

No land will be purchased. What is considered necessary for the common good of the people will be expropriated without compensation.

The Indian councils will take actual possession of the lands that belong to them. The development and strengthening of the Indian communities will be promoted.

Urban Reform

All the inhabitants of houses in the cities and towns will become owners of the houses in which they live. The person who can prove that his sole support is derived from one house will be able to keep it even if he does not live in it.

For every house not in sufficient use, in the judgment of the government, the owner will be fined, and the fines will be invested by the state in housing projects.

Planning

A compulsory plan will be drawn up to replace imported products with substitutes, to increase exports, and to industrialize the country. Every public or private investment will have to follow the national plan of investments. The transactions in foreign money will be made exclusively by the state.

Tax Reform

A progressive tax will be collected from those who receive income higher than that required by an average Colombian family to live decently—for example, five thousand pesos monthly income in 1965. Above this limit, the excess income which is not invested in the sectors stipulated in the official investment plan will pass in their entirety to the state. No institution will be exempt from paying tax. Salaries, up to a certain limit—for example, five thousand pesos monthly in 1965—will not be taxed.

Nationalization

Banks, insurance companies, hospitals, clinics, manufacturing centers, pharmaceutical distribution, public transportation, radio and television, and firms exploiting natural resources will all belong to the state.

The state will provide free education to all Colombians, respecting the ideology of the parents until the end of secondary schooling and the ideology of the student after secondary schooling.

Education will be compulsory until the end of secondary schooling or technical training. There will be legal punishment of parents who do not comply with the obligation to educate their children. Financing of education will be covered by governmental investment programs through increased taxation.

The resources of the subsoil will belong to the state and the exploitation of oil will be done by the state in the interest of the national economy. No oil concessions will be granted to foreign companies except under the following conditions: (1) that the state owns no less than seventy percent of the stock; (2) that refining, distribution and production of fuel are public services under state control; (3) that the companies, their equipment, installations, and plants are returned to the state without compensation, after no more than twenty-five years; (4) that the salaries of the Colombian laborers, both manual laborers and other employees, are at least equal to those of the foreigners in the same job categories.

International Relations

Colombia will maintain relations with all the countries of the world and will engage in commercial and cultural exchange in conditions of equity and mutual benefit.

Social Security and Public Health

The state will put into effect an integral and progressive program of social security to guarantee to the population the right to health and medical care—without jeopardy to the private practice of medicine—and will study all the aspects related to unemployment, illness, disability, old age, and death. All the personnel of the health professions will be functionaries of the government and, up to a limit fixed by law, will be paid according to the size of the families who request to be under their care.

Family Policy

Parents who abandon their children will be punished. The protection of women and children will be guaranteed by law, and punishment will be meted out to those who violate the law.

Armed Forces

The budget of the armed forces will be adequate to maintain them without excessive siphoning off of the funds necessary for health and education of Colombians. The defense of national sovereignty will be the responsibility of all the citizens of Colombia. Women will be obliged to undertake a term of civil service after they reach eighteen years of age.

Rights of Women

On a basis of equality with men, women will take part in the economic, political, and social activities of the country.

The Platform and the Revolution

The United Front of the People is the result of a number of years of experience and reflection. The intended union of the political opposition groups and the other dissatisfied Colombians had to face two main problems. The first is the lack of size, and the second is the lack of a clear definition. The size could easily have been limited by religious motives, traditional political motives, or group and leader loyalties. It was necessary to build a union around concrete objectives which would unify all Colombians regardless of religious beliefs, party, or group and leader attachments. The platform of struggle of the United Front of the People can be realized only after the people have taken power. Its only novelty consists in its seeking the common points of the revolution without entering into religious or party differences. It can be accepted by Catholics and non-Catholics, by poor Liberals and poor Conservatives, by the revolutionary elements of the MRL, the Communist, ANAPO, and Christian Democratic parties, and especially by the revolutionary elements of the nonaligned in these groups. However, it is necessary to explain that this platform leans toward the establishment of a socialist state, that is, "socialist" understood only in a technical and positive sense, not in the ideological sense. We offer practical, not theoretical, socialism.

When a revolutionary platform is talked about, many experts become involved. However, when it is specified that the revolution must consist of a fundamental reorganization of the state by applying science and technology to bring about reforms benefiting the majorities, many bow out.

The platform does not mention tactics for taking power. However, some feel, as does Dr. Alfonso López Michelsen, that this platform is not useful for an immediate electoral struggle; moreover, they feel that the platform is becoming associated with the name of Camilo Torres, and I have clearly given reasons why I will not run for election. Although these reasons may in no way justify any attack by me on the other opposition groups, revolutionary or not, in fact the electoral groups deviate from the platform on any excuse. On the other hand, the followers of the platform, when planning the takeover of political power as an indispensable condition for applying the platform, necessarily have to make a tactical decision—to follow through to the ultimate consequences and use whatever means the oligarchy leaves open to seize power. This attitude has no great ideological consequences because the church itself has established the conditions for a just war. However, many so-called revolutionaries in fact do not wish to follow through to the ultimate consequences.

A platform which plans a socialist state and the liberation of Colombia from American imperialism cannot be indifferent to movements which lean toward socialism and espouse liberation from imperialism. Even though these movements contain ideological elements that have discrepancies in scientific, positive, and practical aspects, they are more akin to us. This solidarity in practice drives away many timid revolutionaries who are more insistent on ideology than on revolution.

There is one fact evident in the movement of the United Front, and that is that it is a mass movement that has formed in little time. Thus, many have recently joined. Their motives for joining differ. Some came to acquire an important position and left frustrated. Others thought a new party was being formed, and they left the way they came—very quickly. As the revolutionary line of the United Front becomes more and more definite and aggressive, the fellow travelers of the revolution will continue to fall by the wayside to return home or wait for the others to complete the revolution and then join it.

The important thing is that the Colombian popular class must continue to move forward, without a single step backwards, in spite of the defections, in spite of the rumors, in spite of the betrayals. The decision of the poor that they do not want their sons to accuse them in the future of having betrayed their historical and revolutionary vocation will be what determines the situation. They know that I will follow through to the ultimate consequences and that even if only a handful of determined men remain with me, we will continue the struggle nonetheless.

Although this is going to be a prolonged struggle, the important thing is that all who have decided to join us have also decided to stay with us to the end.

Message to Colombians from the Mountains

Colombians:

For many years now, the poor of our land have been waiting for the call to arms to throw themselves into the final struggle against the oligarchy. On the occasions when it seemed that the people's desperation had reached the critical point, the ruling class always found the means to deceive the people, to distract them, appeasing them with new formulas that always added up to the same thing—suffering for the people and well-being for the privileged caste.

When the people demanded a leader, and found him in Jorge Eliécer Gaitán, the oligarchy murdered him. When the people demanded peace, the oligarchy sowed violence throughout the country. When the people could no longer withstand violence and organized the guerrillas to seize power, the oligarchy pulled a military coup out of its hat so that the guerrillas, who were tricked, would surrender. When the people demanded democracy, they were tricked once again, this time with a plebiscite and a National Front imposed upon them by the dictatorship of the oligarchy.

But the people will no longer believe, never again. The people do not believe in elections. The people know that the legal means have been exhausted. The people know that armed struggle is the only remaining course. The people are desperate, and they are determined to risk their lives so that the next generation of Colombians will not be one of slaves; so that the children of those who now are willing to give their lives will have an education, a roof over their heads, food, clothing, and, above all, *dignity*; and so that the Colombians of the future will have their own homeland, independent of the might of the United States.

All sincere revolutionaries must realize that armed struggle is the only remaining way open. However, the people wait for their leaders to set an example and issue the call to arms by their presence in the struggle. I want to tell the Colombian people that the time is now and that I have not betrayed them. I have gone from village to village and from city to city, speaking in the public squares in favor of the unity and organization of the popular classes to take power. I have said to the people, "Let us all devote ourselves to these goals until death!"

Everything is prepared. The oligarchy means to organize another force at election time, with candidates who deny their candidacy only finally to be "drafted," with two-party committees. They pretend a new beginning with ideas and people that not only are old but have betrayed the people. What are we waiting for, Colombians?

I have joined the armed struggle.

From the Colombian mountains I mean to continue the struggle, arms in hand, until power has been won by the people. I have joined the Army of National Liberation because I have found in it the same ideals of the United Front. I found the desire and the attainment of unity at the base, a peasant base, without traditional religious or party differences, and without any interest in combating the revolutionary elements of any sector, movement, or party. And without *caudillismo*. This is a movement that seeks to free the people from exploitation by the oligarchy and imperialism, a movement that will not lay down its arms as long as power is not entirely in the hands of the people, and a movement that, in its goals, accepts the platform of the United Front.

All we Colombian patriots must ready ourselves for war. Little by little, we will emerge ready for war. Little by little, experienced guerrilla leaders will appear in all parts of the country. Meanwhile, we must be alert. We must gather weapons and ammunition, seek guerrilla training, talk with those who are closest to us. We must collect clothing, medical supplies, and provisions in preparation for a protracted struggle.

We must carry out small-scale attacks against the enemy where we can be sure of victory. We must put those who claim to be revolutionaries to the test. We must not refrain from acting, but neither must we grow impatient. In a long, drawn-out war, everyone must go into action at some point. What matters is that the revolution finds them ready and on their guard. We must divide the work. The activists of the United Front must be in the vanguard of action and initiative. We must have patience while we wait and confidence in final victory. The people's struggle must become a national one. We have already begun, and we have a long day's work ahead of us.

Colombians: let us not fail to answer the call of the people and the revolution.

Activists of the United Front: let us turn our watchwords into reality:

For the unity of the popular classes, until death!

For the organization of the popular classes, until death!

For the taking of power for the popular classes, until death!

We say "until death" because we are determined to carry on to the end. We say "until victory" because a people that throws itself into the struggle until death will always achieve victory. We say "until final victory," with the watchwords of the Army of National Liberation: NOT ONE STEP BACK! LIBERATION OR DEATH!

9

The Revolutionary Path

Luis de la Puente

In the wake of the Cuban Revolution, Havana became a meeting place of sorts for aspiring revolutionaries from all over the world. A few short months after Batista's departure, Luis de la Puente, a young, middle-class Peruvian lawyer, a member of the social-democratic, reformist APRA (American Popular Revolutionary Alliance) party, attended the First National Agrarian Reform Forum held in Havana. As a result of this visit, de la Puente became convinced that the only way to transform Peru was through armed struggle. A few months after returning from Cuba, he broke away from APRA, and founded APRA-Rebelde (Rebel APRA), which in 1962 became the Movement of the Revolutionary Left (MIR). A follower of Guevara and the Cuban Revolution, de la Puente and other members of the MIR chose to emulate the Cuban rebels and began a guerrilla struggle in the Andean countryside. Aware of the disadvantages of middle-class intellectuals trying to convince the peasants of their good intentions, de la Puente chose the names of traditional Inca heroes with which to baptize the two guerrilla fronts sponsored by MIR. A year before his departure for the mountains, de la Puente delivered a rousing speech, "The Revolutionary Path," in Lima's Plaza San Martín. In the speech, de la Puente exhorted all Peruvians to take up arms against the system. A few months later he went underground, to re-emerge the following year as the head of the guerrilla unit "Pachacutec" in Cusco, while Guillermo Lobatón took command of the "Tupac Amaru" column in the outer perimeter of the rain forest. Ignorant of the peculiarities of the terrain, betrayed by one of his followers, and unable to win the support of the people, Luis de la Puente was killed by the army on October 23, 1965, while pursuing his dream of a revolutionary Peru.

These passages are excerpted from a speech delivered by Luis de la Puente in Lima's Plaza San Martín on February 7, 1964. All notes, unless otherwise specified, have been added by the editors of the original Peruvian edition (MIR, IV Epoca). From *El Camino de la Revolución* (Lima: Ediciones Voz Rebelde-IV Epoca, 1976). Translated by Daniel Castro.

People of Lima:

We have had the opportunity to listen to the electoral platforms put forth during the 1962 campaign and later repeated in 1963. All of Peru is a witness to this, because the then candidate and now president of the republic [Fernando Belaúnde Terry] had the luxury of touring the whole country, using all available means of transportation, including, as he demagogically puts it, a donkey. In all his proclamations, candidate Belaúnde Terry came before the people of Peru pointing out the vices of the *convivencia** and planting new hopes in our long-suffering people. . . .

We believe that Peru's crisis is a systemic crisis. Recent Latin American experience has clearly demonstrated that representative democracy is a farce that supports a system of exploitation, dependence, and misery. There is nothing to be gained from the avenues available through representative democracy. It is a grievous error to entertain any hopes about a system based on deceit and discrimination that uses democracy as a snare.

It is necessary to state clearly to the people that the traditional electoral and parliamentary system, while valuable in the struggle against feudalism in another historical era, is of no use in our time. . . .

Today we can see that elections have become a dance of the millions, and of lies, false promises, and charitable gifts. Universal suffrage is a discriminatory practice, since the majority of our people cannot vote because they are guilty of not knowing how to read or write. Congress has become a den of reactionaries, oligarchs, and servants of the darkest interests of imperialism and the oligarchy.

Elections and Deals: A Dead End Street

Aware of all the aforementioned facts, the MIR abstained from participating in the presidential elections of 1962 and 1963, and in the municipal elections of last year. For maintaining that line, we were called different things, even by members of the Left. Today, more than ever, we are convinced that we are correct.

We once posited that if, in a huge, expensive campaign, the people of Peru became acquainted with and believed in the platform of the different left-wing groups, and gave a majority of their votes to a revolutionary, and if they elected a congress controlled by a majority of revolutionaries;

*The *convivencia* (coexistence) is the term applied to the uneasy and opportunistic alliances between the oligarchy, represented by Manuel Prado, and the formerly leftist-leaning social-democratic APRA party during Prado's presidential regime (1956–1962). (Tr.)

even in this hypothetical case, it would have been impossible to deal with, and much less to solve, Peru's problems.

We talk about this case, and we consider it hypothetical and illusory, since we, the parties of the left, do not have the forty or fifty million soles that each campaign costs.* The bourgeois, landowning parties and the agents of imperialism are subsidized by the Banco de Crédito, the Banco Popular, the National Agrarian Society, the traitor [Romulo] Betancourt's Venezuelan government, International Petroleum Company, Cerro de Pasco Corporation, Marcona Mining, Toquepala, etc., etc. They have the capability of spending forty or fifty million soles in the 1962 campaign, and a similar amount in 1963. There is no competition. Besides, they have everything in their hands; they have the repressive apparatus at their beck and call, and they control the political authorities, the regular police, the secret police, etc. They control all the news media: press, radio, and television. They have the means to move around, the officials to guarantee the safety of their gatherings, the money to hire people, and their thugs enjoy immunity from prosecution. They have everything.

The left commits a grievous error when it chooses the electoral road as the primary form of struggle. We have already seen the consequences of the last two electoral campaigns: uncontrollable ambition, divisions, defeatism, skepticism, confusion, and abandoning our true objectives. . . .

Political power is an expression of economic power, guaranteed by armed force. The present system is perfectly set up with the methods, means, and institutions whose sole function is to defend the interests of a privileged minority. It is illusory, naive, and childish to think that the oligarchy and imperialism are going to allow power to be wrested away from them with smiling faces, pacts, deals, and noble invocations. It is necessary to leave those well-beaten paths of electoral politics and parliamentarism. The Peruvian people now demand a change in the language. Our peasants, despite their low level of education and political awareness, are telling us how to speak. Let us not take the wrong road. Let us not confuse our people anymore. Let us tell them what they are expecting to hear. Let us not fall into the electoral trap set by the oligarchy. Let us have no more illusions about coming to power or sharing it by means of deals and elections.

Fidel's Way

Recently, the Latin American experience has been showing us the way with clarity. Look at Cuba: Fidel's Cuba has demonstrated that it is

*In 1964 this would have been equivalent to $1.48 to $1.85 million. (Tr.).

possible to make an authentic revolution; that it is possible to begin the great Latin American Revolution ninety miles away from North America's shore; that it is possible to nationalize North American refineries in a small country; that it is possible to nationalize the big sugar companies and to establish cooperatives instead; that it is possible to begin the process of industrialization and to accelerate the process of economic development; that it is possible to end the accumulation of land and housing, transforming city dwellers into homeowners and peasants into owners of the land they work; that it is possible to eradicate illiteracy and to make free education available to all; in short, that it is possible to resist the economic, political, propagandistic, diplomatic, and military onslaught of the largest empire in the world, recovering a sense of nation, independence, and nationalism.

Cuba also tells us that all this is possible only on one condition: that the people overthrow the repressive apparatus that guarantees the permanence of privileged and oppressive groups. The destruction of the oligarchic-imperialist system in Cuba, the integral transformation of the country, the endurance and strengthening of the revolution have been possible on the basis of arming the people. And those who still speak of a "Castroite tyranny" and the "communist minority that enslaves and bloodies Cuba" have to be told that Castro's government is supported by the workers who keep their weapons next to the factory, the peasants who keep theirs next to their cooperatives, the students who have their weapons next to their schools; it is based on half a million men and women of the people who have received revolutionary military training and who have in their hands the weapons to defend their revolution and their government. The exponents of representative democracies should be told to arm their people as Fidel Castro has done; then we will find out who enjoys popular support, who is more democratic, or more popular. Let them give arms to the people to see if they can remain in power, to see if they can guide the people as the leaders of the Cuban Revolution have done.

The Latin American Revolution Is On the Move

It is not just the Cuban experience that is valuable. It is good to know that the whole of America is living a revolutionary process. The Venezuelan *guerrilleros* are still fighting in the mountains, and the troops of the traitor Betancourt cannot control the patriots fighting in the states of Falcón, Lara Yaracuy, and Portuguesa. Young men, students, workers, peasants, professionals, honest soldiers, speaking a new language, are showing the peoples of America the path to liberation. All the North American aid and the *yanqui* advisers cannot stop this movement's spreading through the countryside and the cities, reliving the feats of [Simón] Bolivar and [José Antonio] Páez at their zenith.

In Colombia, the *guerrilleros* are fighting in Tolima, Huila, and Vichada. In the mountains of Guatemala, three groups of combatants are defying imperialism and its uniformed puppets. In Nicaragua there are guerrillas following in the footsteps of Sandino. In the Dominican Republic, patriots are fighting in the countryside using guerrilla tactics.* And in Ecuador, the revolution also marches on despite the military repression instigated by the *yanqui* monopolies.

And the revolution also marches on in Brazil, Argentina, and Chile, despite the fact that these countries represent socioeconomic realities different from the rest of Latin America. The peasantry of the Brazilian northeast, grouped in their Peasant Leagues (*Ligas Campesinas*),† and the workers, students, and middle sectors of the south, using their own methods of struggle, are advancing inexorably while the oligarchy is weakened and beginning to crack under the weight of its myriad contradictions. The same thing is happening in Argentina, where the powerful working class increases its revolutionary consciousness daily, while the oligarchy and the military take their turns in power and sink under the weight of their own incompetence.

The Chilean people will soon have, in the course of this year, the opportunity to lose all illusions about the electoral path taken by the left. The Communist and Socialist parties united in the People's Action Front (FRAP) believe that it is possible to come to power by way of elections.‡ They believe that the oligarchy and the imperialists are going to give up their interests peacefully while destroying the yokes that oppress the people. That illusion will vanish very soon in this year's elections, and then the Chilean people will understand, as we Peruvians, Ecuadorians,

---

*A reference to the activities of some political groups that attempted to develop a guerrilla movement but did not succeed.

†Democratic peasant organizations under the guidance of Francisco Julião. The *Ligas* did not survive long after the 1964 coup.

‡In the elections of 1964, FRAP, with Salvador Allende as a candidate, lost the elections. The elections were won by Christian Democrat candidate Eduardo Frei. In 1970 the alliance changed its name to Popular Unity (UP), and it managed to obtain a plurality, but not the majority required by Chilean electoral law. The responsibility of electing the president fell on the Chilean congress, which elected Allende as president. Allende's government was overthrown and the president was assassinated on September 11, 1973. Allende's death shattered the illusion of gaining liberation and, even more so, the illusion of building socialism by peaceful means.

Colombians, Venezuelans, Central Americans, Brazilians, and Argentines understand, that the path of our people's liberation does not pass through representative democracy, because that type of democracy is a trap to tie people's hands and keep them oppressed and vilified.

The Revolution Advances Inexorably throughout the World

It is not only in Latin America that the revolution is taking great strides forward. In other continents too, the peoples are freeing themselves. What we learned, in our school days, about political geography is now useless, the same way that what we learn today might not be useful tomorrow, for new republics are emerging in Africa, Asia, and Oceania. These new republics are the fruit of the great world revolution of our time. Many of them are simultaneously carrying out the task of freeing themselves from the colonial yoke and accomplishing their national liberation, while others escape from the colonial yoke only to fall into the hands of North American imperialism, which is attempting to substitute for the former colonial oppressor. *But the people do not take the wrong path, and the struggle continues.*

We have a glorious Algeria, winning its independence after seven years of unequal and heroic struggle. Peasant guerrillas in the burning Saharan mountains, workers and students in the landlocked Algerian cities, and in Paris, the very capital of the French empire, defeated 500,000 French soldiers armed with the best weapons, North American weapons provided by NATO. Today the new republic is marching firmly along the paths of true democracy, with the certainty of attaining Socialism.

And we have South Vietnam, where the guerrillas are inflicting serious losses on the hundreds of thousands of puppet soldiers, with their North American advisers, North American weapons, ships, planes, and helicopters. Heroism increases, the country becomes stronger, the people become an army, and the enemy trembles and runs away. . . .

We could go on recounting the struggles of peoples to free themselves, and conclude by saying that the world is living one of its most revolutionary and fast-moving stages. *Revolution is inexorably spreading throughout the world, especially through the underdeveloped countries. For the main contradiction existing in our world is that between the oppressed peoples and the imperialist and colonialist countries.*

This is the great contribution of comrade Mao Tse-tung. The revolution marches on through the oppressed countries in Africa, Asia, and Latin America. These liberation struggles are unstoppable. *Peaceful coexistence is the way of transaction and class conciliation on an international* level. *To hope that economic competition will be decided in favor of socialist countries, to stop the people's struggle, to foment the hope that other countries will free us from our yokes, is to fall into new forms of mental colonialism, it is to renege on our position as revolutionaries, as Marxist-Leninists. Revolutions are made by peoples. Each people has to liberate itself by its own resources, and just as there is no conciliation between exploiter and exploited at the national level, this conciliation is unacceptable at the international level as well.*

This shows us that the revolution in Peru is not an isolated revolution. The revolution in Peru is the revolution of America, and the revolution of America is the world's revolution. . . .

Let Us Strengthen Our Faith in the People and the Revolution

Our people, like all peoples, are good and honest but also naive. Our people's capacity for selflessness is wonderful. Much blood and sacrifice has nurtured the tree of the revolution. Our people have believed and have given of themselves one and a thousand times, and one and a thousand times they have been betrayed.

We must prevent our people from falling into the hands of some adventurer and become disillusioned once again. We must make the people see the swindles, in order for them to abandon those who stand on their back in order to serve their exploiters. To avoid new swindles, to prevent the people from believing in things alien to their own destiny, to make them understand that they are being victimized by antediluvian and conciliatory parties, we must continue to insist on making this clear. *Let ideas become our fundamental weapon in this task alongside the masses. Let us make politics our gospel and our pedagogy. Let us raise the revolutionary consciousness of our people by example and clear teaching.*

Comrades, let us be aware that the revolution is a historical fact that nothing and no one can stop. We are convinced that the people are the only source of thought and action for transformation. Let us understand that change under the aegis of the bourgeoisie is impossible. We are certain that only a revolutionary vanguard with the ideology of the proletariat will be capable of leading the process of liberation. Let us discard the electoral and the deal-making processes. Let us speak the new language. Let us demand that our leaders take the lead in the struggle. Let us tell all those exploited and neglected by imperialism and the oligarchy that only a united front under the leadership of the worker-peasant alliance will be capable of leading our people from the depths of the evil pit where it exists.

Finally, let us look at the slogans that will answer the problems that were the object of this gathering.

Halt the Repression!

Let us stop the murderous hand of [President Fernando] Belaúnde's bourgeois government. Let us be ready to stop the repressive arm and cut it off forever. Let us tell Belaúnde and his followers that massacring peasants will not stop the revolution but will accelerate it. Violence against the people has always existed in a variety of forms, and it is now reaching its limit. We are positive that each massacre and each repressive act can only dig a larger and deeper hole where we will bury the oligarchy, imperialism, and all of their servants.

Immediate nationalization of the oil!

The International Petroleum Company must pay what it owes to the government!

IPC installations should be confiscated by the state in payment of the debt!

Let us declare traitors all the people who sell their country!

Let us demand that Belaúnde's government does what it promised. No more swindling of the people. Let us recover immediately the oil from foreign hands. Let us end the ping-pong game played with the oil problem; a game being played between the hesitating bourgeoisie in the executive and the oligarchy entrenched in Congress. The red-hot ball is called oil, and it is passed from hand to hand between the executive and the legislature.

The truth is that there is no need for a special law to make IPC pay the $150 million it owes the government for the rights to extract the oil. It should pay the $150 million that it owes and period. According to the latest report to Congress by the Minister of Development, the value of IPC installations is $90 million. Let the installations be taken over by the state and have IPC pay the balance. According to the constitution and the law, the executive demands payment by an administrative act. It uses force, it confiscates, takes part in the auction as creditor and demands the proceeds as payment. This is the legal way when one wants to make a patriotic demand and to fulfill an election promise. Naturally, the International Petroleum Company and the large monopolies established in Peru must have made all kinds of threats and handed out checks wholesale. And naturally, in a country where moral values are so deeply buried, where corruption, immorality, hypocrisy, opportunism, cowardice, and indifference are rampant, pressures and rewards, threats and money have always produced results. . . .

In the face of this, we declare as traitors to the country all those who hand over the oil, those who come to terms with IPC; those who do not recover the subsoil and the installations for Peru; those willing to condone IPC's debt. And let those who have anything to do with this matter remember that treason to the country is punished according to the laws of the Code of Military Justice.

End the latifundia and indentured servitude!
The land for those who work it!
A peasants' agrarian reform!

As for the agrarian reform, let us demand a peasants' agrarian reform. An agrarian reform that implies the immediate return of the land usurped from the indigenous communities; the expropriation of large landed estates, including the sugar *haciendas*; let there be no exceptions for the sugar barons who become inordinately rich exploiting our workers, hoarding our best lands, taking advantage of free trade and favorable prices in the international market.

An agrarian reform that recovers the collective spirit of our communities in order to build socialism in the countryside; which guarantees small holdings and encourages the creation of cooperatives; which raises the technological levels in all sectors of agricultural production; which increases the amount of arable land to benefit the majority of the people of the country, rather than a few privileged ones, as is the case presently. In short, the country needs an authentic agrarian reform that can free our peasants from all feudal trappings, from primitive agricultural practices and the pauperization in which they live. This will be possible only when the latifundia and all their manifestations are destroyed.

Let us fight for unity!
Unity for the revolution!
Unity in action!

Since MIR emerged into political life in October 1959, it has been fighting for the unity of the Left. We have made every effort to accomplish this unity. In the pursuit of this quest, we have been the victims of dirty maneuvering, misunderstandings, and betrayals. The MIR struggles and it will continue to struggle for unity, but not a unity for electoral campaigns, and let this be clear: no unity, no unity to put forth a candidate for the presidency, Congress, or local government. We do not want unity for that. For that we would rather go our own way, as we have done until now. *If unity is to be to fight alongside the peasants, to fight against the oligarchy, to make the revolution possible, our arms are open to embrace that unity.*

This splendid demonstration can be the beginning of great deeds in our struggle for liberation. *At this time the fundamental objectives of our struggle are as follows: the destruction of the feudal regime and the expulsion of North American imperialism, which in close cooperation oppress our people.* We must channel all our efforts to accomplish these two objectives. That is to say, we propose a democratic revolution of a new type, an antifeudal and anti-imperialist revolution, led by the worker-peasant alliance within a united front that will include all the other sectors of the nation that are suffering the effects of exploitation, oppression, and dependence. When we have accomplished those objectives, we will begin the next stage of our march toward socialism.

The Way of the Revolution Is the Only Way Left Open to Our People

The Peruvian Left is becoming more united every day, despite its present splits. The Left is rectifying its errors through a revolutionary self-criticism that will produce surprising results; we cannot exempt ourselves from this process, since we all have made mistakes, some more, some less. For the self-criticism to be revolutionary, it must be sincere, serious, and without impediments. The most important outcome of this process is that a new attitude will emerge from this process, in order not to take the wrong road and not to encourage the masses to entertain false hopes and dangerous confusion, in order not to allow them to stray from the only way to freedom and justice, which is the way of the revolution.

Yes, compañeros, the way of the revolution is the only way left open to our people. Let us recognize that our peasant brothers, exploited and neglected for such a long time, are telling us the great truth of our time: They are on the move. With their drums and their pipes, their flags and their slings, their women and children, their earthly-heavenly voices are proclaiming the beginning of an epic that will culminate in the multitudinous descent of our people down the millenarian slopes of the Andes.

Long live the Peruvian Revolution!

10

Some Final Notes
[on a Guerrilla Experience]

Héctor Béjar

During the fateful year of 1965, three different guerrilla groups began fighting in the Peruvian highlands against the government of Fernando Belaúnde. Soon after the two columns fielded by MIR were annihilated, a group of guerrillas self-identified as column "Javier Heraud," under the leadership of Héctor Béjar, went into action in Ayacucho. Béjar, a former member of the Peruvian Communist Party, had founded the National Liberation Army after returning from Cuba in late 1962 and surviving an ambush by the Peruvian police that resulted in the brutal killing of most of the would-be guerrilleros. *The list of those killed included poet Javier Heraud, posthumously honored in the name of the column. From the beginning, the poorly armed and badly trained* guerrilleros *were easy prey for an army invigorated by its recent defeat of MIR. A journalist by trade, Béjar reflected on his experiences as a guerrilla, and, during the long years of imprisonment following his capture, he was able to produce several books, one of which,* Peru 1965: Notes on a Guerrilla Experience, *was awarded the prestigious Cuban award* Casa de las Américas *for best essay. Amnestied by the government of General Juan Velasco Alvarado (1968–1975), he worked for Velasco's "revolution" for several years. In this selection, excerpted from his book, Béjar reassesses the guerrilla movements of 1965, pointing out the shortcomings, the rescuable experiences, and the lessons learned for the future.*

B y the end of 1965 the guerrilla movement had been totally liquidated. The cadres who died in battle were the product of many years of struggle and possessed qualities of brilliant leadership for political

From *Peru 1965: Notes on a Guerrilla Experience*, trans. William Rose (New York: Monthly Review Press, 1969), 112–28. © 1970 by Monthly Review Press. Reprinted by permission of the Monthly Review Press Foundation.

persuasion; they were not, however, prepared to deal with the problems created by the revolutionary military movement at this point in Peruvian history.

City and Countryside

The 1965 actions took place almost entirely in the countryside. They didn't affect either the cities or Peru's long strip of coast where important production centers, several mines and oil centers, steel mills, and cane plantations with an agricultural proletariat having a long tradition of struggle are all located.

Two factors contributed to the failure of the urban centers of the coastal and mountain areas to act in support of the guerrillas. They were: a) the guerrillas' conception of the war they were going to initiate, and b) the urban centers' lack of means.

Both for the MIR and the ELN, the guerrilla war had to move from the countryside to the cities. In the first stage, its fundamental purpose was to win the support of the peasant masses and build a strong fighting vanguard, but this led not only to a neglect of the cities, but even to the issue of careful directives so that no premature action would be carried out there.

The goal was to establish a leadership in the countryside. It was feared that if an urban organization began to move too soon it would act on its own, thus creating problems of authority. But two factors worked against the guerrilla unit's retaining command of the movement.

First, one must realize how small both groups were. Opening four fronts in the mountains was already an effort beyond their capacity. It was practically impossible at the same time to set up an organization that would operate in both rural and urban regions. Therefore, almost all of the cadres were in the countryside when the uprising began.

If we add to this the disagreement which existed in the rest of the Left, from the Trotskyists to the Communist Party, as to the timeliness of the insurrection, and the Left's moral "solidarity" but lack of practical help, we will realize why, toward the middle of 1965, the cities remained calm while fighting was going on in the interior. This calm was broken only by the activity of the repressive forces and by some isolated uprisings carried out by elements not under the command of either of the active organizations.

More generally, we must remember the characteristics of Peruvian social life. Our country, which still has not achieved total social, economic, and cultural integration, never reacts as a whole. Strong barriers separate the people who live in the countryside from the city dwellers, the workers from the peasants, those who live in the mountains from those who live on the coast, the north from the south. Powerful actions which take place in certain zones have no repercussions in the rest of the country. That is what has happened throughout our history, and that is what happened in 1965 when the bloody battles in the mountains had no effect on the coast, where the people remained indifferent and did not react to the guerrilla war as the guerrillas had expected them to.

It is true that the guerrillas shook the reactionaries and the oligarchy, since the latter saw quite clearly the danger that our units represented to their stability, above all in a country with as explosive an economic situation as Peru's. But the people did not understand this because they lacked the same power of analysis. Nor did there exist a capable and active political leadership that could take advantage of what was happening for an effective propaganda campaign based on the example of the guerrillas. All the Left did was to publish a few timid messages in support of the guerrillas that did not reach beyond its own small sphere of influence.

However, it must be noted that through their actions the guerrillas in a few months created greater repercussions than had the Left in its entire history. But these repercussions did not include support actions by the people.

The mission that the combatants had given their few activists in the cities was to serve as point of liaison and coordination within our country and with the exterior. They were to supply men, arms, and equipment and to spread propaganda. These tasks were too great for such small groups, which soon lost all contact with the guerrillas when the latter were encircled.

Guerrillas and Peasants

The guerrillas were in a difficult position in regard to the peasant masses. For centuries there has been a tremendous imbalance in Peru between the urban middle and working classes, from which the guerrillas came, and the peasantry.

The man from the city discriminates against and feels superior to the man from the country, especially the Quechua peasant. And inversely, the latter distrusts the man from the city. The peasant has always seen him as the exploiter, the man who has come to take away his land, the master.

A very large proportion of our peasant population speaks only Quechua, and those who are bilingual prefer to speak their native language. They use Spanish only when they have to speak to the landowner. The division also exists in customs. The behavior of city dwellers often seems strange to the peasants and amuses or displeases them.

It is a question, then, of a social division which has deep historical roots in the colonial and republican periods and which can only be overcome by the efforts of the guerrillas themselves.

This may help explain why the process of recruitment of new guerrillas from the places where fighting was going on was very slow. But it could not have been otherwise, since these barriers were compounded by the frugal way in which the people who live in our countryside measure time—not in days, but in harvests.

The guerrillas needed, therefore, action and time to convince the peasants that the method they had adopted was correct: action to show them that they were really prepared to fight against their enemies, and time to carry out a good propaganda campaign to clarify each action both to groups and to individuals.

Meanwhile, the army was acting also. It was an army that knew, through the experiences their U.S. advisors had acquired in other countries, that a guerrilla unit must be smashed at the very beginning if it is to be destroyed at all.

The guerrillas lost this battle against time because most of them lacked the necessary ability to adapt rapidly, not only to the terrain, but also to the daily life, language, and customs of the peasants. This is a process which normally takes years. But anyone who wants to engage successfully in warfare in the Peruvian countryside must accomplish it in months.

The guerrilla unit was defeated before a close relationship had been established between its members and the peasants. This process, which is essential for the future of the revolution, was cut short.

There is a class factor at the bottom of all of this. The petit bourgeois origin of the guerrillas gave them all the virtues and defects appropriate to this social sector of our country.

While they possess daring, imagination, and romanticism, these advanced groups of the petite bourgeoisie have always been susceptible to sectarianism, an excessive love of publicity, the desire to lead, and a tendency to underestimate the adversary. This is why, at the same time that they displayed abundant heroism in battling the enemy and audacity in throwing themselves into a dangerous fight, they were incapable of assimilating themselves in a short period of time into a peasantry that observed their sudden appearance with surprise and bewilderment.

There was another difference. The ideals proclaimed by the guerrillas necessarily appeared remote to the peasants, who were interested above all in their concrete and even local demands. While the guerrillas advocated social revolution, the peasants wanted more tangible things, the realization of small demands that the revolutionaries were not always successful in incorporating into their program—in spite of the fact that these demands are the means for raising the people to a higher level of consciousness. The guerrillas' program was much more complicated and their goals much more distant.

During his entire existence the peasant is separated from the life of the nation and is unaware of the great national problems, even though he suffers their consequences. In general, there is no developed national consciousness in Peru. It has been systematically retarded by the ruling groups. Naturally, this consciousness does not exist in the countryside either. It is true that the peasants understand the meaning of the problems if they are explained in clear and simple language, but they do not feel them in their own flesh, as immediate, pressing issues which would make them fight.

The key problem for us at this stage lies in moving toward the peasantry, in making their worries and desires our own in order then to carry the peasants on toward higher objectives, in making the most of all the issues that arise from the struggle for land and the defense against the large landowners. It is not a question of moving into a peasant zone and calling on the inhabitants to follow us. We must unite ourselves with them and with their leaders and stand by their side in every eventuality. Their immediate local objectives must be incorporated into the general and ultimate objectives of the revolution.

Does this mean that we must modify our position to the extent of temporarily abandoning immediate armed actions?

Not in our opinion. It simply means that the guerrillas must be absolutely clear about the social framework within which they are going to move, and that they must use that framework as their starting point in planning and carrying out their actions. It means that guerrillas must broaden or limit their goals in accord with the social milieu in which they are working.

At the same time, it is necessary to consider the guerrilla struggle in the broadest possible terms, seeing it as part of a national struggle in which numerous revolutionary forces which may employ different methods have come into play. It is still possible that there may be new experiences similar to those of Hugo Blanco, since even the bourgeois agrarian reform, enacted in a timid law, has not been applied. Peru is very large and has many differing realities. The guerrillas must be ready to unite their efforts with those of other revolutionary groups, even though the latter may use different tactics.

The rebels must take into account the characteristics of the Peruvian peasantry. One is respect and obedience to communal authorities. The governor, representative, and mayor of the community represent the will of all its members and their decisions are obeyed without any discussion.

What effect does this have on the guerrillas? The members of the communities react collectively rather than individually, and the opinion of their authorities will determine to a great degree their attitude toward the revolutionaries. The guerrillas are not working with a simple mass but with an organism, a unity possessing its own power structure which must be respected if the outsiders are not to lose the people's trust or even come to be disliked by them. This will also allow the guerrillas, at certain times, to make use of a powerful collective force.

In 1965 the guerrillas were not able to make their methods one with those of the peasantry. The peasants and the guerrillas took separate paths because the guerrillas did not link themselves in time with the social upsurge that had been taking place in the countryside since 1965.

Summing up, we can say that the guerrillas must act and work not only for the distant objectives of the revolution, but also for the immediate ones of the peasants. And not only for the peasants, but with them.

Base and Leadership

The delay in seeing all the factors that were operating against the guerrillas and taking steps in time to correct them was due to the nature of many of the leading cadres.

It is true that the leaders were characterized by great honesty and revolutionary conviction, proven by the fact that they died fighting for their ideals. Nevertheless, they possessed too many other qualities and lacked too many to be able to deal adequately with the circumstances which arose.

We have already mentioned that the qualities of a party leader are not sufficient for the leader of an armed group. Physical adeptness, knowledge of the terrain, and skill in combat are all needed, and they are qualities that not all the leaders possessed in 1965. The decision to fight is not enough to make a man a guerrilla. Many comrades, who could have been excellent cadres in the urban resistance or in a liaison network, went to the countryside inspired by heroic determination but did not have the necessary stamina in spite of their iron wills. Without wanting to, they became a burden for their other, more physically fit, comrades and for the guerrilla unit as a whole. A more objective and pragmatic selection of the personnel would have secured better combat teams.

Meanwhile, hidden in the rank and file of the guerrillas and in the peasant masses were the cadres that a more careful process of selection would have raised to the positions of command that they would surely have earned in battle. But that process, which by its nature is long and slow, did not occur because the struggle was brief and violent.

Survival and Expansion

It is possible, as has been demonstrated in several countries in Latin America, for militarily able cadres who are politically convinced of the correctness of their struggle to survive despite violent and repeated attacks by armies experienced in counter-guerrilla warfare. The guerrilla unit can survive even without adequate "subjective" conditions in the population among which it is operating.

The problem lies in whether the unit can develop to the point at which it really endangers the system and the stability of the regime as a whole. Given all of the social characteristics that we have noted repeatedly—disconnection, imbalances, isolation—it is possible for a guerrilla band to survive for many years without having any effect on the system's vital points.

Guerrilla warfare is not dangerous for the ruling classes so long as it does not exacerbate other social contradictions, giving rise to forms of action that will work in conjunction with it.

In order to do this it is necessary to break with rigid systems of thought and action. Clinging to a single plan of action is always dangerous because it leads revolutionaries to a struggle that is isolated and one dimensional, exclusive and sectarian, closing off any possibilities of growth for the guerrilla unit.

We ought to add that dogmatism is more characteristic of those who carry out propaganda in favor of armed struggle than of those who engage in it.

Arms and Politics

Does armed struggle exclude politics? The answer has always been no, that there can be no contradiction between the two because, under the conditions that prevail in our countries, armed struggle *is* essentially a political struggle.

Our guerrillas must be able politicians at the same time that they are efficient soldiers, but they must not be the only politicians. While the armed struggle is developing in certain zones in the country, the political struggle must be carried throughout the nation in the most diversified forms.

What defines revolutionary conduct and distinguishes it from opportunism are its objectives and the consistent fashion in which they are pursued, and the subordination of all tactics to the only strategic objective which a person who calls himself a revolutionary can have: the seizure of power. When an organization or a group of revolutionaries sets the seizure of power as its objective and does not lose sight of that goal, all forms of action are possible and none should be rejected.

Strikes, passive resistance, public demonstrations, and mass mobilizations all allow guerrilla actions to be felt in the rest of the country and serve to overcome the guerrillas' isolation. Armed struggle in the countryside ought not necessarily to be reflected in terrorist activities in the cities except when it is absolutely necessary, politically clear, explainable to the people, and when it corresponds to the level the masses have achieved in their own action.

The situation in the countryside is similar. If the guerrillas resign themselves only to carrying out armed actions, their position will be more difficult than if they combine them with organizing the peasants and encouraging them to wage mass struggle for clear and concrete objectives.

We should not forget that all the peasant actions recorded in the history of our country have been collective in nature and carried out in the peasants' own name with leaders who have emerged from those same oppressed masses. The guerrilla unit can offer a revolutionary perspective to the peasant struggle through its operations, but it cannot replace that struggle. The guerrilla unit is only part of the whole; it is not the totality of the struggle.

By its mobile nature, the guerrilla band is everywhere and nowhere. When it is not present, the masses must defend themselves by their own means against enemy repression by organizing around the most outstanding leaders of the peasant resistance.

When the guerrillas were liquidated in 1965, the people were left defenseless, completely at the mercy of the army. This was the logical outcome of only organizing the peasants around the guerrilla band, in order to provide it with food and men, without considering the possibility of such a repression. The people were not prepared for this contingency because the guerrilla unit had not had time to prepare them nor had it even thought about the matter. In any case, it would not have been able to ready the people since it was still regarded as an alien body. The resistance must be organized by men who have emerged from the people themselves, the natives of that zone, accustomed to the kind of fight that did not take place here after the defeat of the guerrillas.

Mountains and Forests

It is essential to note that the geography of our country has forced the peasant population to concentrate itself in valleys and high zones, precisely where it is difficult and dangerous to carry on a guerrilla war of the kind known until now.

When we analyze the 1965 experience we see clearly how all of the guerrilla fronts were forced to withdraw into the forest zones of eastern Peru. They are the securest areas from the military point of view, but not from the political, because they have only a minimal population. The most densely populated zones are in the mountains and not the forest.

This is a problem which has still not been solved and which will appear again in future guerrilla actions. It will be overcome only when the guerrillas find ways of operating in the mountains and on the high, open plateaus. This is possible. Our country has a great guerrilla tradition, and the *montoneros* always operated in the Andes.

In short, the rebels will either have to learn how to make war in the mountains or they will have to stay in the forest. In the latter case, they will have to find effective means of influencing the peasantry of the mountains. For a long time those techniques will be political and propagandistic.

Does this mean that a party will have to be formed? At this time it should be, as long as it assures a sufficiently important role to the peasants in the leadership of the struggle, and provided that it does not give birth to a false leadership which becomes an obstacle to the free expression of the masses, and that it favors the growth of new revolutionary cadres arising from the people themselves. Only this way can the guerrilla band lay the foundations for a party through revolutionary action against the enemy.

Why 1965?

Was 1965 the appropriate year to initiate an insurrectional process in our country? Many critics of guerrilla warfare have asked this question, only to respond immediately that it wasn't.

It must be recognized that to the broad masses in our country the Belaúnde government still appeared an instrument of reform, thus creating illusions and hope. The people had not assimilated the experience of the massacres except in the zones that were directly affected, and the administrative corruption and immorality of the government officials had not been revealed in all their reality before the eyes of the urban population. Thus, when the guerrillas burst onto the national scene, shaking the foundations of the reactionary regime, the people were not able to grasp their exact meaning and justification.

We have said that we cannot wait for the proper subjective conditions before initiating the revolution. That is true, but we failed insofar as we did not wait for the guerrillas to have sufficiently obvious justification for beginning their operations, a justification that we needed in order to be able to give the masses the first objective explanations of our position. Despite the fact that the entire people cannot now and will not be able in the near future to understand the necessity of profoundly revolutionizing the system and replacing it with another, the reasons for beginning the rebellion must nevertheless be easily comprehensible.

Ideologically, our attitude was based on an underestimation of the cities. We thought that if guerrilla warfare began in the midst of the peasant population there was no reason to find a justification for it in terms of the bourgeois politics which are foreign, distant, and unknown to the peasantry.

That is completely true as far as the peasantry is concerned, but not in regard to the country as a whole. Thus we closed the road to successful revolutionary agitation among the urban masses. The workers and the poor and middle sectors of the cities were becoming increasingly disillusioned with bourgeois politics, but this was not sufficient to impel them to support actively armed rebellion against the system. Under these conditions, the attitude of the urban population was limited to vague sympathy on the part of some, enthusiasm in small —mainly student—sectors, and indifference on the part of the majority.

There was a powerful and decisive subjective reason for the early initiation of the armed struggle. Our groups were oriented toward action and found in it their only reason for existence. They had to choose very quickly between immediate action and long, gradual development as a party with an uncertain revolutionary future.

This was clearest in the ELN. Every revolutionary body has its own laws of growth and operation which it must fulfill or fall apart. If our organizations, and particularly the ELN, had not risen in arms within a brief period of time, they would have entered a fatal period of disintegration. Through action they bolstered their *esprit de corps* and strengthened themselves; in long passivity, engaged in interminable preparatory work, they ran the risk of collapsing as their members became discouraged.

In view of the process which followed Belaúnde's victory at the polls and determined his fall at the hands of the same people whom he had served so obsequiously, we can say that in later years there will be many opportunities for initiating an insurrectionary action which would have been fully justified in the eyes of the people.

But in 1965 we took up arms guided only by our own sense of readiness.

Lastly, neither organization knew the other's plans due to the reserve which existed between us. When the MIR announced that it was initiating guerrilla warfare at the beginning of 1965, the ELN was not, objectively, ready to do the same, but it had to move up the date of departure for its guerrillas from fear that a general repression would take its militants out of action.

It is possible that something similar occurred on the MIR fronts, this time through a lack of coordination—that, for example, the ambush at Yahuarina in which the first shot was fired on June 9, 1965, caught Luis de la Puente by surprise in Cuzco, where he had not finished his preparations. And it is possible that it took the guerrilla unit on the northern front, which had only just begun to get ready, still more by surprise. The result was that the army faced groups with different degrees of experience, some of which were not fully prepared for combat.

We have been reproached from different points of view for not elaborating a coherent ideological framework and not offering the masses a structured program.

This is partially true. It should not be forgotten that our insurrectionary Left developed from established political parties, and that as a result much of what it has said in regard to ideology and program reflects the transition from old concepts to new ones; this is clear from its statements on the existence and behavior of social classes, the composition of the oligarchy and its relationship with imperialism, the objectives and stages of the revolution, etc.

It is also true that because of insufficient and interrupted theoretical work, the Peruvian Left as a whole has not developed an interpretation of Peruvian reality based on serious study. It has always approached that reality from the point of view of its own preconceived systems. In Peru it has already become a cliché that since the death of Mariátegui, Marxists have ceased to study our reality with precision and a scientific spirit.

We do not deny this. It is partially the result of our ideological heritage, which still keeps us from seeing social changes clearly and leads us into a dogmatism that raises its head on every possible occasion.

But before fixing the program for each stage of the revolution with absolute precision, and at the same time making sure that it works theoretically, practically, and realistically, the Marxist Left ought to decide upon its general and final objectives with complete clarity.

What is the ultimate goal? In our countries it cannot be anything but socialism. "Either socialist revolution or the caricature of a revolution," Che said once. Every day the masses understand more clearly that "revolution" is a synonym for "socialism." We only deceive ourselves by talking about transitional forms that, as far as the enemy is concerned, are just euphemisms to cover up our true ends.

What kind of socialism do we want? The kind that assures the oppressed masses the effective exercise of power, participation in all the affairs of state, and broad control over the decisions affecting their own lives. The dictatorship of the proletariat can only be exercised through that unrestricted participation by the majority of the people which is the ultimate and decisive guarantee of the strength of the revolutionary regime.

In Peru, only an authentic socialism can assure national integration based on the community of interest of the entire people. Our revolution should seek, from the very beginning, political forms that will enable it to retain the support of the masses and avoid bureaucratic rigidity.

We know that this will not be easy in a country which, like ours, has always lived under the worst forms of domination, but we are confident that the revolutionary process, if it is guided by leaders who have sprung from the people and who are conscious of the problems of contemporary socialism, will achieve an effective and real socialism.

Meanwhile, we repeat that the peoples' armed struggle—complex, multiple, rich, and varied—is the only road left for liberating Latin America. The early failures suffered in Peru do not prove that it is futile to fight the oppressor. They simply show that we must correct our ideas, examine reality better, link ourselves to the people, train our fighters more adequately, and eliminate sectarianism and divisions within the revolutionary camp.

To achieve all of this, we must be objective and analytical in order to overcome our errors at the same time that we maintain our determination to continue the road we have undertaken with firmness and zeal.

In these pages we have tried to make a calm analysis of past events, and to invite others to engage in new and promising experiences.

11

Defeat in Bolivia

Inti Peredo

Inti (which in Quechua means "sun") was the fighting name of Guido Peredo Leige, one of the original four members of the Bolivian Communist Party who joined Che Guevara in the ill-fated campaign of the National Liberation Army (ELN), 1966–67. A committed revolutionary, Inti refused to abandon Guevara, even after he was ordered to do so by the secretary general of the party. Throughout the whole campaign he fought alongside Che and eventually became one of the comandante's *most trusted lieutenants. When Che was captured, Inti and five other* guerrilleros *managed to escape. Ironically, on October 8, 1967, Inti had been chosen by Guevara to occupy a position in a suicide detail to engage the enemy and thereby allow Che's column to escape, but the army concentrated on the detachment led by Guevara, allowing Inti and his comrades to avoid capture. Inti, another Bolivian (Darío), and three Cubans (Benigno, Urbano, and Pombo) crossed the border into Chile after successfully eluding an intense manhunt. A year after his ordeal, in "My Campaign with Che," Inti provided the only Bolivian eyewitness account of the* foco *led by Che. In the first segment of the selection that follows, Inti describes the painful last few hours spent alongside Guevara, before the Argentine's capture and execution. In the second, the* guerrillero *relates in vivid detail how he and his comrades were able to break the Bolivian army's encirclement and escape. Inti was in the process of reorganizing the ELN to reinitiate armed struggle when he was captured and executed by the army in 1969.*

From "My Campaign with Che," in *The Bolivian Diary of Ernesto Che Guevara*, ed. Mary-Alice Waters (New York: Pathfinder Press, 1994), 393–40. Translated by Michael Taber. © 1994 by Pathfinder Press. Reprinted by permission of Pathfinder Press.

The Yuro Ravine

The ambush at La Higuera marked a new stage for us, difficult and agonizing. We had lost three men and had virtually no forward detachment. El Médico continued doing poorly, and the column was reduced to only 17 guerrillas who were malnourished due to prolonged protein deficiency. With the question of Joaquín's fate now settled, Che's next steps were directed toward looking for another zone of operations with more favorable terrain. Our immediate need was to make contact with the city to solve logistical problems and receive human reinforcements, since our forces were being spent without being able to replace the men who had fallen.

However, it was first necessary to break out of two encirclements. One of these was practically in our very face, while we learned of the army's other circle from journalists' reports that filtered out and were broadcast on Argentine and Chilean radio. It was no mystery to anyone that our presence had been clearly detected, and this was also announced on international broadcasts. Local stations, however, which were silenced by the regime, gave only very general information.

Between September 27 and October 1 we remained in constant hiding, although some comrades carried out scouting missions to look for a way out along one of the ridges that would enable us to elude the enemy forces. Our rations were considerably reduced and consisted only of three-quarters of a small can of sardines and a canteen of water for the entire day. To make matters worse, the water was bitter. But that was all there was, and we went out looking for it at night, or when it was still dark during the early morning hours. Two comrades carried all the canteens. They climbed down into the ravines taking every precaution, erasing their tracks.

Up until September 30, large numbers of fully equipped soldiers passed in front of us without detecting our presence. On October 1 we began to move a little more rapidly. After days of privation, we ate fritters cooked by Chapaco, and Che ordered that each of us get a small piece of fried charqui. So that the fire would not be detected by the soldiers, we covered it with blankets.

The radio stations began to provide more information. One report of note was that Camba and León, who had deserted on September 26, had turned informer. Another report was that the army's general command had moved its forward post. Our marches were made with extreme caution, although at times we passed by fairly populated areas in broad daylight.

This was the situation as we came to October 8.

The previous evening marked eleven months since Che had gone into the mountains of Bolivia. Up to that point the balance sheet was not particularly unfavorable for us. The army had dealt us only one serious blow, at La Higuera, which on the other hand was accidental. Everything else had been positive on balance. Despite our small numbers, we had captured almost a hundred soldiers, including high-ranking officers; we had put a large number of enemy troops out of commission; and we had captured various weapons and a lot of ammunition.

We now faced a new tactical phase, where it was absolutely necessary to break out of the encirclement in order to reach a new zone of operations. There we would have been able to engage the enemy under conditions set by us, while at the same time making contact with the city, an important question in this period, in order to reinforce our column.

Anyone who reads Che's diary will realize that at no time can one detect desperation or lack of faith, despite the many anguished moments we had passed through. (It should be kept in mind that the diary contains only notations for Che's personal use, primarily reflecting negative aspects, with the aim of analyzing these and later correcting them.) That is why, in reviewing eleven months of operations, Che summed up his thoughts by saying that the time had passed "without complications, bucolically."

The early morning of October 8 was cold. Those of us with wool ponchos put them on. Our hike was slow because Chino walked badly at night, and because Moro's illness was getting worse. At 2:00 A.M. we stopped to rest, resuming our hike at 4:00. We were 17 silent figures, camouflaged in darkness, walking through a narrow canyon called the Yuro ravine.

At dawn a beautiful sun broke out over the horizon, enabling us to carefully scan the terrain. We were looking for a hillcrest we could take to the San Lorenzo river. Extreme security measures were taken, particularly because the gorge and the hill were semibarren, with very low bushes, making it almost impossible to hide.

Che then decided to send out three pairs of scouts: one along the hill to the right, made up of Benigno and Pacho; another along the hill to the left, made up of Urbano and another comrade; and the last one to the area in front of us, assigned to Aniceto and Darío. Benigno and Pacho soon returned with news that left no doubt as to the situation: soldiers were closing off the pass. The problem was to know whether they had detected us or not.

What were the alternatives left to us?

We could not turn back, since the path we had taken, very unprotected, would make us easy targets for the soldiers. Nor could we go forward, since this would mean walking straight into the position occupied by the soldiers. Che made the only decision possible at that moment. He gave the order to hide in a small lateral canyon, and organized the taking of positions. It was approximately 8:30 A.M. The 17 of us were positioned at the center and at both sides of the canyon, waiting.

The great dilemma faced by Che, and all of us, was to know whether the army had discovered our presence, or whether this was simply a tactical maneuver within the broader encirclement they had been putting in place for several days.

Che made a rapid analysis. If the soldiers attacked between 10:00 A.M. and 1:00 P.M., we would be at a profound disadvantage, and our prospects would be minimal, since it would be very difficult to resist for a prolonged period of time. If they attacked between 1:00 and 3:00 P.M., our prospects for neutralizing them were better. If the battle occurred from 3:00 P.M. on, the advantage would be ours, since night would soon be falling, and night is comrade and ally to the guerrilla.

At approximately 11:00 A.M., I went to replace Benigno at his position, but he did not climb down and instead remained there spread out on the ground, since the wound in his shoulder had become infected and was very painful. Benigno, Darío, and I would remain there from then on. On the other side of the ravine were Pombo and Urbano, and in the center was Che with the rest of the combatants.

At approximately 1:30 P.M., Che sent Ñato and Aniceto to relieve Pombo and Urbano. To cross over to their position, we had to cross a clearing that the enemy's position overlooked. The first to try it was Aniceto, but he was killed by a bullet.

The battle had begun. Our exit was closed off. The soldiers shouted, "We got one! We got one!"

From the same narrow gorge, in a position occupied by soldiers, one could hear the regular rattle of machine guns, which appeared to cover the path we had come through the night before.

The group I was in was positioned directly facing one section of the army, at an equal height, which enabled us to observe their movements without being seen. We therefore fired only when fired upon, to not give ourselves away. The army, for its part, believed that all our firing was coming from down below, i.e., from Che's position.

The most difficult situation was that of Pombo and Urbano. Hidden behind a rock, they were under constant fire. They were unable to leave, because if they crossed the clearing they could be wiped out with ease, as happened to Aniceto. Attempting to force them out from that natural fortification, the enemy threw a grenade. The explosion raised a cloud of dust that Pombo and Urbano seized upon. With impressive speed they ran across the clearing as the soldiers fired in their general direction and shouted aggressively. Both of them ended up right where Ñato was waiting for them.

The three of them tried to retreat along a path indicated previously by Che in order to reach a meeting place agreed upon earlier. Nevertheless, they were able to see us, and understood our signal to stay where they were.

The battle continued without interruption. We fired only when fired upon to not give ourselves away and to save ammunition. From our position we put a number of soldiers out of action.

When it got dark we climbed down to meet up with Pombo, Urbano, and Ñato and to look for our knapsacks. We were now in our element. We asked Pombo, "Where's Fernando?"

"We thought he was with you," they responded.

We put on our knapsacks and headed quickly to the contact point. Along the way we found food supplies thrown on the ground, including flour. This troubled us deeply, because Che never permitted anyone to throw food on the ground. When it was necessary to do so, it would be carefully hidden. Farther ahead I found Che's plate, completely trampled. I recognized it immediately, because it was a wide bowl made of aluminum with unique characteristics. I picked it up and stored it in my knapsack.

We found no one at the meeting place, although we recognized footprints from Che's sandals, which left a different mark than the others, making it easy to identify. But these tracks disappeared farther ahead.

We assumed that Che and the others had headed toward the San Lorenzo river, as foreseen, with the aim of hiding out in the woods, far from the army's reach, until arriving at the new zone of operations.

That night the six of us walked along: Pombo, Benigno, Ñato, Darío, Urbano, and myself. Our load was lighter, since at the bottom of the ravine we had thrown out a number of items that seemed unnecessary. Lightening our burden meant we could walk faster.

My knapsack was open and the radio had been taken out. Undoubtedly the person who took it out was Che before retreating. This was natural. A cool-headed man, always looking ahead, Che never organized an unplanned, desperate retreat. On the contrary, at moments of great decision, his stature as a leader, both militarily and politically, grew gigantically. It was therefore obvious that he took out the radio to listen to news, since obtaining information is a very important element in the woods.

We marched silently. None of us could hide our immense concern for the fate of Che and the other comrades.

After losing the tracks of our people, we came once again to La Higuera, a place that brought back painful memories that had still not been erased. We sat down almost in front of the schoolhouse there. The dogs barked persistently, but we did not know whether they were barking at us or were responding to the songs and shouts of the soldiers who were in a state of drunken euphoria that night.

Never did we imagine that so close to us was our beloved commander, wounded but still alive!

Over the course of time, I have thought that perhaps had we known it, we would have attempted a desperate action to save him, even though we would surely have died in the process.

But on that tense and agonizing night, we knew absolutely nothing of what had happened. In low voices we asked each other if other comrades had perhaps been killed in the battle, in addition to Aniceto.*

We continued walking, circling around La Higuera without moving very far away. At dawn, with the first ray of daylight, we hid ourselves in not very dense brush. We had decided to walk only at night, since daytime required rigorous vigilance.

October 9 was calm and peaceful. Twice we saw a helicopter pass overhead. This was precisely the one carrying the still-warm body of Che, cowardly murdered on the orders of the CIA and of the military thugs Barrientos and Ovando. However, we knew nothing of this.

Our only communication with the outside world was a small radio that had belonged to Coco, but was now carried by Benigno. That afternoon Benigno heard a confused report. A local station announced that the army had captured a seriously wounded guerrilla who seemingly was Che. We immediately discounted this as a possibility, since if it were true they would be making a big fuss out of it. We thought the wounded person might be Pacho, and that the confusion resulted from a certain resemblance between the two.

That night we walked through hellish ravines and over steep and jagged cliffs that even goats would not have chosen. But Urbano and Benigno,

*Also killed in the battle were Antonio and Arturo. Pacho was captured, gravely wounded; he received no medical attention and died during the night. Captured and murdered were Chino, Willy, and Che.

with their extraordinary sense of direction and unbreakable resolve, guided us slowly out of the encirclement.

We moved slowly. On October 10 we found ourselves at a spot still close to La Higuera, and we joked that the water we were drinking was the same as the soldiers were drinking down below. We again waited for nightfall to reach Abra del Picacho, through which we hoped to break out of the encirclement.

At approximately one o'clock in the afternoon, Urbano heard a news report that left us frozen: the radio was announcing the death of Che and described his physical appearance and clothing. There was no possibility of a mistake, because in describing his clothing they listed the sandals made by Ñato, a wool poncho that had belonged to Tuma and that Che wore at night, and other details we knew perfectly.

A profound pain came over us, leaving us mute. Che—our leader, comrade, and friend; the heroic guerrilla; the man of exceptional ideas—was dead. The horrendous and lacerating news produced deep anguish.

We remained there unable to utter a sound, with fists clenched, as if afraid of breaking into tears at the first word. I looked at Pombo; tears were streaming down his face.

Four hours later the silence was broken. Pombo and I spoke briefly. The night of the ambush at the Yuro ravine, the six of us had agreed that he would assume command of our group until we met up with Che and the rest of our comrades. It was necessary at that very special moment, to make a decision that would honor the memory of our beloved leader. We exchanged some ideas, and later the two of us spoke to our comrades.

It is difficult to recall exactly, in minute detail, a moment filled with so many emotions, with such deep feeling, with such intense pain, and with such a desire to cry out to revolutionaries that all was not lost, that Che's death was not a burial of his ideas, that the war was not over.

How can one describe each of our faces? How can one faithfully reproduce all the words, the gestures, the reactions made amid that awesome solitude, under the constant threat of the military cannibals seeking to assassinate us, offering rewards for our capture "dead or alive"?

All I remember is that with a very great sincerity and an immense desire to survive, we swore to continue the struggle, to fight until death or until reaching the city, where we could begin again the task of rebuilding Che's army, in order to return to the mountains and continue fighting as guerrillas.

With firm voices, but laden with emotion, we made our pledge that afternoon—the same pledge that hundreds of men in all parts of the world have now taken—to turn Che's dream into reality.

Thus, on the afternoon of October 10, Ñato, Pombo, Darío, Benigno, Urbano, and I stated out loud, in the jungles of Bolivia:

"Che: Your ideas have not died. We who fought at your side pledge to continue the struggle until death or the final victory. Your banners, which are ours, will never be lowered. Victory or death!"

Breaking the Encirclement

How did we survive the encirclements placed around us after the battle at the Yuro ravine, against forces vastly superior in both numbers and weapons?

Some may think it was solely the result of the elemental factor called the "survival instinct" or the desire to continue living. I sincerely believe this was not the only reason.

It is true we wanted to continue living, but that was not all. In essence, we maintained our aggressiveness and were ready to engage in combat at any moment, as we had always been.

Was it impossible, then, to break out of the tight enemy encirclement and return to the city in search of contacts to continue the struggle?

On the afternoon of October 10, after pledging never to desert the revolutionary process, we made plans to break out of the encirclement and decided to look for the other survivors. Through radio reports we learned that the army knew that only ten guerrillas remained alive. Our group was composed of the six already mentioned. The other group, whose direction we did not know but assumed to be the same as ours, was composed of Chapaco, Moro, Eustaquio, and Pablito. The deserters Camba and León collaborated with the army in identifying us and giving the exact number of those remaining.

We had already realized how the enemy's encirclement was organized, and we knew how the soldiers were proceeding. We therefore decided to break through at the most abrupt point. Unfortunately, on October 11 Moro, Pablito, Eustaquio and Chapaco were killed at the mouth of the Mizque river.* These comrades would surely have made the same decision we did to never give themselves up, and they died in combat with dignity. They

---

*Moro was killed in the fighting. The three others were wounded (Chapaco gravely) and captured; they were subsequently murdered. The fighting took place in the early morning of October 12.

chose a route in the opposite direction from ours (to the south), obviously attempting to reach the city, as we were. The only ones remaining now were us.

We were in poor physical condition. We had eaten little and had exerted great efforts during the previous days. In addition, the great tension we had been under also left its mark on us.

We lightened our load once again. Ñato, who carried all the medical supplies, buried them, since these would be of no use to us in the future. The metal box that had been used previously for sterilization was turned into a cooking pot. The flour soup we prepared after so many days of privation served only to "fool our insides," but did not restore our strength.

In the early morning hours of October 12, we began walking in the direction of one part of the circle. At 3:00 A.M. we crossed the road to La Higuera at the Abra del Picacho, just as we had done earlier with Che. It was completely silent all around. When it got light we were at the other side of the pass. We came upon a hut and decided to go ask its inhabitants for the exact location, reorient ourselves, try to stock up on food supplies, and continue on. We looked for the peasants but found no one. Remaining in the hut was too dangerous, so we decided it would be better to hide ourselves in the bushes surrounding the house.

Two totally opposite events marked the day. A boy about twelve years old, very alert, identified our exact location for us. He pointed out the direction of the river, offered us a pot to cook in, and began to milk a cow for us. Unfortunately, a peasant passing by saw us and ran off toward the pass to denounce us to the soldiers, large numbers of whom were concentrated there as part of the strategic encirclement around our dwindling column. Owing to our physical weakness, we were unable to catch up with him. And because he was a peasant, we did not want to shoot him.

In this emergency situation, we were compelled to leave immediately, without cooking and without waiting for the milk. We circled around a steeply sloped creek that emptied into the San Lorenzo river. Then Urbano, who was walking at the front, saw soldiers who were already in position. Possessing all the technical resources, they had passed ahead of us and were there waiting for us.

Urbano, who had rapid reflexes, opened fire immediately. The soldiers returned the fire.

This was the last time we carried knapsacks. Forced by circumstance to escape the enemy at great speed, we took only the ration of sugar and our respective wool ponchos. The rest we threw away.

We climbed a hill beside us that was very steep and dangerous, as one could fall to the other side of the creek. Since the ravines were the only place in the area with trees, we were forced to get out any way possible to seek a better position. We dragged ourselves to a type of wooded "island," with an area of approximately 50 square meters. The situation was relatively worse than before, because the small grove was surrounded by open plains where the soldiers could easily kill us. We hid and kept silent, hoping they would not spot us, waiting for nightfall, when we could leave.

Some peasants began to circle around the area, and the army began to surround it. At approximately 4:30 P.M. on October 12, a tight circle of soldiers was moving in on the "island." This was their best opportunity to eliminate us, but the final word had not been spoken.

The six of us resolved to group ourselves in the highest part of the small wood, and to respond to enemy fire only when we were sure of hitting the mark. The soldiers opened fire, insulting us and calling on us to surrender. We kept our silence, aware of their movements.

These were extremely difficult moments. We thought our last moment had arrived, and prepared ourselves to die with dignity. At one point I proposed that we bury the remaining money and watches, to avoid having these fall into the hands of the soldiers. Pombo, however, with much assurance, stated that we would be able to break out of the circle at night. We all kept our respective belongings.

Our silence disconcerted the army. Some soldiers, showing their fear, shouted, "There's no one here. Let's go." Others insulted us.

A new operation was soon begun. Groups of soldiers began to "comb" the little island, an easy task given its small size. When they were close, we opened fire. Three soldiers and a guide fell dead.

The troops retreated, but immediately began to fire bursts of machine gun fire and grenades, since our position was now located. They also changed their insolent tone. Now they no longer insulted us, but shouted, "Guerrillas, surrender! Why continue fighting when your leader is dead?"

As Pombo had foreseen, the firing stopped when night fell. But to our misfortune, there appeared a beautiful moon, showering its light on every corner. To try to leave under such circumstances was too risky.

We remained vigilant. A terrible chill had fallen and went right through one's clothing down to the bone. We shivered as we watched the sky, waiting for the moon to be obscured.

At 3:00 A.M., clouds came down over the entire area. This was the moment we had been waiting for with impatience. We crawled slowly. To our surprise, the soldiers had pulled back a bit. Apparently the four losses they suffered during the afternoon drove them to take precautions. Soon we were close to enemy positions. The soldiers were posted five meters apart from each other. The weather and the wait had affected them as well.

We continued advancing until suddenly one of the soldiers, instead of firing, shouted, "Halt! Who goes there?"

That was our salvation. We threw ourselves at one of the trenches, killed a few of the soldiers, and crouched together there. An intense exchange of fire broke out on all sides, lasting approximately 15 minutes or longer. When it ended, we began to leave. The army's encirclement had been broken.

Our escape from the mountains has been utilized by writers and journalists to concoct fantastic tales. Some day—because now is not the time, since we would be hurting the peasants who helped us—we will relate the details of this action, which in truth did have its incredible and fascinating aspects. We will only say that had it not been for this solidarity, our survival would have been extremely difficult.

Beginning in the early morning of October 13, we walked only at night, trying to avoid contact with the population, except when this was absolutely necessary for acquiring food or obtaining information. We were somewhat wary, since some peasants—not all and not the majority—motivated by the 10-million-peso reward for our "heads," as the radios announced, would run off to denounce us to the soldiers. But there were many peasants who helped us leave this vulnerable area, guiding us to Vallegrande, providing us with food, giving us valuable information, and remaining silent despite the beatings, threats, and even robbery they suffered at the hands of the army.

For a month we walked toward the Cochabamba-to-Santa Cruz highway. On November 13 we made our first serious attempt to head toward the city. Ñato and Urbano reached Mataral to buy sandals and clothes, to change our threadbare "suits" and modify our sinister appearance. At the store in town, they obtained information that the soldiers were aware of our presence and were preparing for combat against us. They immediately returned to warn us. In the afternoon we noticed several patrols persistently looking for us. We remained in hiding all day. That night we started walking again, crossed the highway, and tried to leave the area. However, on November 14 the army discovered us, and once again we engaged in unequal combat. At the top of a hill, when we were close to escaping the enemy forces, Ñato was struck by a bullet. We formed a line of defense and dragged him toward our position, but he was already dead.

Ñato was a man dear to all, firm in his convictions, courageous, ready to find solutions to the small domestic problems that sometimes accumulate and lead to so many unpleasant consequences. He died in our last battle, after having faced greater dangers than this one in which he lost his life. Such are the fortunes of war. As a simple tribute to this prototype of a man of the people, one can only say: He was a complete guerrilla and a man loyal to the ideas of liberation.

From Mataral we marched parallel to the highway, hoping that our people in the city, who had received hard blows, would realize our maneuver and come to help get us out of the mountains. However, fierce repression had destroyed the weak organization we still had left, and the remaining cadres found themselves in a difficult situation, making it very hard for them to operate. Our movements were easily detected by the army, since we inevitably left signs of our passage. Therefore, until December we had many other skirmishes with the soldiers, inflicting new casualties on them.

We have deliberately never told how we emerged from the mountains, because this would endanger the lives of a number of peasants and their families who risked everything for us, along with honest revolutionaries from the city.* They understood the meaning of our struggle and risked what little they had to create the conditions for us to be able to initiate the stage of rebuilding the ELN. Some day in the not-too-distant future, we will be able to acknowledge them. It is necessary to state, however, that this type of generous solidarity gives the categorical lie to those who hold that the rural population is immune to revolutionary ideas and that "nothing can be done." Fortunately, we can proudly say the opposite. Moreover, we are certain that in the next stage of the guerrilla struggle, the peasants will sooner or later come over massively to our side, since our army represents their aspirations of social, economic, and political progress.

As a brief epilogue, we can state the following: Urbano and I were the first to reach the city. There we made contact with other comrades and organized the arrival of Pombo, Benigno, and Darío.

The rest of the story is known, although it has not yet ended. The second part will soon be written, with new guerrilla actions in the jungles of Bolivia.

---

*An account of this escape, written by Peredo's father-in-law, at the time a prominent member of the Communist Party, is contained in Jesús Lara, *Guerrillero Inti* (Mexico City: Editorial Diógenes, 1972).

12

Problems and Principles of Strategy

Carlos Marighella

*Unlike other revolutionaries of his time, Carlos Marighella was already
a middle-aged man when he quit the orthodox Communist Party of Brazil
to found the Revolutionary Communist Party of Brazil (PCRB). An admirer of the Cuban Revolution, he attended the Organization of Latin
American Solidarity (OLAS) conference in Havana in 1967 and returned
to Brazil a convinced and dedicated revolutionary. After the PCRB,
Marighella started the Action for National Liberation (ALN) guerrilla
group that went into action in 1968. Throughout his short career as a
revolutionary—he was gunned down by the army in 1969—Marighella
advocated the creation of armed fronts in the cities and the countryside.
A revolutionary strategist like Che Guevara and Luis de la Puente,
Marighella produced a significant body of work including the* Minimanual
of the Urban Guerrilla, Letters from Havana, *and* For the Liberation of
Brazil. *All of his writings, with the exception of his forays into poetry and
fiction, dealt with preparing a viable plan to carry out urban guerrilla
struggles throughout Latin America. From Marighella's perspective, Che's
death in Bolivia had not signified the end of the revolutionary struggle in
Latin America; it had instead posited the need to reevaluate and readapt
his theories to different settings, such as the cities of the most urbanized
countries of Latin America. In "Problems and Principles of Strategy" he
lays out a step-by-step directory of how to maximize the effectiveness of
urban guerrillas working in concert with their rural equivalent.*

The most important problem of the Brazilian revolution is that of strategy, and regarding this—the sense in which it should be directed—
there exists no complete accord among revolutionaries. Our organization has adopted a determined strategic concept through which it has

From *Urban Guerrilla Warfare in Latin America*, ed. James Kohl and John
Litt (Cambridge, MA: MIT Press, 1974), 81–86. © 1974 by MIT Press. Reprinted
by permission of MIT Press.

been oriented, but it is evident that other organizations have different viewpoints.

The concepts and principles expressed here refer, therefore, to those questions about which our organization can give an opinion acquired from experience. For us the strategy of the Brazilian revolution is guerrilla warfare. Guerrilla warfare forms part of revolutionary people's warfare. In "Some Questions About the Brazilian Guerrillas" we have already established the principles that orient our strategy, and for those who wish to know them it is sufficient to refer to the mentioned work. To the principles already enumerated there, we would like to add some others which will help form an idea of our strategic concepts regarding the Brazilian revolution.

Study and application of these principles by revolutionary groups combined with the personal experience of militants will contribute to a better comprehension not only of the desired objectives of our struggle, but also of the fundamental means to reach them. The following are the strategic principles to which we refer:

The Strategy of the National Liberation Action

1. In a country like Brazil, where a permanent political crisis exists resulting from a deepening of the chronic structural crisis together with the general crisis of capitalism and where, as a consequence, military power has been established, our strategic principle is to transform the political crisis into an armed struggle of the people against military rule.

2. The basic principle of revolutionary strategy under the conditions of a permanent political crisis is to release, in the city as well as in the countryside, such a volume of revolutionary action that the enemy will be obliged to transform the political situation into a military one. Then dissatisfaction will reach all the strata of society, and the military will be held absolutely responsible for all failures.

3. The main aim of revolutionary strategy in the transformation of the permanent political crisis into an armed struggle and of the political situation into a military solution, is to destroy the bureaucratic-military machine of the state and replace it with the people in arms.

4. To destroy the bureaucratic-military apparatus of the Brazilian state, revolutionary strategy starts from the premise that that apparatus, within the conditions of the permanent political crisis that characterizes the national situation, entails ever closer relations with the interests of North American imperialism. This machine cannot be destroyed unless the main blow is aimed against North American imperialism,

which is the common enemy of humanity and primarily of the Latin American, Asian, and African peoples.

5. Our conception of revolutionary strategy is global both in the sense that its main function consists in countering the global strategies of North American imperialism and in the sense that the political and military strategies exist and act as one, rather than as two separate entities. At the same time, tactical functions are subordinate to strategy, and there exists no possibility of their employment outside of this subordination.

6. Given the global character of our strategy, in undertaking the struggle for the overthrow of the military, we must take into account as a strategic principle the radical transformation of the class structure of Brazilian society toward the goal of socialism. North American imperialism is our principal enemy and we must transform the struggle against it into a national liberation and antioligarchic action.

Thus, in the face of revolutionary attacks, the military will be compelled to come to the defense of North American imperialism and of the Brazilian oligarchy and will become publicly discredited. On the other hand, with the overthrow of military power and the annihilation of its armed forces, we shall expel the North Americans and destroy the Brazilian oligarchy, eliminating the obstacles in the road to socialism.

Strategies of Urban and Rural Struggle

1. The urban struggle acts as a complement to the rural struggle, and thus all urban warfare, whether from the guerrilla front or from the mass front (with the support of the respective supply network), always assumes a tactical character.

2. The decisive struggle is the one in the strategic area (i.e., the rural area) and not the one that evolves in the tactical area (i.e., the city).

3. If by some mistake, urban guerrilla warfare were to be conducted as the decisive struggle, the strategic conflict in the rural area of the peasantry would become relegated to a secondary level. Noting the weak or nonexistent participation of the peasantry in the struggle, the bourgeoisie would take advantage of such circumstances to suborn and isolate the revolution; it will try to maneuver the proletariat which, lacking the support of its fundamental ally, the peasantry, will try to preserve untouched the bureaucratic-military apparatus of the state.

4. Only when the reactionary armed forces have already been destroyed and the military-bourgeois state cannot continue to act against the

masses, can a general strike in the city be called which, in combination with guerrilla struggle, will lead to victory. This principle, derived from that which affirms that the primary end of revolutionary struggle is the destruction of the military-bureaucratic apparatus and its substitution with the people in arms, is employed to prevent the bourgeoisie from subverting the general strike and resorting to a coup d'état in order to seize the initiative from the revolutionaries and cut their road to power.

Strategy of the Urban Guerrilla

1. Because the city is the complementary area of struggle, the urban guerrilla must play a tactical role in support of the rural guerrilla. We must make of the urban guerrilla therefore an instrument for the destruction, diversion, and containment of the armed forces of the dictatorship in order to avoid their concentration of repressive operations against the rural guerrilla.
2. In the process of unleashing the urban guerrilla, the forms of struggle that we employ are not those of mass struggle, but those of small armed groups supplied with firepower and dedicated to the battle against the dictatorship. Seeing that the firepower of the revolutionaries is directed against their enemies, the masses, who until then were powerless before the dictatorship, will look upon the urban guerrillas with sympathy and lend them their support.
3. The forms of struggle that characterize the urban guerrilla are guerrilla tactics and armed actions of all types, actions of surprise and ambush, expropriations, seizure of arms and explosives, revolutionary terrorist acts, sabotage, occupations, raids, punishment of North American agents or police torturers, in addition to flash meetings, distribution of leaflets, painting of murals by armed groups, etc.
4. The infrastructure of the urban and rural guerrillas have common points: the training and specialization of the guerrilla; physical conditioning; self-defense; the utilization of professional skills; the technical preparation of homemade weapons; the development of firepower and training for its handling; information networks; means of transportation and communication; medical resources and first aid. Our aim is to rely on both infrastructures, in order not to be reduced to one or the other guerrilla forms, and to combine the two correctly.
5. Revolutionaries engaged in guerrilla warfare give enormous importance to the mass movement in the urban area and to its forms of struggle, such as acts of restitution, strikes, marches, protests, boycotts, etc. Our strategic principle with respect to the urban mass move-

ment is to participate in it with the objective of creating an infrastructure for armed struggle by the working class, students, and other forces: to employ urban guerrillas and to unleash their operations through the use of armed mass groups.

Strategy of the Rural Guerrilla

1. Peasant struggles resulting from demands against landlords, or from the organization of rural syndicates, will develop into armed clashes and in this sense are positive. However, without firepower the peasants will be crushed by the forces of reaction. It is unlikely that rural guerrillas will emerge, in a strategic sense, out of peasant conflicts. The Brazilian peasantry has a very limited political consciousness and its tradition of struggle does not reach farther than mysticism or banditry; its experience of class struggle under the direction of the proletariat is recent and limited.

    Under the present conditions of the country, dominated by the dictatorship, the strategic struggle in the rural area will develop from a guerrilla infrastructure emerging among the peasantry. Seeing in their midst the emergence of a firepower that combats the landlords and does not violate their interests, the peasants will support and participate in guerrilla warfare.

2. The main strategic principle of guerrilla struggle is that it can neither have any consequence nor any decisive character in revolutionary warfare unless it is structured and consolidated in an armed alliance of workers and peasants united with students. Such an alliance, supplied with growing firepower, will give the guerrillas firm foundations and advance their cause. The armed alliance of the proletariat, peasantry, and the middle class is the key to victory.

3. Rural guerrilla warfare is decisive because, in addition to the extreme mobility possible in the interior of the country, it leads to the formation of the revolutionary army of national liberation which can be built from an embryo constituted by the armed alliance of workers and peasants with students. The peasants, without whom the revolution cannot reach its ultimate consequences, are impossible to incorporate into the urban guerrillas.

4. In no event should the Brazilian guerrilla defend areas, territories, regions, or any base or fixed position. If we were to do such, we would permit the enemy to concentrate its forces in campaigns of annihilation against known and vulnerable targets.

5. The Brazilian rural guerrilla should always be mobile. Similarly, the urban guerrilla ought to be extremely mobile and never stage an

occupation without meticulously organizing a retreat. Revolutionary warfare in Brazil is a war of movement, whatever the circumstances.

6. The guerrilla plays the principal strategic role in revolutionary warfare, and his political objective is the formation of a revolutionary army of national liberation and the seizure of power. In the revolutionary struggle we must avoid the distortion of this political objective and prevent the guerrilla, urban or rural, from transforming himself into an instrument of banditry, or unifying with bandits or employing their methods.

Organizational Strategy

1. The continental size of the country, the varying strategic importance of its areas, and the principle of diversity of revolutionary action combine with other factors to determine the existence or emergence of multiple revolutionary centers with regional coordination. Such revolutionary centers will dedicate themselves to implementing a guerrilla infrastructure to unleash the revolutionary struggle and dispose freely of political and tactical action at the regional level.

2. The strategic direction and global tactics of our organization—i.e., the unified political and military direction—will not emerge at once. Such leadership is formed through a permanent process in which armed struggle assumes the fundamental form of guerrilla warfare, going from the strategic field to the tactical and vice versa, until affirming itself in a group of men and women identified with revolutionary action and capable of carrying it to its ultimate consequences.

3. The revolutionary unity of our organization exists in terms of the strategic, tactical, and organic principles that we have adopted and not in terms of names or personalities. It is this identity of ideology, theory, and practice which will ensure that unconnected revolutionaries in various parts of the country will perform acts that will identify them as belonging to the same organization.

13

Thirty Questions to a Tupamaro

*Originally founded in 1963, the National Liberation Movement (MLN-Tupamaros) became one of the most romantic and romanticized guerrilla groups in Latin America. Characterized by their strict discipline and the mathematical precision of their actions, they were led by Raúl Sendic, who had extensive experience as an advocate of the agricultural workers in the Uruguayan countryside (*peludos*). The name Tupamaros came from the pejorative term used by Spaniards during colonial times to designate rebels after the fall of the Peruvian leader Tupac Amaru II. Despite the overwhelming number of middle-class members, not surprising in an eminently middle-class country, the Tupamaros also counted many industrial and rural workers in their ranks.*

The interview "Thirty Questions to a Tupamaro" started circulating as an internal document. The identities of the interviewer and the respondent remain unknown. From the answers provided by the interview, it appears that at the beginning the MLN seems to have been more concerned with exposing the weaknesses of the government than with overthrowing it. Years later, after the imposition of a military dictatorship in 1973, the overthrow of the government became their main objective. The Tupamaros, unlike more doctrinaire revolutionary groups, relied more on their praxis than on involved and complex ideological and theoretical discussions. They hoped to join with members of other revolutionary organizations in other countries to stage a widespread continental revolution. Their dreams never came to pass, as the organization did not survive the repressive measures adopted by the government. When a semblance of normalcy returned to Uruguay in 1984, those Tupamaros who were still alive realized that the time had come for them to seek incorporation into the political mainstream.

1. What has been the fundamental principle on which you have based the activity of your organization until now?

From *Urban Guerrilla Warfare in Latin America*, ed. James Kohl and John Litt (Cambridge, MA: MIT Press, 1974), 227–36. © 1974 by MIT Press. Reprinted by permission of MIT Press.

The principle that revolutionary action in itself, the very act of arming oneself, preparing, equipping, and pursuing activities that violate bourgeois legality, generates revolutionary consciousness, organization, and conditions.

2. What is the fundamental difference between your organization and other organizations of the left?
The majority of the latter seem to place their faith in making declarations and issuing theoretical statements about revolution in order to prepare militants and revolutionary conditions; they do not realize that fundamentally it is revolutionary action which precipitates revolutionary situations.

3. Could you give me any historical example illustrating the principle that revolutionary action generates revolutionary consciousness, organization, and conditions?
Cuba is an example. In place of the long process of forming a Party of the masses, a guerrilla *foco* of a dozen men was installed, and this deed generated revolutionary consciousness, organization, and conditions. Given the revolutionary fait accompli, authentic revolutionaries saw themselves as obliged to follow in its path.

4. Do you mean to say that once revolutionary action is launched, the famous unity of the left can develop in the struggle?
Yes, the forces calling themselves revolutionary will find themselves obliged to choose between support or disappearance. In Cuba, the Popular Socialist Party[1] opted to support the struggle, which it had neither initiated nor led, and survived. But Prío Socarrás,[2] who called himself the principal opponent of Batista, did not support it and disappeared.

5. This is with respect to the left, but what of the people in general?
For the people—those who truly disagree with the injustices of the regime—the choice is much simpler. They want change, and they must choose between the improbable and remote change which some offer through proclamations, manifestos, or parliamentary action and the direct road embodied by the armed group and its revolutionary action.

6. Do you mean to say that the armed struggle, at the same time that it is destroying bourgeois power, can create the mass movement an insurrectional organization needs to make the revolution?
Yes, without considering as lost that effort used to create a Party or Movement of the masses before beginning the armed struggle, it must be recognized that the armed struggle hastens and precipitates the mass

movement. And Cuba is not the only example; in China, too, the mass Party was created in the course of the armed struggle. That is to say that the rigid formula of certain theoreticians "first create the Party, then begin the Revolution," is historically more the exception than the rule. At this stage of history nobody can deny that an armed group, however small, has more possibility of becoming a people's army than does a group limited to issuing revolutionary "positions."

7. Nevertheless, a revolutionary movement needs a platform, documents, etc.
Of course, but one should not be confused. It is not only by polishing platforms and programs that the Revolution is made. The basic principles of socialist revolution are given and tested in countries like Cuba—there is nothing more to discuss. It is sufficient to adhere to those principles and to show in action the insurrectional road to their application.

8. Do you believe that a revolutionary movement should prepare for armed struggle even when conditions for the armed struggle are not present?
Yes, for at least two reasons. Because an armed movement of the left can be attacked by repression at any point in its development, it should be prepared to defend its existence . . . remember Argentina and Brazil. Also, because if each militant is not instilled with the mentality of a fighter from the very beginning, we shall be building something else—a support movement for a revolution others will make, for example—but not a revolutionary movement in itself.

9. Can this be interpreted as denigration of all other activities except preparing oneself to fight?
No, work among the masses which leads the people to revolutionary positions is also important. What the militant must remember—including those at the head of the masses—is that on the day the armed struggle is launched he is not going to stay at home awaiting the outcome. And he should prepare himself as a result, even though his present militancy may be on other fronts. Moreover, this will give authority, authenticity, sincerity, and seriousness to his present revolutionary message.

10. What are the concrete tasks of a militant in the mass movement who belongs to your organization?
If a militant in a union or a mass movement is involved, his task should consist of creating a circle, whether a group in the union or the entire union, where support can be organized for the activities of the armed apparatus and preparations made to join it. Theoretical and practical training and recruitment will be the concrete tasks within that circle. In addition,

there is propaganda for armed struggle. And where possible, the union should be impelled toward more radical struggles and more definite stages of the class struggle.

11. In general, what are the fundamental objectives of the movement at this stage?
To have an armed group, as well prepared and equipped as possible, and tested in action.

To have good relations with all popular movements which support this type of struggle.

To create propaganda organs to radicalize the struggle and raise consciousness.

To have an efficient apparatus to absorb militants by offering opportunities for theoretical training, and to absorb groups within the mass movement that fulfill the above-mentioned functions.

12. Does the importance that the movement gives to preparation for armed struggle imply that a combatant cannot improvise?
The armed struggle is a technical act which requires, then, the technical knowledge, practice, equipment, and mentality of a fighter. Improvisation in this area is very costly in terms of lives and failures. The spontaneity promoted by some who speak vaguely of either the "revolution which the people will make" or "the masses" is either mere stalling or else it means leaving to improvisation the culminating phase of the class struggle. Every vanguard movement must, to preserve that vanguard character at the culminating moment of the struggle, intervene in it and know how to give technical guidance to the popular violence against oppression in such a manner that the objective is attained with the least possible sacrifice.

13. Do you believe that parties of the left can achieve that preparation for armed struggle by maintaining a small body of shock troops or a self-defense force?
No Party complies with the revolutionary principles it enunciates if it does not seriously face up to this preparation at every level of the Party. Otherwise it will not achieve the maximum possible efficiency with which to confront reaction at each stage, which can lead to fatal negligence (remember Brazil and Argentina) or to wasting a revolutionary conjuncture.

If they are not prepared for their specific objective, the small armed Party groups can become a sad mess of political maneuverings. A miserable example to recall in this regard is the incident which occurred at the demonstrations of last May Day: some armed groups were reduced to the task of protecting the distribution of a leaflet in which other groups of the left were attacked, and yet other armed groups confined themselves to the task of preventing the handing out of leaflets.

14. What do you think that militants of the armed Party apparatus can demand of their respective leaderships?
That their action be directed solely against the class enemy, against the bourgeois apparatus and its agents. No armed group can fulfill its specific objective if its leadership does not meet these minimum requisites:

   a.   That it be responsible and demonstrate by deeds its unwavering adherence to the principle of armed struggle, giving it importance and supplying the material means necessary for its preparation.
   b.   That it offer the necessary conditions of security and discretion to those militants who carry out illegal tasks.
   c.   That, through its scope and correct line, it should have a chance—as immediate as possible—of becoming the leader of the proletarian masses.

15. Do you not believe that an armed apparatus should depend on a political party?
I believe that every armed group should form part of a political apparatus of the masses at a certain point in the revolutionary process, and that, in case such an apparatus does not exist, it should contribute to creating one. This does not mean that it should be obliged, in the present situation of the left, to adhere to one of the existing political groups or that it should launch a new one. This could serve only to perpetuate the mosaic or to add to it. It is necessary to combat the current meager idea of a party as being identified by a headquarters, meetings, a newspaper, and positions on everything around it. It is necessary to get over the idea that the other parties of the left will dissolve before its verbal broadsides, that all their base units and the people in general will one day come to it. This is what has happened for sixty years in Uruguay and the result is plan to see. It is necessary to start with reality. It is necessary to recognize that there are authentic revolutionaries in all parties of the left, and that there are many more who are not organized. To take these elements and groups wherever they are and to unite them is a task for the left in general, in preparation for the day when sectarianism will be left behind, something which does not depend on us. But the Revolution cannot stop and wait until this happens. Each revolutionary, each revolutionary group has only one duty: to prepare to make the revolution. As Fidel Castro said in one of his recent speeches ". . . with a Party or without a Party." The Revolution cannot wait.

16. Can you give me details of the strategy for seizing power in Uruguay?
No, I cannot give you a detailed strategy. On the other hand, I can give
you some general strategic lines, and even these are subject to change
with circumstances. That is to say, strategic lines valid for the day, month,
and year they were mentioned.

17. Why can you not give me a detailed and definitive strategy?
Because a strategy is elaborated on the premise of basic real facts, and
reality changes independent of our will. You understand that a strategy
premised on the existence of a strong and organized union movement is
not the same as one based on the fact that the movement has been scattered, to give an illustrative example.

*18. On what basic real facts does your organization premise its general
strategic lines at this time?*
To cite only the most important ones:

—The conviction that the crisis, far from having been overcome, is
becoming worse by the day. The country is established on a capitalist plan
of development to increase the production of exportable items, which if
applied will yield only very minimal returns and only after several years.
This means that we have several years ahead in which the people will
have to tighten their belts. And with $500 million in foreign debt it is not
foreseeable that sufficient credits will be coming from abroad to allow
those sectors of society whose standard of living has fallen to return to
their former level. This is a basic concrete fact: there will be economic
hardship and popular discontent in the coming years.

—A second basic fact for a strategy is the high degree of unionization of the workers of Uruguay. Even if all unions do not have a high
degree of militancy—either because of their composition or because of
their leaders—the mere fact that virtually all the basic services of the
state, banking, industry, and commerce are organized constitutes by itself
a highly positive fact without parallel in Latin America. The possibility
of paralyzing the state services has created and can create very interesting conjunctures from the viewpoint of insurrection because—to give an
example—it is not the same to attack a state at full strength as it is to
attack one half-paralyzed by strikes.

—Another strategic factor to take into account, this one negative, is
the geographic factor. We do not have impregnable locations in Uruguay
where we could install a guerrilla *foco* which could hold out, although we
do have places in the countryside where access is difficult. To compensate, we have a big city with more than 300 square kilometers of buildings, which allows for the development of an urban struggle. This means
that we cannot copy the strategy of those countries where geographic con-

ditions permit installation of a *foco* in the mountains or woods with a chance of stabilizing itself. On the contrary, we must elaborate a strategy suitable to a reality different from that of most countries of Latin America.

—In addition, in any strategic survey, we must always take into account the forces of repression. Our armed forces, some 12,000 men sketchily equipped and trained, constitute one of the weakest organizations of repression in America.

—Another important strategic factor is our powerful neighbors and the United States, always potentially disposed to intervene against revolution on the continent.

—And finally, a fundamental strategic factor is the degree of preparation of the revolutionary armed group.

19. How do the present crisis and popular discontent enter into the strategy?
In the objective and subjective conditions for the Revolution. It is fundamental that the majority of the population, although not in favor of throwing themselves into an insurrection, at least not be prepared to kill for a regime which holds them down. This, among other things, reduces the strategic calculations regarding the forces of the enemy, in all practicality, to its organized armed forces, and raises the possibility of a favorable climate for the first stages of revolutionary government.

20. And as regards the forces of repression?
They should be evaluated by taking into account their level of combat preparation, their means, and their distribution in the country. In the interior there is one military unit (200 men) about every 10,000 square kilometers, and a police commissariat about every 1,000 square kilometers. The armed forces have to cover all the objectives that might be attacked by an insurrectionary movement with 12,000 military personnel and 22,000 police, of whom half of the former and 6,000 of the latter are concentrated in the capital. Of the police, only about 1,000 have been trained and equipped for truly military action.

21. Can the possibility of foreign intervention be a reason for postponing all armed struggle in Uruguay?
If that were so, Cuba would not have carried out its revolution 90 miles from the United States; nor would there be guerrillas in Bolivia, a country which borders on Brazil and Argentina, as does ours. Foreign intervention can constitute an immediate military reverse but also a political advantage which in time will become a military advantage. Imagine the city of Montevideo occupied by foreign troops, with the resulting outrage to nationalist feeling and harassment of the population, and imagine that

force being confronted by an armed revolutionary group within the city
. . . You can get a perfect idea of what the so greatly feared foreign intervention means politically and militarily.

Besides, in any case, our strategy is contained within the continental
strategy of creating many Vietnams, and the interventionists will have a
lot of work on many scattered fronts.

*22. How does the high level of unionization figure in a revolutionary
strategy?*
The trade unions, even with their present limitations, have committed and
can involve the majority of the working population in a direct struggle
against the government, a sort of situation which the government has often resolved by calling out the armed forces. Through the existence of an
armed revolutionary group capable of raising the class struggle to a higher
stage, we can conduct the struggle under better conditions, with a large
part of the population behind us and with the basic services of the State
deteriorating.

23. Is our geography completely adverse to a struggle in the countryside?
That is not strictly so. We do not have impregnable spots like other countries, but there are accidents of nature which allow temporary refuge to
an armed group. The latifundio is a great ally. In latifundio areas, that is
to say, in two-thirds of the country, the population density is less than
0.6 inhabitants per square kilometer, which facilitates the clandestine
movement of an armed contingent; compare that with the overall average
of Cuba, more than twenty inhabitants per square kilometer, and even
with the regions of small farms in our country, like Canelones and the
south of San José, with the same average density.

At the same time, the livestock-breeding latifundio solves the tricky
logistical problem of food supplies that in other places requires a supply
line, which can be achieved only with great complicity on the part of the
population.

In addition, the frightful living conditions of the rural wage earners,
some already organized into unions, have created a spontaneous rebel
sector which can be very useful in the rural struggle. If our countryside
cannot be used to shelter a permanent *foco* at least it can serve to disperse
the forces of repression.

24. And for the urban struggle, do the conditions exist?
Montevideo is a city sufficiently large and polarized by social struggles
to give cover to a vast active commando contingent. It constitutes a far
better framework than that which other revolutionary movements have
had for the urban struggle. To be sure, any organization which hopes to

last in the urban struggle should patiently construct its material bases and the vast support network which an armed contingent needs to operate or subsist in the city.

25. How does the fact of the existence of a prepared armed group figure in strategic planning?

If there is not a reasonably prepared group, the revolutionary conjunctures are simply wasted or not taken advantage of for the revolution. Things like the *Bogotazo*[3] happen.

The armed group goes about creating or helping to create the subjective conditions for the revolution from the very moment at which it begins to prepare itself, but especially after it begins to act.

26. What will be, then, the general strategic lines for the present moment?

To form an armed force with the greatest possible speed, with the capacity to take advantage of any propitious conjuncture created by the crisis or other factors. To create an awareness in the population, through actions of the armed group or other means, that without revolution there will be no change. To strengthen the trade unions and to radicalize their struggles and link them with the revolutionary movement.

To link up with the other revolutionary movements of Latin America, for continental action.

27. Is this a blueprint of your organization exclusively?

No, it is one for all authentically revolutionary organizations and for all the individuals who really desire a revolution.

28. Do you consider all these tasks to be equally revolutionary?

Yes. Some believe that we are doing a revolutionary task only when we are training to fight or when we go into action, but all the tasks which help the strategic plan are equally important for the revolution.

29. Can you give me an illustrative example?

Whoever runs an errand to acquire equipment necessary for a base of operations, whoever obtains money, whoever lends his automobile for mobilization, whoever lends his house is running as much risk, and sometimes more, than the member of the action group. It must be realized that the majority of the revolutionaries have spent most of their time on these small practical things without which there is no revolution.

30. Does that mean that a strategic possibility can open up with our daily effort?

Yes. Our strategy for revolution depends partly on the conditions which we may be able to create through our efforts aimed at the seizure of power and partly on not losing sight of the conditions which reality presents to us.

Notes

1. The Moscow-line Communist Party.

2. A former president and leading politician who aided Castro during the early years of the guerrilla movement but went into opposition soon after the seizure of power.

3. The *Bogotazo* was a spontaneous urban riot in Bogotá, Colombia, in 1948. Triggered by the assassination of populist Jorge Gaitán, it led to a civil war called, simply, "La Violencia."

14

Questions to a Militant
of the PRT-ERP

James Petras

Like Uruguay and Brazil, Argentina in the late sixties and early seventies was buffeted by several revolutionary urban guerrilla movements. One of the most prominent and dynamic of these groups was the Trotskyist Revolutionary People's Army (ERP), the armed wing of the Revolutionary Workers Party (PRT). The ERP burst into prominence when it executed Augusto Vandor, a labor representative heavily identified with the repressive policies of the government of General Juan Carlos Onganía. The ERP blamed him for the confrontation between government forces and masses of workers and students in the province of Córdoba, on May 30, 1969—the Cordobazo left fourteen demonstrators killed and hundreds wounded. This event and the killing of Vandor marked the initiation of open warfare between the guerrillas of the ERP and the military government. As a result of its successful armed activities the ERP gained a great deal of respect and credibility among the Argentine people, but the wave of revolutionary success was soon stemmed by the onset of the repressive period known as Argentina's "Dirty War." James Petras, a political scientist, frequent contributor to the New Left Review, *and author of numerous articles and books about Latin American politics and U.S.-Latin American relations, allows us a rare opportunity to learn about Argentine guerrillas by interviewing one of the participants and probing into his motives for fighting. In the interview, the ERP's militant attempts to provide a rationale for the existence of the organization. More important, the militant argues in favor of the existence of an organization capable of creating a revolutionary structure to accomplish long-term goals to avoid the letdown that occurs after cases of spontaneous combustion like the* Cordobazo.

From *New Left Review*, no. 71 (January–February 1972): 51–57. Reprinted by permission of *New Left Review*, 6 Meard Street, London W1V 3HR, United Kingdom.

What are the origins of the PRT-ERP?

In the early 1960s a number of groups fused together—Fidelistas, sugar workers from the North of Argentina and a Trotskyist group led by Moreno.[1] In 1968 and 1969, a number of groups—including Moreno—split off as we oriented our cadres toward armed struggle. We rejected the rural guerrilla strategy: the war is where the masses are and Argentina is mostly urban. It is false to dichotomize between the city and the country. We formed the PRT as a party of cadres; the ERP is the army of the masses. In 1970, we decided to form this army as an anti-imperialist group. We have drawn on the experiences of Vietnam in forming an army of the people; an insurrection in the Russian style is not possible. Our process is a prolonged war. The insurrection in the Dominican Republic [the assassination of dictator Rafael Trujllo in 1961 and the U.S. occupation in 1965] and the *Cordobazo* show that spontaneous insurrections are not capable of winning.

What is the relation between the Party (PRT) and the Army (ERP)?

The party contains the best cadres of the working class. The Army, based on the great combativeness of the masses, is an intermediate organization which links the masses to the Party. The Army is only one of many organizations that link the Party to the masses. The Army is necessary because of the prolonged nature of the struggle. The Party directs the ERP. The PRT always has a majority in the leadership of the ERP. As of now there are no differences in the membership and politics of the PRT-ERP.

What events shaped the development of the PRT-ERP?

[General Juan Carlos] Onganía's dictatorship put an end to legal struggle, the trade unions were intervened. The PRT had some influence in the trade union movement and led some of the mobilizations of the sugar workers in Tucumán. The *Tucumanos* asked for arms—we were not prepared at the time. The guerrillas are a result of pressure of the masses; to give a violent response to a military dictatorship.

What is the tactical orientation of the PRT-ERP?

We are based in industrial centers of the interior: Córdoba, Rosario, Tucumán, because the conflict between the working class is more intense and the level of class consciousness is higher than in Buenos Aires, which is most underdeveloped politically.

How is the PRT-ERP evolving?

Few old leaders remain. Many new cadres have been incorporated. Many contacts with the masses. We have a crisis of growth. More people want to join than can be absorbed. We want to avoid populist deviations, adventurist militarism. We want control of the military cadre. In one year, we have tripled our membership.

What events have helped your growth?
The second *Cordobazo* (March 1971) was a qualitative leap. It was organized and not spontaneous. People took over the *barrios* and put up barricades. We disarmed the police, contributed to the defense of the *barrios*, and distributed food from supermarkets.

Some "leftist" groups have criticized your food distribution activity as paternalistic.
It is not paternalistic: we recruit cadres. In each *barrio* there are *comités de resistencia*; there are neighborhood committees to distribute food. The distribution of food is well received in the *barrios*. Workers and taxi drivers cooperate. When we stop a meat truck now, we don't have to pull out a gun—we tell the driver who we are and he only asks, "What *barrio* this week?"

How do you explain the growth of the ERP?
The ERP grows as the class struggle grows. It offers the masses an option—an alternative to Peronism. Our armed action receives publicity from the bourgeois press. The dictatorship closes legal channels. Our violence is linked to the masses—that causes us to grow. The so-called insurrectional groups are politically and militarily incapable of opposing the government. The other left groups are in disintegration.

There are three alternatives to the dictatorship: the bourgeois "Hour of the People" (a coalition of Peronist, Radical, and Liberal electoral parties); the reformist "Encounter of the Argentines," directed by the Communist Party; and the guerrilla alternative—the ERP. The left will choose one of these alternatives. The ERP is inserted in the working class—it orients the war toward working-class struggle.

What type of problems have you faced?
Lack of political material; decline in theoretical work, lack of analysis. However, these weaknesses are not due to a militarist approach. Since February 1971, we have begun to raise the quality of our political work. At first we were not lined up with the trade unions. Then we began to work in Fiat and other industries—now we are with the working class. With students we are discussing how to work with intermediary groups.

What are the politics of the PRT-ERP?
The ERP is a national liberation organization that struggles for the people. The PRT is based on the working class and fights for socialism. There is a difference in emphasis.

How do you view the guerrilla action within the revolutionary struggle?
The action of the guerrilla is linked to the masses; we participated in the
barricade fighting in the *Cordobazo*. The political struggle reaches its
highest point in arms. The guerrilla struggle is thus political. There are
two types of activity: organized action, linked *indirectly* to the masses by
its content—bank assaults; and action linked to the masses through participation in their struggles—the case of Sylvester. This latter is more
effective and squares with the level of mass awareness. Action against the
police is not our line. Torturers are something else. . . . Military action is
not the only form of struggle; there is trade union action; the struggle is
multiple—it depends on the masses.

How do you conceive the revolution in Argentina?
Argentina is capitalist and semicolonial. The bourgeoisie is a junior part-
ner of U.S. imperialism—there is no "national" bourgeoisie to promote
independent capitalist development; the fight is for socialism.

The bourgeoisie cannot lead the revolution—only the working class
can make the revolution. The Revolution must be worker and popular
(*obrero y popular*)—"popular" means that it embraces petit bourgeois
employees and students. There can be no "intermediary stage" and no
participation of the bourgeoisie—the anti-imperialist struggle must be
under working-class leadership. For our prolonged war, an army is needed,
located not in rural areas, as in China, but in the cities, especially those of
the interior. The insurrection will occur at the end of the process, with the
disintegration of the army. The struggle will build up from small to big
battles and be made up of thousands of conflicts and clashes.

What is the political situation today in Argentina?
Polarization is becoming acute. Peronism as an ideology is losing prestige, the workers in Córdoba are abandoning the Peronist leaders. The
electoral agreements between the "Hour of the People" and Lanusse are a
means of avoiding *Cordobazos* and preventing the people from joining
the guerrillas.

How do you view the trade union struggle in Argentina?
The trade union movement is mainly Peronist—it has evolved from state
sponsorship (under Perón) to resistance directed by the bureaucrats. The
trade unions have a limited role in the struggle of the masses—they are
not an instrument of revolution, but reach the broadest mass of workers.
The Party is the instrument of revolution. The PRT is only the embryo of
the Revolutionary Party. Against the trade union bureaucracy, we support
the formation of rank-and-file committees (*comités de base*). We hope
that the Fiat unions become the basis for a new national labor union. We

have political, not organizational, links with the revolutionary class unions (*sindicatos clasistas*).

How do you view the Peronist movement?
It is an alliance of three classes: the bourgeoisie, the petite bourgeoisie, and the working class. Ideologically, its politics are national-capitalist. The Peronist guerrillas, FAR, FAP, and Montoneros, are the popular sectors of the movement. The political apparatus is petit bourgeois.

As the class struggle intensifies, Peronism will divide. Perón is a centrist: between the bourgeois and proletarian sectors of the movement. The revolution in Argentina will be made with Peronist workers, but the leadership will not be Peronist but Socialist. The mass of workers will get rid of the bourgeois Peronists. We do not have a sectarian position toward Perón: the PRT carries on an ideological struggle with Peronism; the ERP does not engage in ideological debates with Peronists—some are in the ERP.

How do you view the other guerrilla groups (the FAR, FAP, FAL, and Montoneros)?
Despite ideological differences, we maintain fraternal relations. We are all embryos of any army of the people. When we liberated political prisoners we freed four ERP members and one Montonera.

What political ideas have influenced the PRT-ERP?
The PRT is primarily influenced by Marx and Lenin. Trotsky's works on Permanent Revolution and the Soviet Bureaucracy have also been influential; and we defend his political role in the Russian Revolution. Also Mao and Giap's work on the idea of a party-army. From Che, two basic lessons: first, all objective conditions need not be given to begin armed struggle; second, there is a need to create the New Man in the course of the struggle for socialism.

Is guerrilla struggle compatible with Leninism?
We base ourselves on Lenin's theory of the Party; armed struggles are compatible with the Leninist party. What is central is the construction of the party of the working class directed by Leninists. Lenin's criticism was directed against terrorism—action dissociated from the masses. We work to make the masses conscious, to mark a road for the masses.

The guerrillas do not distract the masses—they show a method of struggle that raises consciousness more effectively than does distributing leaflets. The guerrillas are not a substitute, but a stimulator of the masses. The working class feels that the guerrillas support its actions.

How do you evaluate the revolutionary experiences in Russia, China, and Cuba?

In the Soviet Union, the revolution occurred in a backward country—these conditions produced Stalinism. In China, you have a workers' party with a peasant base that is in the process of continuous change. Cuba is the best product of revolution; in content it is closer to socialist man.

How do you evaluate the new experiences in Peru, Chile, and Bolivia?

Each is different. In Peru you have a nationalist bourgeois government which is very lucid—more so than the bourgeoisie. But you cannot end imperialism while the bourgeoisie heads the revolution. The Peruvian experience influences some Argentinian military officers but not the Argentinian people.

In Bolivia you have a Bonapartist regime in special conditions.[2] The Bolivian working class is the most conscious in Latin America. What they lack is a Party. The trade unions are combative and antibourgeois, but they are no substitute for a Party. The Bonapartist regime is shaky—the class struggle will lead to civil war. Regarding Chile, we maintain fraternal relations and support the position of the MIR.

How do you view the position of the United States in Latin America?

The United States has pushed Brazilian development and tried to push Argentinian—but has failed. The United States exercises hegemony in twenty countries and denationalizes industries. We do not discount U.S. military intervention directly or through the Argentinian or Brazilian armies. Defeat and internal problems are forcing the United States out of Vietnam, in order to strengthen its position in Latin America. The United States will intervene—it will not allow a revolution in Argentina.

How do you view the revolutionary process in Latin America?

Two or three Vietnams . . . acute crisis in general, of which the bourgeois reformists cannot take advantage . . . socialist revolution is on the agenda . . . imperialism is taking a tactical retreat . . . in some countries there are guerrillas, in others, movements of masses, as in Bolivia and Chile . . . the confrontation will take place against imperialism and the national bourgeoisie, which is counterrevolutionary. The situation is complex: the routes to revolution are different in different countries. Revolution is in the Southern Cone [of South America—J.P.]. Between 1960 and 1967, Venezuela and Colombia were in the vanguard—now the vanguard is the working class of the Southern Cone. Uruguay and the Tupamaros, Argentina and the ERP, the Chilean government and the MIR, Bolivia and the Popular Assembly, are the key countries for leadership in the revolutionary struggle.

How do you view the possibilities of the United States and the national bourgeoisie imposing a Brazilian-type system in Argentina?
In Argentina, the bourgeoisie has no viable programme. To impose a Brazilian-type solution in Argentina will lead to a civil war. The Brazilian experience is possible in Argentina only after defeat in a civil war.

Notes

1. Manuel Moreno was the person most associated with the antiguerrilla line in the PRT. He split before the 1970 conference that endorsed armed struggle, and has since become a leading spokesperson for his position in the Fourth (Trotskyist) International. In 1973, he and some other dissidents joined to form the Partido Socialista Argentino, which is now the official Trotskyist party in Argentina and is quite anti-ERP and antiguerrilla.

2. This answer was, of course, made before the counterrevolutionary coup in Bolivia of September 1971.

15

In the Shining Path of Mariátegui, Mao Tse-tung, or Presidente Gonzalo? Peru's Sendero Luminoso in Historical Perspective

Daniel Masterson

Sendero Luminoso (Shining Path), as the Communist Party of Peru is commonly known, first erupted into the Peruvian consciousness on May 17, 1980, when it declared war on the Peruvian state. For the better part of twelve years the Shining Path held the initiative, and for a brief time it seemed as if it were on the verge of accomplishing its goals of taking over power and creating a state of "New Democracy." Despite the fact that Sendero has traditionally been associated with unparalleled violence, there are many complex areas of its ideology and praxis that bear close examination but are often ignored because of the immediacy of the war. The complexity of Sendero can only be understood by examining the roots from which the organization sprang. Historian Daniel Masterson, author of Militarism and Politics in Latin America: Peru from Sanchez Cerro to Sendero Luminoso, *probes the historical, ideological, and praxeological foundations of Sendero, from the interpretation of Peruvian reality by the founder of the Communist Party of Peru, José Carlos Mariátegui, to the adaptation of Mao Tse-tung's philosophy to Peru, to the crisis experienced by Sendero as a result of the arrest of its founder, leader, and chief ideologue, Abimael Guzmán, better known among his followers as Presidente Gonzalo.*

This article originally appeared in an earlier form as "In the Shining Path of Maraiátegui, Mao Zedong, or Presidente Gonzalo?" *Journal of Third World Studies* 11, no. 1 (Spring 1994): 154–77.

S hortly after the capture by a special police unit on September 12, 1993, of the leader of Peru's infamous Sendero Luminoso, Abimael Guzmán Reynoso, the London-based Maoist newspaper *A World to Win* appealed to its readers in a front-page headline: "Move Heaven and Earth to Defend the Life of Chairman Gonzalo." Known to his followers in Peru and the world Maoist movement by this nom de guerre, Guzmán, after his trial, conviction, and sentencing to solitary confinement for life without parole, made one last public appeal to his followers with these words:

> Listen to this! We see worldwide Maoism is marching relentlessly forward in its task of leading the new wave of the world proletarian revolution. Listen well and understand. Those who have ears, use them. Those who have understanding, and we all have it, use it well. Enough nonsense! Enough confusion! Understand this! We need Maoism as a living force, and this is happening.
>
> We need Maoism to generate new Communist Parties to direct the next great wave of world proletarian revolution that is upon us.[1]

Nowhere in this rambling message is there any mention of the Peruvian peasantry that Sendero Luminoso purported to be liberating during the first phase of its "People's War" in the early 1980s. Indeed, in his only public statement articulating Sendero Luminoso's ideology, a July 1988 interview in the Maoist newspaper *El Diario*, Guzmán rarely referred to his nation's impoverished and embattled peasantry. The focus of that interview as well as the bulk of Sendero Luminoso's literature is Maoist theory. Seemingly lost in the mass of Maoist rhetoric are the ideas of Peru's leading Marxist intellectual and the man whose name Sendero Luminoso incorporated into its party title, José Carlos Mariátegui.

The Partido Comunista del Perú en el Sendero Luminoso de José Carlos Mariátegui (Communist Party of Peru in the Shining Path of José Carlos Mariátegui) of today diverges sharply from the unique Marxist/Andean communalism advocated by Mariátegui in his *Seven Interpretative Essays on Peruvian Reality* published in the late 1920s. Guzmán attempted to explain this contradiction in his *El Diario* interview with the claim that, "in synthesis, Mariátegui was a Marxist-Leninist. Thus as I see it, today Mariátegui would be a Marxist-Leninist-Maoist. This is not speculation, it is simply the understanding of the life and work of José Carlos Mariátegui."[2]

Given the intense debate among scholars regarding Sender Luminoso's links to the peasantry and the fundamental importance of a peasant base for revolutionary Maoism, a clear understanding of this revolutionary group's ideological foundations is critical if we are to comprehend the implications of the capture of its messianic leader and principal ideologue. Will Sendero Luminoso's ideology, heretofore inseparable from

"*Pensamiento Gonzalo*" (Gonzalo Thought), sustain the organization and provide it with the same revolutionary zeal that characterized the movement before the capture of Guzmán in September 1992? This question can only be studied usefully if Sendero Luminoso's evolution is examined within the long-term historical context of Peruvian radical leftist politics and peasant mobilization.

The roots of the modern Peruvian Left can be found in the often vague and frequently iconoclastic writings of the early twentieth-century social critic, Manuel Gonzales Prada.[3] This frequently bitter commentator's call for a complete restructuring of Peruvian society drew the deep intellectual interest of the young journalist and writer, José Carlos Mariátegui, in the years immediately following the First World War. Deeply distrustful of politics, Mariátegui never developed a comprehensive body of political thought in the tradition of the contemporary Western radical Left. Although he drew heavily upon Marxist theory, Mariátegui's ideas were grounded firmly in the reality of Peruvian poverty, race, class conflict, and neocolonialism. Before he met an early death at the age of thirty-five in 1930, Mariátegui articulated far better than any previous countryman the fundamental problems impeding Peru's social progress and national unity.[4] In his *Seven Interpretative Essays on Peruvian Reality,* Mariátegui observed: "The Peru of the coast, heir of Spain and the Conquest, controls the Peru of the Sierra from Lima; but it is not demographically or spiritually strong enough to absorb it. Peruvian unity is still to be accomplished . . . what has to be solved is a dualism of race, language and sentiment born of the invasion and conquest of indigenous Peru by a race that has not managed to merge with the Indian race, eliminate it, or absorb it."[5]

From the perspective of the 1920s, Mariátegui saw Peru's "reality" as semifeudal and neocolonial. He argued that his nation's rich Indian heritage was subverted by the Spanish Conquest and the exploitative colonial system established in the aftermath of Pizarro's defeat of the Incas. Since the Spanish colonial state was fundamentally precapitalist and primarily interested in extracting mineral wealth from the colony, the economic legacy of the colonial era was overwhelmingly negative. With the defeat of the Incas, the Spanish destroyed one of the most bureaucratically efficient states ever to exist. Nevertheless, Mariátegui recognized that the bond holding the Inca state together—the tradition of communalism and reciprocity based on the clan-like structure known as the ayllu—was sufficiently resilient to have survived the political collapse of *Tawintinsuyu* (Inca Empire).

Indeed, the ayllu was the social foundation of Andean civilizations for centuries before the rise of the Inca Empire. Thus, although like many of his contemporaries, Mariátegui did not fully comprehend the historical roots of the ayllu, he did understand how important communalism was as a societal alternative to the exploitative socioeconomic structure of Hispanic Peru. As a creative Marxist, Mariátegui believed that Peru offered an interesting model for an innovative form of socialism. At the same time Mao Tse-tung was beginning to enlist the Chinese peasantry in building his revolutionary base, Mariátegui saw in the reciprocal communalism of Andean social tradition a form of "communism" that was preferable to the exploitative, individualistic, and foreign-dominated policies that had submerged the Indian in poverty and robbed Peru of its vast economic potential. On this point Mariátegui wrote: "Communism has continued to be the Indian's only defense. Individualism cannot flourish or even exist effectively outside a system of free competition. And the Indian has never felt less free than when he has felt alone."[6]

Mariátegui dismissed criticisms of the Inca state as despotic with the argument that Inca "communism" was agrarian based and the communism of Marx and Sorel was rooted in the industrial sector.[7] Liberal concepts of individual liberty and free will thus had no meaning for the "Man of *Tawantinsuyu*." Therefore, while Mariátegui viewed the alienation of the Peruvian peasantry in a Marxist perspective, he saw the solution to their desperate plight not in modern Marxist terms, but rather in the application of traditional Andean social models to a contemporary socialist Peruvian state. Mariátegui insisted that the Incas created their complex state with the ayllu as its "nucleus." He argued that the same approach could be taken with the modern socialist state if an efficient educational system emphasizing primary schooling for the masses, technical training, and a free and accessible university system was established as a foundation.[8]

The key to understanding the importance of Mariátegui's contribution to modern Peruvian thought is to recognize his unique willingness to use the traditional Andean social norms as a workable model for creating a more just society. He expressed great faith in the innate capability of the Peruvian indigenous population to function as a productive force for state building. Like Marx, he emphasized the dignity of labor as a key element of the human condition, but unlike Marx, he did not view labor in exclusively economic terms. Instead of wedding himself to the concept of "surplus value," Mariátegui viewed Andean labor in its variety of reciprocal forms as a means of maintaining values and community solidarity. These labor systems also helped transfer wealth on a communal rather than an individual basis. Shared tasks such as planting and harvesting for the ayllu, and road building, military service, and weaving for the state were not individual obligations to be rewarded as paid labor. Rather, these tasks were what established an individual's place in the community. For Mariátegui, faith in the renaissance of the Indian was not associated with "westernizing" Quechua (Indian) society. He argued that "the community (ayllu) is a system of production that keeps alive in the Indian the moral incentives that stimulate him to do his best work." Quoting the Peruvian social theorist Hildebrando Castro Pozo, Mariátegui concluded, "the Indian community preserves two great economic and social principles that up to now neither the science of sociology nor the empiricism of the great industrialists have been able to solve satisfactorily: to contract workers collectively and to have the work performed in a relaxed and pleasant atmosphere of friendly competition."[9]

Mariátegui's faith in the innate ability of Peru's indigenous population to rebuild the nation within the traditional communalist framework is very rare among twentieth-century Peruvian intellectuals. As we shall see, that faith has never been expressed by the self-styled intellectual leader of Sendero Luminoso, Abimael Guzmán Reynoso.

Unlike Guzmán, who clearly relished directing Sendero Luminoso's "People's War" before his capture, Mariátegui preferred the realm of ideas to revolutionary activism. Near the end of his life he did found the newspaper *Labor,* and as a member of the so-called Secret Cell of Seven, Mariátegui established the Socialist Party of Peru in 1928. But he soon categorically denied that the Socialist Party had links with Moscow. Subsequently, he and his socialist colleagues were criticized by Latin American Communists for creating a party "open to the middle classes and the unorganized masses."[10] Mariátegui also broke with Peru's emerging populist movement, the Alianza Popular Revolucionaria Americana (APRA) party, when it sought to build a political base in Peru during the late 1920s.

Characteristically, Mariátegui turned his back on APRA and its leader, Víctor Raúl Haya de la Torre, because of what the Marxist idealist termed its "vulgar" political aspirations. Ironically, APRA would not achieve national political power until more than five decades after Mariátegui's death. For most of this half century, APRA was viewed by the nation's conservatives and the military leadership as a far more potent threat than Peru's weak Communist Party. Only in the late 1970s would the military accept APRA's political right to govern the nation, thus opening the way for the election of Alan García Pérez in 1985.

Fundamentally important for understanding Sendero Luminoso's revolutionary outlook and tactical approach to its People's War is a comprehension of APRA's formative years from 1930 to 1948. APRA's often violent struggle for power during these early years involved conspiracy, assassination, and terrorism led by revolutionary cells of activists known as *Bufalos*. The early APRA unquestionably provided a native model for Senderistas to follow once they launched their People's War in May 1980. Abimael Guzmán clearly learned from the failures of APRA's revolutionary campaign, most particularly the abortive Callao Naval Revolt of October 3, 1948.

When in 1948 dissident Apristas allied with rebellious enlisted personnel of the Peruvian navy to topple the government of José Luis Bustamante y Rivero in an attempt to establish a socialist government, APRA's leadership lost its nerve and refused to support the party's rank and file. After the rebellion was suppressed, Peru's Left was crushed by a right-wing reaction led by army general Manuel A. Odría, which effectively ended organized revolutionary activism in Peru until the 1960s. Significantly, Guzmán directly alluded to the Callao Revolt of 1948 as a defining event in his life as a revolutionary. In the *El Diario* interview he claimed the Callao insurrection helped mold his early revolutionary consciousness. In Guzmán's words: "I had the occasion to see the uprising in Callao in 1948. To see with my own eyes the people's courage, how the people were brimming with heroism, and how the (APRA) leadership betrayed them. . . . These things exerted an influence on me. I believe like every communist, I am the child of the class struggle and the party."[11]

After APRA's abandonment of revolutionary politics following the abortive Callao Revolt, Peru's radical Left remained dormant until three guerrilla cadres with ties to Castro's Cuba began operating in the nation's central Sierra in 1965. Mirroring most other Latin American Communist parties, Peru's Partido Comunista Peruano, using various names from 1930 to the mid-1960s, generally shunned violence. Indeed, Peru's Communists, following Moscow's line, often sought accommodations with Peru's conservative governments. Despite the inaction of Peru's Communists, APRA nevertheless sought to exploit Cold War fears for its own benefit by portraying itself as the leading anti-Communist force in Peru.[12] Thus, for more than thirty years after Peru's Marxists organized, their political impact remained minimal and their ranks factionalized. For example, in the 1962 presidential elections, three parties of the Left shared the very modest total of only 60,000 votes of more than 1.1 million cast.[13]

Characteristically, the three guerrilla cadres that began operations in 1965 were only peripherally linked to Peru's Moscow-line Marxists. The most significant of these guerrilla fronts was the Movimiento de Izquierda Revolucionaria (Movement of the Revolutionary Left, MIR), and its leader, Luis de la Puente Uceda, owed more to support from Castro's Cuba and Communist China than he did from Peru's Communist Party.[14] These cadres were suppressed quickly and brutally by the Peruvian army because they were so poorly coordinated and out of touch with Peru's urban Left. These *focos*, as they came to be called after the revolutionary success of Castro's small band of guerrillas in Cuba's Sierra Maestra, lacked the secure internal cell structure, the intelligence-gathering capabilities, and the utter ruthlessness of Sendero Luminoso.

When Sendero Luminoso launched its extremely violent People's War in the small highland village of Chuschi in the Department of Ayacucho in May 1980, the guerrilla front consciously sought to avoid the past failures of Peru's weak and fragmented Left. This effort may well explain why Sendero Luminoso looked more to the teachings and tactics of Mao Tse-tung than it did to the unique mix of *indigenismo* and Marxism espoused by Mariátegui. Still, before the capture of Guzmán, Sendero Luminoso demonstrated marked similarities to Peru's only popular mass movement of the twentieth century, APRA. With its messiah-like leader, its secretive and highly disciplined organization, and its single-minded conviction that only Sendero Luminoso could save Peru, the guerrilla front closely resembled the early APRA. But the APRA leadership's lack of revolutionary zeal and its penchant for political compromise and intrigue, especially after 1948, repelled Guzmán. The Sendero leader vehemently emphasized this point in the *El Diario* interview when he compared APRA with Chiang Kai-shek's Kuomintang: "Haya de la Torre proposed the formation of a front similar to the Kuomintang, claiming that the proletariat was too tiny and immature to be able to give rise to a Communist Party. This was nothing but sophistry. . . . Haya de la Torre was never a Marxist-Leninist. Never! He always opposed Lenin's theories. . . . This is really the bottom line, the rest, cheap hoaxes."[15]

Guzmán further claimed that, like the Kuomintang, which he characterized as the attempted "executioner" of the Chinese Communist Revolution, APRA had consistently attempted to destroy Peru's Marxist parties in order to broaden its base among Peru's popular masses. This assessment is largely accurate. Clearly, Guzmán recognized that APRA's strength was its ability to survive. Thus, it is comprehensible that Sendero Luminoso would emulate APRA's early organizational model. But for an understanding of Sendero Luminoso's ideological perspective, it is necessary to briefly review the organization's evolution before 1980.

Only the nearly successful rebellion of Tupac Amaru II against Spanish colonialism in the early 1780s compares in scope and violence with the fourteen-year People's War conducted by Sendero Luminoso. Within five years of launching their "armed struggle" with the symbolic action of burning ballot boxes in the Andean market town of Chuschi in May

1980, Senderistas were active in all of Peru's administrative departments, and their armed columns were operating in sierra and *selva* provinces containing nearly half of Peru's population.

Like no previous resistance movement in modern Peruvian history, Sendero Luminoso successfully exploited the glaring vulnerabilities of Peruvian society to its revolutionary advantage. The ignorance and neglect of Peru's poorest sierra provinces by the nation's modern coastal sector, the cultural dualism of a long-divided social fabric, and most of all the lack of hope of young Peruvians for a better future explained Sendero Luminoso's remarkable success during the first decade of its "armed struggle."[16]

Sendero Luminoso's initial success during the armed phase of its revolutionary struggle was, however, a result of more than a decade of organizational planning and recruitment. Abimael Guzmán, a member of Peru's Communist Party from his student days at the University of Arequipa in the mid-1950s, began building his distinct mission of the class struggle almost immediately after obtaining a position on the philosophy faculty at Ayacucho's University of San Cristóbal de Huamanga in 1962. Throughout the early 1960s, Guzmán began to dominate the university's discussion groups during which he argued that only a complete revolutionary restructuring could "redeem" Peru.[17] After visiting China in the midst of the Cultural Revolution in 1965, Guzmán returned to San Cristóbal de Huamanga to continue the creation of revolutionary cells and to implement the expertise gained in the land of his ideological mentor, Mao Tse-tung. Guzmán's time in China shaped his views on the nature of the "armed struggle," and provided practical training in organizational techniques, tactics, and the use of explosives.[18] After assuming the post as personnel director at San Cristóbal de Huamanga, Guzmán effectively controlled the hiring for an institution of fifteen thousand students as well as high-school extension programs for the departments of Ayacucho, Huancavelica, and Apurimac in Peru's south central sierra.[19]

With a firm organizational base in Ayacucho and adjoining departments, Guzmán declared his independence from Peru's already factionalized Communist Party and formed the Partido Comunista del Perú en el Sendero Luminoso de Mariátegui in February 1970. Throughout the ensuing decade, Guzmán and his immediate leadership cadre, operating largely in secret, organized the broader infrastructure of Sendero Luminoso or what they termed the party's "generated organisms." These included students' and women's groups, trade unions, teachers' unions, and the Movimiento de Campesinos Pobres (Movement of Poor Peasants). According to Sendero Luminoso, these generated organisms were created as part of "a broad mobilization to get deep into the heart of the masses, to agitate, to open the party and to prepare for the people's war."[20]

Peru's reformist military government under General Juan Velasco Alvarado (1968–1975) and its conservative successor headed by General Francisco Morales Bermúdez (1975–1980) unwittingly aided Sendero Luminoso's efforts by ignoring the desperate, poverty-stricken, and remote Ayacucho region. Moreover, Velasco's attempt to mobilize the traditional Peruvian Left behind his radical reformist agenda allowed Sendero Luminoso great latitude during its formative organizational years. The inability of the conservative Morales Bermúdez government to identify the threat from the emerging insurgency can only be explained as a major failure of Peruvian military intelligence. Indeed, Guzmán was arrested by Peruvian police in 1979, but was soon released when it was determined that he did not pose a serious security threat to the state.[21]

When in 1980 the weakened and discredited military leadership returned the reins of government to Fernando Belaúnde Terry, the civilian president whom they had deposed twelve years before, Guzmán saw this as the opportune time to launch the People's War. Reasoning that an exhausted and divided military would be very reluctant to initiate an active counterinsurgency or to again depose Belaúnde Terry, the leader of Sendero Luminoso began the first phase—"agitation and armed propaganda"—of the five-stage program for revolutionary victory in Peru.[22] The insurgency was soon able to progress to the second and third stages, "sabotage against Peru's socioeconomic system" and "generalization of the People's war," because Guzmán's assessment of the Peruvian military was substantially correct. The Belaúnde administration and the armed forces leadership refused to acknowledge the severity of the threat from Sendero Luminoso or take consistent action against the insurgency until mid-1983. Only after Peru's ineffectual Guardia Civil counterinsurgency units, known as the Sinchis, proved to be spectacular failures in the field did the army and naval infantry enter the campaign against Sendero Luminoso. The insurgency's armed cells, which always totaled fewer than five thousand during the formative years of the People's War, were still able to advance to Sendero Luminoso's fourth stage, "conquest and expansion of the revolution's support base and strengthening of the guerrilla army," throughout the remainder of the 1980s. This progress was possible because the armed forces never established a coordinated strategy to deal with the insurgency.

Carlos Tapia, in his recent analysis of the countersubversive war, *Las fuerzas armadas y Sendero Luminoso,* argues correctly that the Peruvian military was conducting the war against the brutal insurgency between

1983 and 1987 with the same outdated strategic outlook as in its success-ful campaign against the Cuban-style guerrilla *focos* of the mid-1960s. A national security advisor to the Peruvian government commented in 1996 that the Peruvian military simply was forced to "throw away its counter-insurgency manuals" and try to establish a new, more effective approach to combating the terrorist front.[23]

Nevertheless, no comprehensive strategy was ever successfully de-veloped to confront Sendero Luminoso because the three armed services refused to integrate their efforts. Moreover, army commanders in the main emergency zones were rotated every December, thus depriving the anti-insurgency campaign of experienced commanders. This policy seems to have been a result of the unwillingness of army officers to risk their ca-reers in a war with no easily identifiable enemy. As evidence of the wide-spread human rights abuses of the military in the emergency zones began to mount, armed forces officers were also clearly concerned that they might eventually be held accountable for these abuses. Thus, from 1983 to the end of the decade, army commanders rarely initiated aggressive patrols to counter Sendero Luminoso's armed columns. Rather, the com-manders generally limited themselves to protecting their base camps and conducting short-range sweeps.[24] The armed forces' approach to the counterinsurgency campaign changed little under Belaúnde Terry's suc-cessor, Alan García Pérez (1985–1990). When García's failed economic policies brought the Peruvian economy to the brink of ruin by the end of the decade, Sendero's attacks on the "incompetent and corrupt" state gained increasing acceptance in Peru's urban setting.

As the Peruvian economy spiraled toward an inflation rate of over eight thousand percent during García's last year in office, the despair of the Peruvian people aided the violently radical cause of Sendero Luminoso. The crippled economy further impeded the still uncoordinated armed forces campaign against the insurgency. Still primarily committed to the mission of border defense, the Peruvian army and air force never aggres-sively emphasized counterinsurgency operations in Sendero Luminoso's original strongholds in Ayacucho and the newly opened high jungle the-ater in the coca-rich Upper Huallaga Valley in the Department of San Martín. Scarce funds for defense led the commander of the Peruvian Navy in 1989 to estimate the "readiness" of his institution at less than forty percent.[25] Army commanders were also forced to furlough their troops for days at a time because of a lack of funds for basic necessities. Poor sala-ries and low morale also led to high desertion rates among the Peruvian officer corps. Adding to this malaise within the armed forces establish-ment was the mounting international criticism of the military's human rights abuses in the war against the insurgency. Clearly influenced by the

Argentine military's success in the "Dirty War" twenty years before, elements of the Peruvian military had adopted the same methods after taking control of the counterinsurgency campaign in 1983.[26]

With the abject failure of democratically elected civilian presidents and the military establishment to resolve Peru's dire economic and social problems, Sendero Luminoso seemed to be unquestionably advancing toward the fifth and final phase of its fanatical campaign to create the "People's New Democracy" in Peru. The final stage, calling for "general civil war, the siege of the cities, and the final collapse of state power," seemed to be occurring soon after the surprise election of the virtually unknown Nisei, Alberto Fujimori, to the presidency in April 1990. With a vastly expanded war treasury funded by its alliance with narco-traffickers in the Upper Huallaga Valley, Sendero Luminoso was actually able to provide funds to extend its international support network and, most importantly, vastly expand its previously limited terrorist operations in Lima. While it is clearly premature to make a definitive assessment, it now seems apparent that Sendero Luminoso's decision to concentrate its efforts in Peru's capital city reflected Guzmán's rejection of both the teachings of Mariátegui and the strategic model of Mao Tse-tung.

Sendero Luminoso was never a peasant-based insurgency. In the words of noted Peruvian anthropologist Carlos Iván Degregori, Sendero Luminoso is "primarily a movement of intellectuals and young people without hope."[27] The work of Cornell anthropologist Billie Jean Isbell on Sendero Luminoso in Chuschi, Ayacucho, confirms this assessment. Rather than attempt to understand and cooperate with the Ayacucho peasants through their complex system of reciprocity and the ancient ayllu structure, Senderistas in Chuschi in the early 1980s forcibly imposed a "war planting" schedule upon the villagers that seriously disrupted their intricate agricultural cycle. Furthermore, the Senderista cells operating in the vicinity of Chuschi were never able to maintain control of the area or protect the villagers from the retaliatory abuse of the brutal Sinchis. One eyewitness to terrible violence inflicted upon the villagers by both Sendero Luminoso and government forces claimed that the Chuschinos were "left between the sword and the wall."[28] As early as 1983, Chuschinos were forced to choose between these two grim alternatives. Significantly, Chuschinos rejected an open alliance with Sendero Luminoso and requested that a Guardia Civil post be constructed in the village.[29]

The most convincing evidence of Sendero Luminoso's failure to create a peasant base is the widespread emergence of peasant self-defense brigades known as Rondas Campesinas. Originally appearing in northern Peru in the early 1970s as a form of vigilantism to deal with cattle rustling, these Rondas soon became the Peruvian peasants' first, and often only, means of defense against the increasing terrorist violence of Sendero Luminoso. Unable to sustain a broadly based counterinsurgency presence in both Lima and the sierra, the army and naval infantry relied heavily on poorly armed Rondas to augment the government's campaign against Sendero Luminoso from 1982 onward. The work of Duke University anthropologist Orin Starn on the Rondas offers important insights into the emergence of these self-defense brigades. Noting that the number of Rondas grew from approximately two hundred in 1984 to fourteen hundred by the end of 1991, Starn concludes that Peru's peasantry initially became alienated from Sendero Luminoso because the insurgency's destruction of Peru's rural infrastructure was sharply at odds with the peasantry's increasing desire for modernization in the sierra. Starn specifically noted that "the gradual withdrawal from the countryside of government and development groups in the face of assassinations and threats from the Shining Path meant a cut-off of modest outside support for projects like clinics, schools and small irrigation projects."[30] Sendero Luminoso's failure to understand the peasantry's ties to traditional Andean planting patterns and limited access to outside markets was thus compounded by the insurgency's fanatical commitment to destroying the very modest improvements in the poverty-stricken lifestyles of Peru's rural poor.

The field work of Starn and Peruvian anthropologist José Coronel in the city of Huanta, Ayacucho, confirms the abject failure of Sendero Luminoso to follow the paths of Mariátegui or Mao Tse-tung to incorporate the peasantry in its so-called People's War. Violence against the people of Huanta by Sendero Luminoso initiated the creation of some of the most successful Rondas in rural Peru. Not only have Huanta's self-defense units reduced the threat of the insurgency, but these Rondas have recently initiated small public works projects.[31]

The successful campaign of the Rondas in the Apurímac River Valley mirrored that of the civil defense patrols in Huanta, motivated in many cases by the zeal of Protestant evangelicalism. Almost half of the Apurímac Valley's peasants are evangelicals. The struggle in the valley became a holy war between the peasants and the "anti-Christ," as Sendero Luminoso came to be seen. One Pentecostal pastor in the town of San Agustín who also headed a civil defense brigade mixed Andean mythology and biblical terminology when he declared: "The Shining Path is like a demon, worse than the devil. There is no name for them because they eat human flesh . . . the liver, they suck human blood." By the late 1980s the evangelicals in the Apurímac Valley were fighting Sendero Luminoso fiercely with the motto: "For every Christian, one hundred *terrucos* [terrorists] will die." Ironically, the evangelicals were also protecting drug traffickers in the valley in order to gain funding and arms to combat the insurgency.[32]

The largely spontaneous emergence of the Rondas throughout rural Peru in the last decade is seen by Starn as a phenomenon of significant importance. With more than 300,000 peasants enlisted in these Rondas by 1992, the self-defense units seemed to Starn to embody the type of communal activism idealized in the Marxist perspective by Mariátegui.[33] Moreover, it now seems apparent that Sendero Luminoso's decision to concentrate on a Lima-based terrorist campaign during Fujimori's first eighteen months in office was a sign of the insurgency's failure in the countryside.

Sendero Luminoso's misdirected campaign in the sierra was over-shadowed by the more highly visible terrorist offensive in central Lima and the capital's sprawling *barriadas* during this time period. Neverthe-less, Fujimori was compelled to augment the armed forces' over-extended counterinsurgency operations by placing greater emphasis on the Rondas in the antiterrorist campaign. The Nisei president armed 526 peasant com-munities by the end of 1992 and made highly visible visits to sierra vil-lages where effective Rondas were operating.[34] Clearly, the president's aid was still more symbolic than substantive. These gestures sought to cement the alliance Fujimori was creating with the leadership of the armed forces. Without an established political base of his own, Fujimori was forced to rely upon the military's support to a greater extent than any civilian president in Peru since Augusto B. Leguia (1919–1930).

The authoritarian posture of the Fujimori regime became apparent when in early 1992 he issued the so-called *decretos-bomba* (decrees bomb). This series of measures would have privatized Peru's largely state-dominated economy, further centralized the nation's administrative struc-ture, and vastly strengthened the role of the armed forces in the counter-insurgency campaign. At the heart of this decree package were measures to increase the powers of military commanders in Peru's emergency zones, place restrictions on journalists covering the war, and most importantly, create the so-called Unified Pacification Command. This last measure would have given the president the power of appointment over all top posts within the Peruvian armed forces. In return, the military command-ers would have had extraordinary access to the president and nearly com-plete autonomy in the conduct of the war against Sendero Luminoso.

When the Peruvian Congress refused to accept Fujimori's full pack-age of decrees and instead added amendments that the armed forces considered detrimental to the war against Sendero Luminoso, the strong-minded Nisei staged an *autogolpe* (self-coup) on April 5, 1992, and dissolved the Peruvian congress. President Getulio Vargas of Brazil employed the device of the self-coup to establish his authoritarian Estado Novo in 1937, and it now appears that President Fujimori had the same intentions until pressure from the international community forced him to hold new congressional elections and a national referendum on a new constitution. The subsequent congressional elections established a compliant legislature that facilitated the amending of the national constitution and assured Fujimori's reelection in 1995.

The capture of Guzmán and most of Sendero Luminoso's administrative leadership (Comité Central) in Lima immensely influenced the future of the insurgency's campaign and vastly strengthened Fujimori's political position in Peru. Occurring in the midst of Sendero Luminoso's furious attempt to bring down the Peruvian government with brutal bombings that targeted schools and Lima's fashionable suburbs, Guzmán's capture deprived the insurgency of its leading strategist and ideologue. In many ways, Guzmán was the author of his own capture. The nearly total shift of strategic emphasis from the sierra to Lima after 1989 represented a capitulation by Sendero Luminoso of the rural-based campaign that is the central dynamic of Maoist doctrine. In reality it manifested a premature attempt to achieve the collapse of the Fujimori government by means of traditional urban terrorist tactics employed in previous eras by the Algerian revolutionaries against the French in the late 1950s and the Irish Republican Army since the mid-1960s. The Lima bombing campaign of July through September 1992 was Sendero Luminoso's "Tet Offensive," representing a desperate attempt to end in a matter of months what Guzmán once declared could be a "fifty-year people's war."

Thus, the "strategic equilibrium" that Sendero Luminoso hoped to attain in the countryside was never achieved because of the insurgency's misunderstanding and terrible abuse of the peasantry. The decision to shift the campaign to Lima clearly alienated some of the Senderista leadership and may have led to the betrayal of some of its high-ranking members, such as Osman Morote, who opposed the strategy. Unquestionably, Guzmán's presence in Lima allowed the National Directorate against Terrorism (DINCOTE), under the command of police General Antonio Ketín Vidal, to track the terrorist leader down through careful surveillance work that included matching Guzmán's discarded psoriasis medicine packages and cigarette butts to a suspected "safe house" in the Lima suburb of Surco.

Assessing the impact of the raid by the special antiterrorist unit (DINCOTE) on Sendero Luminoso's Surco safe house seven months later, retired Peruvian army colonel José Bailetti Mac-Kee concluded: "Given the high level of organization and cohesion within the party, Sendero already had emergency replacements capable of taking over for the captured national and regional leadership. However, it is highly unlikely that the Sendero command could have envisioned the degree of police infiltration or the capture of so many leaders at once. The Party was beheaded, its political structure noticeably hit, and its overall apparatus weakened."[35]

With Guzmán's subsequent conviction and imprisonment for life in an underground cell supervised by the Peruvian navy, Sendero Luminoso is now deprived of its chief ideologue and political and spiritual leader. Guzmán has compounded this loss by seeking to negotiate the end of the People's War in return for better prison conditions. The rapid submission of a leader who once proclaimed that Senderistas must be prepared to wage fifty years of struggle, if necessary, to win the People's War has disillusioned the insurgency's rank and file. Some Limeños have derisively contrasted the Sendero leader's capitulation to the long heroic prison struggle of Nelson Mandela against apartheid in South Africa. It also seems to have strengthened the position of Oscar Alberto Ramírez Durand, who is now recognized as Sendero Luminoso's new operational commander. Ramírez Durand, whose nom de guerre is "Comrade Feliciano," was Sendero Luminoso's third in command before the capture of Guzmán. A highly revered "war leader" and member of the insurgency's Politburo, Ramírez Durand was Guzmán's personal link with Sendero Luminoso's popular guerrilla army. Like Ramírez Durand, many of Sendero Luminoso's regional military commanders were not captured in the October 1992 police raids. Ramírez Durand and these regional commanders thus hold the key to the insurgency's future. Peruvian military observers assessing the future of Sendero Luminoso note that the insurgency must immediately confront the following problems.

1) Permanently resolving the party's leadership dilemma;
2) Rethinking its comprehensive strategy as it confronts a coordinated offensive from the nation's armed forces;
3) Rebuilding a secure and effectively functioning chain of command; and
4) Regaining the strategic offensive.[36]

All of these objectives will be increasingly difficult to accomplish because of the legacy of Presidente Gonzalo. Abimael Guzmán's inability or unwillingness to understand the mentality of Peru's peasantry deprived Sendero Luminoso of the political base envisioned by Mariátegui and realized by Mao Tse-tung. Sendero Luminoso's decision to make war on the nation's campesinos violated the most fundamental precepts of Maoist doctrine and left Senderistas to rely solely on the abstract and often contradictory body of thought known as *Pensamiento Gonzalo*. With Guzmán as their active leader, Senderistas confidently portrayed themselves as a "new type of Marxist-Leninist-Maoist, Gonzalo Thought Party."[37] Few Senderistas were troubled by the clear divergence from classical Maoist principles while the insurgency was nearly paralyzing the Peruvian state before 1990. Guzmán mollified those that were by claiming that his urban campaign in Lima was being initiated because the Maoist concept of "strategic equilibrium" in the countryside had been achieved. The success of the Rondas Campesinas, of course, offered strong evidence to the contrary and explains why members of the Rondas were singled out for the most brutal atrocities perpetrated by the insurgency.[38]

Now Sendero Luminoso's new leaders will be forced to recognize how damaging the legacy of Presidente Gonzalo's complex blend of Maoism, violence, mysticism, and *personalismo* has become to their cause. They must adopt a new revolutionary paradigm distinct from Gonzalo Thought. This change must be accomplished even while the international Maoist movement denies the validity of Guzmán's peace proposals and characterizes President Fujimori as an "unprincipled, crafty and deformed cretin stuck on the points of the military's bayonets."[39]

Sendero Luminoso's cause is now being undermined by Peru's slowly improving economy. The abject despair of the García years is no longer the pervasive mentality of the Peruvian citizenry. Nevertheless, for every six Peruvians in the workforce, five do not earn a subsistence income. Any major downturn in the Peruvian economy could draw new adherents to the now dwindling ranks of the insurgency. In addition, because the scope of the war has drastically slowed, human rights abuses by the military have declined. The navy has recently addressed this issue in its main service journal, the *Revista de Marina*. The article, entitled "Terrorism and Human Rights in Peru," while largely criticizing international human rights organizations for underplaying the abuses of Sendero Luminoso, still represents a significant departure from the official silence of the military on the rights issue in the past.[40] For the military to gain the mass support of the Peruvian people in defeating the insurgency, however, its commanders must drastically revise their perception of the "rules of war" in Peru. At present, there is little indication that this rethinking is happening.

Despite the spectacularly successful release of all but one of the hostages held by the Movimiento Revolucionario Tupac Amaru in their early 1997 siege of the Japanese Embassy in Lima, the Peruvian armed forces' morale is still poor. The armed forces are not unified or properly led. The military's commander in chief, General Nicolás de Barí Hermoza Ríos, has been discredited by allegations of ties to drug traffickers and is strongly opposed by an "institutionalist" element within the armed forces that wants the military to emphasize increased professionalism and distance itself from Fujimori. Estimates by the army senior staff are that Sendero Luminoso is now 75 percent defeated and primarily localized in the Upper Huallaga Valley. However, this report is not necessarily cause for confidence. There is increasing evidence that Senderistas operating in the Upper Huallaga are not only being sustained by funds from the drug trade, but in fact have shifted their focus from revolution to lucrative criminal activity. As in the case of Colombia's Revolutionary Armed Forces of Colombia (FARC), the distinction between drug trafficking and revolution has all but disappeared. Sustained by $500 million in drug revenues in 1995 alone, FARC seems to have become the model for the surviving elements of Sendero Luminoso.

The war begun by Sendero Luminoso claimed more than 25,000 lives, displaced 600,000 rural Peruvians, and is not yet over. The ideological path taken by the founders of the insurgency bears little resemblance to the vision of socialist communalism articulated by José Carlos Mariátegui. Abimael Guzmán, the quintessential representative of the frustrated mestizo class that swelled the ranks of the insurgency, attempted to mold the Maoist revolutionary model to the Peruvian "reality." He failed because, while he sought to wage a class war on the Maoist model, his understanding of the importance of race, and especially *indigenismo,* was sadly lacking. "Presidente Gonzalo" forged his own revolutionary path largely independent of the teachings of Mariátegui and Mao Tse-tung and without an understanding of the complexity of his native Peru's diverse culture. Indeed, Sendero Luminoso's principal public spokesman since the capture of Guzmán, Luis Arce Borja, has declared that "[Andean] cultural tradition has nothing to do with the war and the revolutionary struggle." Arce Borja characterizes Andean traditions as "irrationalities" and "whining nationalisms" that should be regarded as the "residue of moribund bourgeois ideology."[41] Clearly the legacy of Mariátegui has been lost by Sendero Luminoso as it has traveled a brutal path to its peculiar vision of a "New People's Democracy."

Notes

1. Statement of Abimael Guzmán, "We Will Win and You Will See It," *Revolutionary Worker* 14, no. 37 (January 17, 1993): 8–9.

2. "Interview with Abimael Guzmán Reynoso," conducted by Luis Arce Borja, *El Diario,* July 24, 1988 (author's transcript copy).

3. Gonzales Prada's biting social commentary drew important attention to the issues of race, social inequality, and militarism in Peruvian society.

4. For an excellent discussion of Mariátegui and the evolution of the Peruvian Left see Jorge Basadre, *Historia de la República del Perú, 1822–1933,* 17 vols. (Lima, 1983), 10:7–34.

5. José Carlos Mariátegui, *Seven Interpretative Essays on Peruvian Reality* (Austin, TX, 1971), 163–64.

6. Mariátegui, *Seven Interpretative Essays*, 57–58.

7. Ibid., 74.

8. Ibid., 77–124.

9. Ibid., 61.

10. Basadre, *Historia*, 10:28.

11. *El Diario* interview (author's transcript copy).

12. For a discussion of APRA's political evolution within the context of Peruvian politics and civil-military affairs see the author's *Militarism and Politics in Latin America: Peru from Sánchez Cerro to Sendero Luminoso* (Westport, CT, 1991). A useful but brief review of the traditional Communist Party of Peru's position as of the mid-1980s can be found in the pamphlet "Que es el Partido Comunista Peruano y que se propone?" (Lima, 1985).

13. *Las fuerzas armadas y el proceso electoral de 1962* (Lima, 1963).

14. These guerrilla *focos* and the counterinsurgency campaign by the Peruvian armed forces are discussed in *Militarism and Politics*, 210–20.

15. *El Diario* interview (author's transcript copy).

16. The best discussion of the origins of Sendero Luminoso is in Carlos Iván Degregori, *El surgimiento de Sendero Luminoso: Ayacucho, 1969–1979* (Lima, 1990). Also among the growing literature on this topic are the informative analysis by Gustavo Gorriti Ellenbogen, *Sendero: Historia de la guerra milenaria en el Peru* (Lima, 1990), and the valuable collection of essays edited by David Scott Palmer, *The Shining Path of Peru* (New York, 1991).

17. Confidential interview with a former professor at the University of San Cristóbal de Huamanga, July 11, 1990, Ithaca, New York.

18. Peruvian military intelligence documents made available to the author stress the operational aspects of Guzmán's training in China. Nevertheless, the ideological impact of his visit during this tumultuous time in modern Chinese history clearly was equally important.

19. David Scott Palmer, "The Sendero Luminoso Rebellion in Peru," in *Latin American Insurgencies*, ed. George Fauriol (Washington, DC, 1985), 67–96. While a Peace Corps representative in Peru in the 1960s, Palmer was a teaching colleague of Abimael Guzmán at San Cristóbal de Huamanga.

20. *El Diario* interview (author's transcript copy).

21. Confidential interview with a staff member of the Centro de Altos Estudios Militares (Peru's National War College), May 30, 1990, Chorrillos, Peru. The arrest and release of Guzmán in 1979 has become common knowledge in Peru.

22. *El Diario* interview (author's transcript copy).

23. Carlos Tapia, *Las fuerzas armadas y Sendero Luminoso: Dos estrategias y un final* (Lima, 1997), 37–44, and confidential interview with a Peruvian government national security advisor, April 16, 1996, Washington, DC.

24. Confidential interview with a member of Peru's naval infantry (Marines), May 26, 1990, Lima, Peru, and Enrique Obando Arbulu, "La situación de la subversion hoy," unpublished paper.

25. Confidential interview with a Peruvian naval officer, May 27, 1990, Lima, Peru.

26. As early as 1983, retired army general Edgardo Mercado Jarrín, former chief of staff and interim president during the 1968–1980 military government,

warned the armed forces of the dangers in "Argentinizing" the war. He argued publicly that such an approach would undermine the counterinsurgency campaign and enhance Sendero Luminoso's recruiting. The same position was adopted by General Adrian Huamán, army commander in Ayacucho in the mid-1980s. Their arguments never received enthusiastic support within the ranks of the officer corps.

27. See Degregori, *El surgimiento de Sendero Luminoso*, and discussions with the author, New Brunswick, New Jersey, October 1992, and Washington, DC, June 1993.

28. Billie Jean Isbell, "The Emerging Patterns of Peasant Responses to Sendero Luminoso," unpublished paper, 1988; and confidential interview with a former resident of Ayacucho Department, July 11, 1990, Ithaca, New York.

29. Isbell, "The Emerging Patterns of Peasant Responses to Sendero Luminoso," and discussions with the author, July 1990, Ithaca, New York.

30. Orin Starn, "Peasants at War: Rural Defense Committees in Peru's Highlands," unpublished paper, 1991.

31. Orin Starn, "La resistencia de Huanta, Quehacer," no. 84 (July–August 1993): 34–41.

32. Poinciano del Pino, "Peasants at War," in *The Peru Reader: History, Culture, and Politics*, ed. Orin Starn, Carlos Iván Degregori, and Robin Kirk (Durham, 1995), 379–81.

33. Deborah Poole and Gerardo Renique, *Peru: Time of Fear* (London, 1992), 156–58; and Obando Arbulu, "La situación de la subversion hoy."

34. Colonel (ret.) José Bailetti Mac-Kee, "Subversion and Countersubversion: Sendero Luminoso in the Post-Guzmán Era," in *Prospects for Democracy and Peace in Peru* (Washington, DC, 1993), 21.

35. Ibid., 21–22.

36. Bailetti Mac-Kee, "Subversion and Countersubversion," 21–22; and confidential interview with a senior DINCOTE commander, Lima, Peru, July 14, 1997.

37. "People's War Will Crush the Fascist Beast!" *El Diario*. This English-language version of *El Diario*, which is undated, was sent to the author unsolicited in January 1994.

38. For a graphic account of Sendero Luminoso's violent campaign in Ayacucho see Alberto Valencia Cardenas, *Los crimenes de Sendero Luminoso en Ayacucho* (Lima, 1992). The documentary literature on the issue of human rights abuses is growing. A particularly well-researched account of Peru's *desplazados* (displaced persons) is Robin Kirk, *The Decade of Chaqwa: Peru's Internal Refugees* (Washington, DC, 1991).

39. "Is a Peace Accord Possible in Peru?" *El Diario* (insert). This undated supplement to the newspaper was received by the author in January 1994.

40. Capitán de Navio Alfredo Palacios Dongo, "Terrorismo y derechos humanos en el Peru," *Revista de Marina* 85, no. 1 (January–March 1992): part 1, and 85, no. 2 (April–June 1992): part 2. For the Peruvian government's position on the human rights situation as of mid-1992 see "Peru: 1992 Obligaciones Internacionales de Estado y gobierno de facto," Informe de la Coordinadora Nacional de Derechos Humanos (Lima, 1992).

41. Luis Arce Borja, *El Diario*, January 1994.

16

The Iron Legions

Daniel Castro

One of the defining characteristics of the Shining Path is the level of in-fluence that women have played in the creation and development of the movement. In this conflict initiated by the Shining Path, women have shared equal responsibility and equal status with their male counterparts. What is more, they have occupied an unusually large number of important po-sitions from the level of local subcommittees all the way to the Central Committee. Daniel Castro, a historian and the author of " 'War Is Our Daily Life': Women's Participation in Sendero Luminoso," establishes the fact that the women of the Shining Path are the repositories of a long tradition of struggle among Andean women. Thus, the revolutionary women of Sendero faced a dichotomous quandary: in order to transform the present and turn the world upside down, they had to reach into the past. Despite the fact that Sendero is almost extinct, the war has brought a new awareness of the combative potential of Peruvian women in gen-eral, and of Andean women in particular.

The active role played by women in the uprising led by the Communist Party of Peru (Sendero Luminoso), 1980–1992, should be seen not as a surprising development, but rather as the culmination of a long tradi-tion of Andean women's participation in movements of resistance and re-bellion in Peru going back to colonial times. This latest incursion of women into the realm of revolutionary guerrilla violence, in a society long domi-nated by an economically and politically powerful patriarchal elite, rep-resents only another facet of Peruvian women's ongoing struggle for recognition and equality.

As the purported repository of a long tradition of Andean resistance and rebellion, Sendero Luminoso managed to successfully articulate spe-cific problems affecting women throughout the country in general and the Andean region in particular. Despite the plurality of cultures in Peru, for all practical purposes the whole society can be divided into two distinct ethnic groups, Indians and non-Indians.[1] This division along ethnic lines separates an upper from a lower world; the Indians inhabit the lower world while non-Indians enjoy the privileges of the upper world. By extension, the same distinction could be made applicable to women who, because of gender and economic class, are condemned to inhabit the lower world.

The prominent Peruvian writer José María Arguedas, recognizing the existence of a dichotomous world inhabited by Indians and *mistis* (white overlords), posited a situation where no meaningful dialogue other than that of violence between these two components of society was possible. This violent confrontation was bound to take place when the Indians managed to transform their passive hatred of the *mistis* into a collective flood of rage.[2] By concentrating its activities in the predominantly agricultural Andean region and its Indian population, Sendero Luminoso came closer than any other movement, save the Great Andean Rebellion of the eighteenth century, to transforming the collective hatred of the Indians into an unstoppable flood of rage.

Unlike other revolutionary movements in Latin America, Sendero's preoccupation with the woman question resulted in the active recruitment and participation of large numbers of women as rank-and-file members and as leaders of the movement. The historical roots of this preoccupation can be found in the writings of the founder of the Communist Party of Peru, José Carlos Mariátegui, and a small but vocal group of women writing in *Amauta*, the journal created by Mariátegui as a vehicle of expression for the revolutionary aspirations of a generation coming of age in the wake of the Soviet Revolution. These ideological postulates later became inordinately important in the reemergence of the "reconstituted" party in the Andean context of Ayacucho between the closing days of 1979 and the beginning of 1980.[3]

Writing in 1924, Mariátegui celebrated the gains made by women in the twentieth century, an optimistic outlook that led him to prematurely proclaim that "gradually we have come to the juridical and political equality of both sexes."[4] In the mid-1960s the People's Feminine Movement (Movimiento Feminino Revolucionario, or MFP), one of Sendero's "mass organizations," chose the works of former Soviet commissar Alexandra Kollontai as texts for studying and discussing the woman question.[5]

The MFP began as a group representing the women of the Revolutionary Student Front (Frente Estudiantil Revolucionario, or FER) at the University of San Cristóbal de Huamanga (Universidad Nacional San Cristóbal de Huamanga, or UNSCH).[6] The main focus of the MFP was to educate and to incorporate peasant women from the surrounding areas into the revolutionary movement that was beginning to be articulated at

UNSCH under the leadership of philosophy professor Abimael Guzmán Reynoso.[7]

Ayacucho provided fertile ground for the development of a revolutionary movement. Ranked next to last in a map of national poverty, it was characterized by Cynthia McClintock as a "Fourth World" enclave in a "Third World country." At the time of the creation of the Ayacucho Regional Committee, the direct antecessor of Sendero, in the early 1970s, Ayacucho lacked the most elementary services; it reputedly had one physician per 18,000 inhabitants, while the caloric intake of its inhabitants was less than half of the World Health Organization's prescribed minimum of 850 calories.[8] The department also led the nation in illiteracy, in adult and infant mortality; in the twenty years between 1961 and 1981 its population decreased from 4.1 percent to less than 3 percent of the country's total, while it received only 1 percent of the national budget earmarked for domestic expenditures.[9]

Accepting Mariátegui's characterization of Peruvian society as semifeudal and semicolonial, and recognizing the success of the Chinese Revolution under the guidance of Mao Tse-tung (Mao Zedong), Guzmán posited that the peasantry in Peru represented the truest revolutionary force in the country. Thus, all political work by the nascent organization was oriented toward the political preparation and development of the peasantry for the unavoidable revolutionary war destined to resolve, once and for all, the contradictions of class struggle.[10]

In adhering to the ideological stream flowing from Marx to Lenin to Mariátegui and Mao, and ultimately, to Guzmán, the incorporation of women into its program of preparation for the armed struggle continued to be one of Sendero's main priorities. Women were included not just as supporters but also as actual combatants.[11] The party's analysis of objective conditions concluded that Peruvian women and particularly peasant women bore the quadruple brunt that, according to Mao, characterized all semifeudal and semicolonial societies: the brunt of political, societal, marital, and religious oppression.[12] From this perspective it followed that women could be truly liberated only when the capitalist structures of class exploitation were destroyed. This conclusion was in line with Mariátegui's perception that women were first and foremost members of a class rather than members of a particular sex, and consequently their goal was to gain total social and political emancipation rather than partial liberation along gender lines.[13]

In 1975 a split occurred inside the MFP. The "democratic" faction of the MFP, favoring emancipation, won out in the ideological struggle against the faction favoring "bourgeois" liberation along gender lines. The MFP published a manifesto calling for the development of the women's movement along class lines, insisting on the view that the conditions of women's oppression were a result of the relations of ownership of the means of production rather than a sole question of gender, much in the way that Marx, Engels, and Lenin had posited the same question.[14] From this reasoning it followed that women, "who are half of the world," will develop a popular movement that will obtain the emancipation of women by women under the leadership of the party, while constantly fighting against increases in the cost of living that affect the physical integrity of the masses and struggling against the bourgeois thesis of woman's liberation.[15]

By addressing the problems faced by women—specifically peasant women—from a class perspective, Sendero provided a platform where women could be seen and heard, as well as an opportunity to participate in the war against the official Peruvian state. Sendero had chosen its target carefully, for at the time participation of women in the official political parties, including the electoral Left, was purely nominal. In 1985 three women were elected to the senate, as opposed to 57 men, while in the lower chamber women occupied 10 out of 180 seats, yet during the elections women represented 20 percent of the senatorial candidates and 10 percent of the candidates to the lower chamber.[16]

In Sendero, on the other hand, women occupied positions of leadership and responsibility in the higher ranks of the political and military arms of the organization. Such was the case of Augusta la Torre, who together with Catalina Arianzén had founded and developed the MFP. When the party went underground in 1979, La Torre became one of the most influential members of the party's Central Committee, successfully arguing in favor of initiating and developing the war on the countryside as opposed to prematurely transferring it to the urban centers of the country. It is entirely possible that her unyielding position favoring the countryside over the city as a theater of operations might have figured in her mysterious death in 1988 or 1989.[17] Catalina Arianzén was arrested and tortured by the police in 1982 and subsequently transferred to a psychiatric hospital, where she learned of her husband's death in the prison massacre of Senderistas by the armed forces and the police in 1986. This event caused her to fall into a deep state of depression, which justified her being confined to a mental hospital.[18]

Given the clandestine nature of Sendero, it is difficult to calculate with exactitude the number of women active in the organization at its point of highest activity, 1990–1992. There are estimates that 35 percent of the military leaders, particularly at the level of underground cells, were women.[19] The police placed the proportion of women members of Sendero at 33 percent, while Sendero made a larger claim of 40 percent.[20] Essays and articles appearing in Peru's press set the percentage of women members of the extended Central Committee at 56 percent.[21]

Although the exact number of women in Sendero will remain a mystery, at least for a while, it is eminently clear that with the exception of the Great Andean Rebellion of the eighteenth century, never had the role of women in a rebellion been as prominent as in this case. An illustration of the extent of women's participation in the conflict is provided by the number of women arrested by the government in its attempts to stem the tide of violence. In 1985 there were only 100 women arrested by the police, but in 1986 this number increased to 790.[22] In later years, as the armed struggle intensified, there was an exponential increase in the number of women arrested, with as many as 600 being detained in a single day.[23]

The importance of the role played by women of Sendero is also evident in the policies adopted in the "liberated zones," where strict moral guidelines were established and severe punishment meted out to those guilty of such crimes as domestic violence and the abuse of women.[24] The participation of women in Sendero generated a heroic mystique surrounding some of the better-known female fighters: Edith Lagos, Laura Zambrano, Carlota Tello, Augusta la Torre, Nelly Chavez, Sybila Arredondo, and innumerable others who became part of a unique revolutionary pantheon easily recognized by most people in the country·

Very few members of Sendero, living or dead, attained the level of recognition and admiration awarded to nineteen-year-old Edith Lagos, killed by the police on September 3, 1982. The mysterious circumstances surrounding her death added to the mythical stature of the young revolutionary and to the cult of her memory. It was never made clear whether she was shot by the police during a confrontation or killed while in police custody after being wounded and captured. Upward of thirty thousand people attended her funeral in Ayacucho in an act of open defiance to the authorities' ban on a public funeral.[25] The frail-looking, petite Edith Lagos became a tragic and romantic rallying figure. An active cadre of Sendero from the age of sixteen, Lagos symbolized the aspirations of many of the Sierra youth who were then still trying to understand the full significance of the bloody rebellion initiated only two years earlier in the remote Sierra village of Chuschi.[26] More significant still, the posthumous tribute paid to Edith Lagos was a clear recognition of the vital role that women played in the existence and survival of the organization.

Another Senderista who made a deep impression in the popular imagination was Laura Zambrano, the former leader of Sendero's Political-Military Bureau of Lima.[27] Prior to the war, she earned a reputation as a fiery leader of Peru's National Teachers Union (Sindicato Unico de

Trabajadores de la Educación del Perú, or SUTEP) in the general teachers' strikes of 1978 and 1979. In 1984 she was arrested, tortured, and raped by her captors.[28] Public outrage prompted her release soon after; she was rearrested shortly thereafter and confined to the Miguel Castro Castro high security prison in Lima, together with another seven hundred suspected women Senderistas. After serving seven years she was released in 1991 and resumed her tasks as head of the Lima Metropolitan Committee until her arrest on September 12, 1992.

Despite Sendero's avowed commitment to work for the emancipation of all women, it did not hesitate to extend its deadly violence to those women who opposed its ideological and strategic postulates.[29] This was demonstrated on February 13, 1992, when María Elena Moyano—deputy mayor of Villa El Salvador[30]—was shot to death and blown up in front of her family, one day after she had organized a march of thousands denouncing Sendero's actions in Lima's poor neighborhoods.[31]

The escalating violence of the war, exacerbated by Moyano's assassination, provided Peru's president, Alberto Fujimori, with an excuse to dissolve Congress and suspend the constitution, assuming dictatorial powers on April 5, 1992, for the alleged purpose of combating and eliminating Sendero.[32] A month later, on May 9, police commandos attacked the Miguel Castro Castro prison during an alleged prison riot, killing thirty-five members of Sendero's leadership, eight of them women. Janet Talavera and Eivia Zanabria, party members in charge of press and propaganda, and Yovanka Pardavé, in charge of the People's Support Committee, were among those selectively eliminated.[33]

Five months later, on September 12, in a remarkable combination of good police work, information from "repentant" members of the party, carelessness and overconfidence by some of the leaders, and a great deal of good fortune, Abimael Guzmán, the secretary general and "supreme commander" of Sendero Luminoso, was captured in a middle-class suburb of Lima.[34] In the same "safe house" the police arrested the number two member of the Central Committee, Elena Iparraguirre Revoredo, along with Martha Huatay Ruiz, Laura Zambrano, and one of Peru's prima ballerinas, Maritza Garrido Lecca.[35] After a summary trial all those arrested in the raid and suspected of being tied to Sendero were sentenced to life in prison in various isolated prisons in the Andes mountains. The only exception was Abimael Guzmán, who is serving time in an underground prison in Callao built especially to house him.

The arrest of the leaders of the Communist Party of Peru-Sendero Luminoso and the subsequent trial sent the Peruvian press into a feeding frenzy. Sensationalism monopolized the front pages and the "teasers" of the yellow and not so yellow electronic media. The news was filled with allusions to sexual orgies and the imminent last dance of an "AIDS-infected ballerina," and "the women of Gonzalo" filled the headlines.[36] Those covering the events of the day chose to ignore the fact that a significant segment of Peruvian women had stopped being the passive, enduring, sexual objects they were expected to be, and, through their incorporation into an armed resistance movement, sought to establish their identity as equal members of society, ready and willing to pay with their lives for their role in transforming the world. Regardless of the patriarchal implications of Guzmán's attitude toward both the men and women of the organization, the women of Sendero exemplified a unique resolve that has been absent in the majority of the population for a very long time. The determination of Senderista women and their willingness to fight to the end in order to gain total emancipation is evident in the words of Laura Zambrano, who characterizes revolutionary women as constituting the invincible "iron legions" that "are the half of the world that support the sky" and who is convinced that "the success of the revolution depends on the level of participation of the women."[37]

By mid-1997 the civil war in Peru appeared to be grinding to a halt, yet, for the war to end forever, it is necessary that an all-out effort be made by the government and the citizenry to eradicate the contradictions that bred the war. In the course of the war and its aftermath, Peruvian women rebels have demonstrated the resilience and the capacity of the human spirit to overcome even the most trying of calamities of war and death. Their participation in this war has changed forever the perception of Peruvian women as passive objects of economic, social, sexual, and political oppression. If a lesson has been learned from the violence and destruction of the immediate past, it is that any attempt to reconstruct Peru and move forward is destined to fail without the full emancipation of women and their active participation in conditions of ultimate equality.

Notes

1. Rodrigo Montoya, "Cultura y democracia en el Perú (algunos elementos para la discusión)," in *El Perú en una encrucijada* (Lima, 1988), 145–46.

2. José María Arguedas committed suicide in 1969. As a mestizo born and raised in the Andes, he, more than any other writer of his generation, captured the true spirit of the Peruvian Indian in his novels and short stories.

3. After 1964 the main priority of the pro-Chinese wing of the Communist Party was "to reconstitute the Party of the masses and to recapture Mariátegui," a task they considered accomplished prior to the initiation of armed struggle, May 17, 1980.

4. José Carlos Mariátegui, "La Mujer y la política," in *Temas de educación*, sixth ed. (Lima, 1980), 123.

5. Carol Andreas, *When Women Rebel: The Rise of Popular Feminism in Peru* (Westport, CT, 1985), 179.

6. Established in 1657, the university was closed following the War of the Pacific, 1879–1883, but it reopened in 1959. The FER's publication *Por el Sendero Luminoso de Mariátegui* (On Mariátegui's Shining Path) gave the party its nickname.

7. Abimael Guzmán began teaching philosophy at UNSCH in 1962. He was in charge of the Education Program designed to train teachers. This was particularly significant at a time when nearly 55 percent of all Peruvian women pursuing a professional career trained as teachers.

8. Some observers working in Ayacucho place the ratio at one physician per thirty-nine thousand inhabitants.

9. Carlos Iván Degregori, *Sendero Luminoso: I. Los Hondos y mortales desencuentros. II. Lucha Armada y utopia autoritaria*, sixth ed. (Lima, 1988), 9–15.

10. Luis Arce Borja and Janet Talavera "Presidente Gonzalo rompe el silencio: Entrevista en la clandestinidad," *El Diario*, July 24, 1988.

11. Juan Lázaro, "Women and Political Violence in Contemporary Peru," *Dialectical Anthropology* 15, nos. 2–3 (1990): 241.

12. José González, "Sendero de mujeres," *Si* (April 6, 1987): 83. See also Gabriela Tarazona-Sevillano with John B. Reuter, *Sendero Luminoso and the Threat of Narcoterrorism* (New York, 1990), 77.

13. José Carlos Mariátegui, "Las reivindicaciones feministas," in *Temas de educación*, 130.

14. Catalina Arianzén, "El marxismo de Mariátegui y el movimiento femenino," in Rosa Mavila León, "Presente y futuro de las mujeres de la guerra," *Quehacer* (September–October 1992): 46–47.

15. "Bases de discusión: El pensamiento Gonzalo y los trabajadores," *El Diario,* January 8, 1988.

16. *Programa Nacional de Promoción de la Mujer* (Lima, 1990), 163–64.

17. With the exception of a captured videotape showing her husband, Abimael Guzmán, reciting an elegy in front of her body, there is no available evidence fixing the time or cause of death with any degree of certainty.

18. Gustavo Gorriti, *Sendero: Historia de la Guerra Milenaria en el Perú* (Lima, 1990), 360. The last official report lists her as still being in the hospital as late as 1987. An estimated 250 Senderistas were killed in the prison uprisings of June 1986. Prominent among them was Arianzén's husband, Antonio Díaz Martínez.

19. Lázaro, "Women and Political Violence," 234.

20. Orin Starn, "New Literature on Peru's Sendero Luminoso," *Latin American Research Review* 27, no. 2 (1992): 218. The 33 percent figure was provided by Starn, who cites statistics furnished by Robin Kirk in an unpublished essay on the women of Sendero scheduled to appear in English. The Spanish version of Kirk's monograph, *Grabado en piedra: Las mujeres de Sendero Luminoso* (Lima, 1993), provides both the police's and Sendero's estimates.

21. Mavila, "Las mujeres de la guerra," 45. See also "Partido Comunista del Perú-Sendero Luminoso," *La Republica*, Lima, September 13, 1993. The newspaper carried an organizational chart of Sendero's "directorate," listing twelve women and eleven men.

22. González, "Sendero de mujeres," 81.

23. Carol Andreas, "Women at War," *Report on the Americas* 24, no. 4 (December/January 1990–91): 21.

24. Ibid., 21. See also Tarazona-Sevillano, *Sendero Luminoso*, 77–79.

25. Lázaro, "Women and Political Violence," 243.

26. Gorriti, *Sendero*, 362–63.

27. González, "Sendero de mujeres," 80, 82; "Las caras del terror: La cúpula senderista," *Caretas* (March 4, 1991): 32–33.

28. Andreas, *When Women Rebel*, 184.

29. Virginia Vargas, "Women: Tragic Encounters with the Left," *Report on the Americas*, 25, no. 5 (May1992): 30.

30. Located in the outskirts of Lima, Villa El Salvador was transformed from a straw-mat squatter settlement into a model of urban planning and development.

31. Simon Strong, "Where the Shining Path Leads," *New York Times Magazine*, May 24, 1992.

32. James Brooke, "A Lethal Army of Insurgents Lima Could Not Stamp Out," *New York Times*, April 17, 1992.

33. Nathaniel C. Nash, "Peru Routs Rebels in 4-Day Prison Fight," *New York Times*, May 11, 1992; *Notimex* Wire Service, May 11–13, 1992.

34. James Brooke, "The Snaring of Guzmán: 'Bingo—We Got Him,'" *New York Times*, September 15, 1992.

35. Nathaniel C. Nash, "Peru Rebel Group Seen as Potent," *New York Times*, September 15, 1992. Martha Huatay was assumed to have been in charge of the People's Support Committee to assist suspected Sendero members in preparing legal defenses.

36. Mavila, "Las mujeres," 44.

37. "Nuestra vida cotidiana es la guerra: Entrevista exclusiva a Laura Zambrano Padilla," *El Diario*, March 14, 1988.

17

Tunnel to Canto Grande

Claribel Alegría and Darwin J. Flakoll

Despite the hegemonic claims of Sendero Luminoso, in 1983 a different guerrilla group, the Tupac Amaru Revolutionary Movement (MRTA), erupted onto the Peruvian political landscape. Unlike Sendero, the MRTA was born out of a coalition of leftist groups that were not totally opposed to participation in mainstream politics. Led by former APRA sympathizer Victor Polay, the MRTA concentrated its activities in the northeastern region of the country and in Lima. Within a few short years, most of its leaders had been imprisoned in the Canto Grande prison complex in Lima. For almost three years, their comrades dug a tunnel from the outside, and on July 9, 1990, a scant nineteen days from the presidential inauguration of Alberto Fujimori, the MRTA completed the work. Forty-eight of its members, including Polay, escaped. Claribel Alegría and Darwin Flakoll, longtime collaborators in fiction and reportage projects, authors of Ashes of Izalco *and* The Death of Somoza, *were preceded to Peru by their reputation as trustworthy reporters, and for a week they were granted the rare opportunity of interviewing a wide array of leaders and members of the MRTA. Their book,* Tunnel to Canto Grande, *is the result of their investigative work with the MRTA.*

The only MRTA prisoners inside Canto Grande who knew the tunnel project was under way could not understand why the digging went so slowly. Rodrigo described the psychological tensions that afflicted them:

> A prisoner always yearns for his freedom. We on the inside felt a constant anguish at the snail-like progress that was being made, whereas the compañeros on the outside had a cooler, more dispassionate view

From *Tunnel to Canto Grande* (Willimantic, CT: Curbstone Press, 1996), 138–58. Reprinted by permission of Curbstone Press. Distributed by Consortium.

of the project and a better understanding of the obstacles and security problems that were encountered and the time it took to overcome them. It's not that we didn't understand these delays, but we became more and more exasperated with the passage of time. After all, nearly three years had gone by since the inception of the plan. Also, we only had rudimentary information as to how the work was progressing outside. The visitors who passed us information couldn't go into detail. Just as one example, Ciro came to me one night and told me how he had sneaked into the "no-man's-land" between Pavilions 1-B and 2-A and pressed his ear to the earth to see if he could hear any sounds of underground digging that would indicate the tunnelers were drawing near. I decided to break the news to him that the tunnel hadn't even passed under Tower No. 8 and penetrated into the prison compound. It nearly broke his heart.

Meanwhile, the work of mapping the underground passageways in minute detail continued. The crucial routes that had to be opened were from Pavilion 2-A to the admissions building, where the women prisoners were locked in on the floor above the clinic, and from Pavilion 2-A all the way around to Pavilion 6-B, adjoining Victor Polay's third-floor cell in the *venusterio*. Some of the locked gates and steel doors along these two subterranean passageways had proven recalcitrant and efforts to make keys for the locks had failed. A breakthrough was finally achieved when the prisoners discovered the virtues of caustic soda. When this was applied to the bolt heads atop the door hinges and the application was renewed every several days, the bolt heads slowly melted, and the entire door or gate could simply be lifted up and removed from the hinges. Facsimiles of the bolt heads were smuggled into Canto Grande and secured to the bolts with Epoxy glue.

Another important preparatory measure undertaken months in advance was the construction of an enclosed latrine in the open patio of Pavilion 2-A. It was announced that this was to be closed except on days when women visitors were allowed into the prison, as it was intended for their exclusive use. In reality, the women's latrine served a double purpose: first, it added to the impression that the MRTA prisoners were constantly improving the conditions of their living area to make their lengthy incarceration as comfortable as possible. Much more important, however, it was intended as the possible prison end of the tunnel. The entire patio of Pavilion 2-A was cemented over to discourage any tunneling attempts from the patio itself. It had always been envisioned that the tunnel would have its outlet in the patio, but due to its length and its various twists and turns, it would be a veritable miracle were it to surface at an exact predetermined point. Armando anticipated that when it reached the surface, the diggers would find themselves somewhere under the cemented floor of the patio, where it would be impossible to break through the concrete rapidly and noiselessly. Hence the need for the women's latrine, where the concrete had been perforated and the necessary escape hatch already existed. The other possible exit point lay in the triangular patch of "no-man's-land" where the fronts of Pavilions 1-B and 2-A nearly abutted. This area was fenced off but was not paved with concrete, so a tunnel exit at that point could be opened almost noiselessly.

Still another necessary preparatory measure for the escape was to make sure that all the prisoners were in tip-top physical condition and able to make the 350-meter dash for freedom in a hunched-over, crouching position without collapsing. Well before the time arrived, Rodrigo ordered the leaders of the morning exercises to make sure that everyone did fifty deep knee bends every day. The purpose, of course, was to get their leg muscles in shape for the coming ordeal.

"Forty-five, forty-six, forty-seven, forty-eight, forty-nine, and . . . fifty." Victor Polay grunted as he pushed himself erect after the last knee bend and exhaled explosively. Months of sedentary prison life and excessive carbohydrates in the daily diet had girdled his midriff with extra pounds, and now the time had come to work them off. He was subjecting himself to the same physical-fitness campaign that he had prescribed for the other MRTA prisoners, and besides the setting-up exercises he performed in his cell on awakening, he jogged for an hour each morning and each afternoon in the small patio behind the *venusterio*.

He had also gradually changed his sleeping habits in preparation for the forthcoming escape. Whereas he had previously turned in with the other prisoners on the third floor after the evening television programs ended, he now went downstairs at midnight and chatted with the general until they set out the pieces on the chessboard and continued their endless nightly tournament. The general was an inveterate night owl who usually went to bed near dawn and slept through the morning When their chess match ended at 3:30 or 4, Victor would stretch, yawn, and bid the general goodnight, then go clattering up the stairs to his own cell, taking care to make enough noise so that the Republican guard on the first floor would sleepily make a mental note that Polay was on his way up to bed as usual.

To make up for the lost hours of sleep, Victor took a substantial siesta after lunch each day. He knew that when the tunnel opened, the escape would have to take place before dawn, after the guards changed shifts at 3, and the new watch had been given enough time to grow somnolent. It was also clear to him and Rodrigo that the escape could not be scheduled after a visitors' day at Canto Grande, because the common prisoners, having received cash or food from their family, would exchange it for liquor or cocaine paste and frequently stay up celebrating all night long.

Jaime and Paloma had known each other casually before they were thrown together at close quarters, night and day for eighteen months. Paloma knew that Jaime had been involved in a relationship with another woman before he was sent to prison and then had come directly from prison to work on the tunnel.

We interviewed Paloma and Jaime separately about their participation in the project, and then—after Jaime blurted out something to the effect that the Canto Grande excavation had also turned out to be the backdrop of a budding romance—we interviewed them together late one evening in the Lima safe house.

"We felt attracted to each other from the beginning," Paloma confessed, "but it's natural to feel a warm affection for all those with whom you share dangers and difficulties. Also, I'd heard about the 'other woman,' and I was careful to behave in a neutral manner as one does when a man is committed to someone else. But still, I felt there was something supernatural at work."

"The other thing was all over. It was in the past, but Paloma wouldn't believe me," Jaime protested.

"That's because you don't have a trustworthy face," Paloma retorted.

"It all started in the house," Jaime said. "We were together all the time. Paloma had to learn her job, and I helped her as much as I could when I wasn't digging."

"I thought things over for a long time," Paloma volunteered. "I was worried that if we fell in love we wouldn't do our jobs properly, that somehow it would be an undisciplined, unrevolutionary thing to do. But at the same time, I believe one has to make a revolution happily, smiling and looking into each other's eyes, because at any moment you can die, or be captured, tortured, and sent to prison for years."

"Wasn't the problem with Jorge another complication?" Claribel asked.

"Of course. Jorge saw that we were becoming very close, and he was jealous. He declared himself to me one day, saying he had always dreamt of falling in love with a girl like me, and he begged me to please stop flirting with Jaime.

"I told him I wasn't flirting—well, not very much—but the fact is that Jaime is volatile and full of life, and I get along very well with him because he's a happy person and always bubbling over with new ideas. But Jorge started pressuring me, and I had no idea how he felt until then. I told him: 'I want to clear things up. Jaime isn't my *compañero*, but neither are you, so you have no right to dictate to me.' At that point, he said he thought we were both behaving badly and he was going to call a meeting to complain."

"That was an immature reaction on his part," Jaime broke in. "Jorge should have realized that sentimental relations are involuntary and can't be negotiated, but he was young and bullheaded, and he insisted on making a complicated, noisy issue of it."

"Was this a meeting of the whole group?" we asked.

"No, it was just Antonio and the three of us," Paloma replied, "but I wanted to sink through the floor, because Jorge accused Jaime of betraying his previous girlfriend, who was also a member of the organization, and said that Jaime's opportunistic conduct disappointed him. His words implied that I was a loose woman, and that really wounded me. Then Jaime spoke up and said the other affair was a thing of the past, and he admitted he was in love with me.

"Finally, I told them that I had come here to do a job and that was my principal objective. The party had chosen us to accomplish this task, and we were wasting time with these emotional squabbles. In the end, we all agreed that the closed environment and our own emotional immaturity were to blame for the incident, and that we should put it behind us and get on with the job."

But it wasn't easy, Paloma admitted, because they still felt strongly attracted to each other. She particularly recalled the incident of the rose.

"One day Jaime gave me a rose from the garden, and I put it in a glass of water in the kitchen. Some days later he came up from the tunnel to ask me for some medicine because his stomach was bothering him, and he saw the rose was still there. Go ahead and tell them what you told me."

Jaime was visibly embarrassed, but he replied: "Something about how a rose that once blossomed was now withering and fading away, and how could we permit that to happen? After that our relationship kept on developing in an inevitable way."

"But how did you find a chance to talk to each other with so many people in the house?" Claribel was curious about practical details.

"We talked to each other normally in front of the others," Jaime replied, "and none of the *compañeros* knew that. . . ."

"And besides, we'd go down to the library late at night where we could talk and read," Paloma interrupted, "because Jaime loves to read. That was our way of getting away from the others."

"The tunnel, of course!" Claribel exclaimed. "Wonderful! It turned out to be a tunnel of love as well as a freedom tunnel."

The two of them blushed and exchanged complicitous smiles.

When Paloma's back began to bother her in November 1989, Jaime helped her in the kitchen when he finished his work shift.

"I scoured pots and pans, swept and mopped, and cleaned up the kitchen," Jaime grinned. "I washed clothes and the household linen, and I peeled thousands of potatoes. By January her pain was unbearable, and we had to bring in a 'cousin' to take over the job."

Paloma's sciatic nerve was affected, and she had to sleep with a board under her thin mattress. She was also in a state of deep depression, because the muscles in one of her legs were visibly atrophying, and she feared she would become paralyzed or even lose the leg.

The MRTA doctor who came to the safe house periodically to examine her agreed that palliatives were not helping, and she would have to submit to a delicate and dangerous operation. Luis Angel drove her to the hospital and registered her, and the following day she underwent the operation. It was successful, and by the fifth day she was walking.

"While she was in the hospital, I was delegated to come to Lima and buy the big truck," Jaime said. "It took several days to find one the right size, in good condition, but not flashy enough to draw attention. Because of that, I was able to come and visit her with Luis Angel as soon as she awoke after the operation."

"I came to, and there they were," Paloma recalled. "I was deeply touched by those two wonderful people, closer than brothers, who seemed to be the only ones concerned about my condition at that moment."

Paloma left the hospital after eight days and spent the next two weeks convalescing at the home of a friend. When she returned to the operational base, she was walking normally and relieved of pain, and she gradually resumed her share of the household duties. The only limitation on her activities was a prohibition against lifting weights.

But Paloma's brush with disfigurement and paralysis had led her to think deeply about her relationship with Jaime, and she came to the conclusion that it was hypocritical to continue dissembling before the other members of the team. Jaime heartily agreed.

"When I returned, there was an evaluation session to analyze how the work was going, and Jaime and I took the opportunity to announce to everybody that we were now *compañeros*. We did that to dispel any doubts or possible misunderstandings."

"And how did the others react to the news?"

"Nobody was really surprised," Jaime said. "They had all seen it coming, and they accepted it as something natural."

"And what was Jorge's reaction?"

"He had no visible reaction. Life went on as before," Jaime recalled.

"He was finally convinced," Paloma said, "and we kept on being friends to the very end."

"That's wonderful!" Claribel exclaimed, to bring the evening session to a close.

Meanwhile, for what seemed like the first time since the inception of the project, the digging proceeded smoothly and steadily and the tunnel steadily crept forward beneath the Canto Grande prison compound at the rate of three meters a day.

Armando was able to visit the safe house more frequently during the excavation of the "Heroes and Martyrs of Los Molinos" leg and he often spent the entire night there. Armando had an obsession about tunnels, and during one of our conversations he waxed eloquent on the subject.

> I was always happy to go down in the tunnel. I got used to it, and some-times I worked down there at night. It's a bit gloomy, dark and damp, but it has a certain charm. There's nothing more amazing than total dark-ness. When you turn out the lights, you feel a complete solitude and absence of light. I would do this frequently and lie down, feeling a tran-quil, agreeable sensation. They say it's a psychological technique using sensory deprivation that is very relaxing. I always felt calm working at night. And it's beautiful when you've been down below for a long time to come out and look up at the starry sky.

Nevertheless, Armando's mind was troubled. The tunnel now extended more than 200 meters underground and included two sharp curves, one to the left and another to the right. The fact that the diggers had hit their first objective—the water tower—squarely on the nose gave him a sense of confidence. But that had been a simple calculation, because the water tower was visible from the roof of the operational base, and he had only to calculate for the displacement created by the first, "Che Lives," leg of the tunnel. The MRTA had secured several general architectural plans of Canto Grande, each of which showed its geographical orientation with respect to due north. The problem that gnawed at his mind was that these maps disagreed with each other as to the true orientation of the prison compound, and an error of a few degrees in setting the direction of the final leg of the tunnel could lead to a mistake of twenty or thirty meters in arriving at the predetermined exit point. His only instrument for setting the course to be followed was a surveyor's theodolite, which was difficult to use in the cramped underground space, and he had no way of double-checking the accuracy of his calculations. The MRTA prisoners had un-successfully taken various compass readings from different points inside Canto Grande to try to establish the prison's orientation with respect to magnetic north, but their results contradicted each other.

I visited Canto Grande myself—he told us—and took surreptitious com-pass readings and made observations which led me to conclude that the plans in our possession were skewed by between fifteen and thirty degrees, which is a tremendous error. The *compañeros* inside had an ordinary, nonprofessional compass, but there is such a maze of iron reinforcing bars in the walls that the compass was thrown off and we couldn't trust the results. In the end, they took about thirty readings from different positions, and I drew up an average reading which I felt was more or less correct. We set our course inside the compound by that reading, but I knew we were flying blind and would have to make another correction before setting off on the final leg.

~

I was awakened one morning by the sound of a heavy tractor motor in the outer patio—Victor recounted.—From the corridor window a narrow slice of the no-man's-land next to Tower No. 8 was visible, and there I could see a heavy Caterpillar bulldozer digging a trench parallel to the wall of the outer enclosure. A prison trusty was standing next to me, watching the activity, and I asked him: "What's happening out there? Are they finally putting in a water reservoir?" "No," he said, "they're looking for a tunnel. Last night the guards in the tower heard digging noises. They think it's coming from Pavilion 6-A, and now they're trying to uncover it."

An icy hand clutched at Victor's heart. He knew, of course, that the tunnel had penetrated beneath Tower No. 8 and the water tank and was now aimed at the patio of Pavilion 2-A. One of the diggers had been careless, and the guards had heard him. The MRTA chief watched helplessly as the bulldozer relentlessly pushed sand out of the trench and slowly disappeared from sight below ground level. As he watched, a heavy steamroller chugged into the enclosure and started trundling ponderously back and forth parallel to the trench in an attempt to cave in the tunnel with its sheer weight. Later, it was joined by a third piece of heavy construction equipment: a mechanized trencher that started banging its heavy excavating shovel against the ground in the area between the bulldozed trench and Pavilion 6-A.

The occupants of 6-A were drug traffickers—Victor continued—and it was natural to think they were the tunnelers because they were closest to where the digging sounds had been heard. Besides, they were the richest group of prisoners and had the money to bribe guards and smuggle digging tools into Canto Grande. It was also natural for the authorities to assume that the tunnel originated under Pavilion 6-A and was heading toward the outer wall. It never occurred to them that the tunnel originated outside the walls and was aimed inward. And it never crossed their minds that the MRTA could be digging a tunnel, because our group was on the fourth floor of Pavilion 2-A, and the lower floors were occupied by common prisoners, with a generous sprinkling of stool pigeons. An excavation could never be hidden from them.

Inside the tunnel itself, the diggers were first paralyzed by the sounds of the bulldozer's engine and its clanking treads passing back and forth overhead, and then by the dull, booming explosions every time the trenching tractor banged its shovel against the earth.

"They've found us." Jaime was desperate as another thud freed a shower of sand particles above his head. He and Armando were at the tunnel face where the overhead had not yet been stuccoed with cement gruel. Armando, his jaw clenched with anxiety, listened to the noises above that carried clearly through the earth.

"They've heard us," he corrected Jaime, "but they haven't found us yet. Stop the digging, and let's get back to the base."

One of the diggers was posted at the turn where the second leg of the tunnel merged into the new "Heroes and Martyrs of Los Molinos" leg. His task was to report to the safe house if any cave-ins occurred. Armando and Jaime scurried the length of the tunnel and climbed the vertical ladder. Paloma and her "cousin" María busied themselves outside the house as lookouts in case a guard patrol started making a house-to-house search of the neighborhood, while the entire team busied themselves inside to remove all evidence that the base was occupied by eighteen people rather than four. Bedrolls, sleeping bags, changes of clothing, as well as extra plates and cutlery were stowed in the underground library and the cover of the tunnel shaft was poised for instant lowering as soon as the last digger disappeared into the earth in the event of a police raid.

Armando sat at the dining-room table and reviewed the situation. During the past week, the underground terrain through which the tunnel was advancing had changed from a compact sand and dirt mixture with only occasional large rocks, to a difficult, boulder-studded composition of soil. Undoubtedly, one of the diggers had banged the wedge end of his crowbar into a boulder and the sound had carried up to the surface. What was done was done and couldn't be corrected now, but Armando felt confident that the tunnel could not be uncovered by overhead trenching because, according to his calculations, it was at least fifteen meters below the surface, and no bulldozer could dig that deep without caving in the sides of the trench.

Canto Grande is located at the upper edge of an alluvial plain that slopes imperceptibly downward to the plain of Lima from the first escarpments of the Andean foothills. To the naked eye, the terrain appears level, but Armando's calculations with the theodolite informed him that the ground level of the Canto Grande compound was at least nine meters

higher than ground level at the safe house, and he had made sure that the
tunnel kept to a dead-level horizontal course despite its twists and turns.
This ensured that by the time the diggers penetrated beneath the outer
wall of the prison they would be at least fifteen meters below the surface.
Armando closed his eyes and imaginatively placed himself inside the mind
of any Canto Grande prison official. It was against all logic and incon-
ceivable to the prison mentality that would-be escapees should dig straight
down for fifteen meters before leveling off to a horizontal course and
heading for the nearest outer wall. If they dug down fifteen meters—and
where would they hide all that dirt?—they would have to dig upward the
same distance to get back to the surface when the tunnel reached a safe
exit point. And where, to reiterate, would the tunnelers hide all that dirt?
No, Armando shook his head. He was confident that the tunnel was safe
from discovery.

Victor Polay tells of his reaction to the suddenly increased tension:

It took us two days to get word to the safe house about what was happening inside the prison, but of course they already knew from the sounds of
the bulldozer and trencher overhead, and they had suspended digging. It
was during that time that the new prison commandant visited the *venusterio*
and spoke to Victor.

"What do you think we're doing out there, *Señor* Polay?" he asked
me.

"I imagine you're putting in a water reservoir," I said.

"No," he told me, "we're hunting for a tunnel that the narcos are
digging."

"If you're so worried about tunnels," I suggested, "why don't you dig
a moat five meters deep running all the way around the outer wall?"

"You know, that's not such a bad idea," he said thoughtfully.

Actually, every prison official always suffers from tunnel psychosis.
While I was in Canto Grande they discovered two tunnels being dug by
common prisoners, not to mention the first tunnel the MRTA tried to dig.
And the current flurry of activity deepened that psychosis.

I remember one day I was in the *venusterio* patio talking to Major
Jara and Captain Castillo, and Major Jara said: "You aren't looking well,
Mr. Polay; you're losing weight. What's wrong? Aren't your *compañeros*
feeding you properly?"

"No," I replied. "I'm dieting to lose weight so I can escape through
your tunnel over there."

They nearly died laughing.

"It's true," I went on. "I read about the tunnel escape in Chile several
years ago, and there was a fat man who got stuck halfway through. He

deserved it, of course, but the worst part was that all the prisoners behind him were prevented from completing their escape. So I'm taking no chances."

They all thought that was terribly funny, and it never entered their minds that it might be true. After all, they knew that I was counting on negotiating an amnesty with Vargas Llosa after the elections. And here I was, cooped up with captains, majors, colonels, and generals in the maximum-security ward. There was more army brass around me than if I'd been imprisoned in a military fortress.

The bulldozer dug a trench five meters deep and some twenty-five meters long in two days, while the steamroller and trencher moved ponderously back and forth over the area where the digging noises had been heard. Their efforts were in vain, and, to Victor's immense relief, on the third day they were withdrawn. Republican guards continued hammering iron probes into the soil, but to no avail. Armando's calculations had been vindicated, and the tunnel kept on advancing at a depth of fifteen meters.

The patch of rocky soil cleared up, almost miraculously, and the diggers now found themselves penetrating into an area of hard, compacted sand that was ideal for excavation. The tunnel walls and overhead were so firm that timbering was unnecessary and only the overhead was stuccoed. Despite the precautions taken to work silently, the two shifts were now progressing steadily at the rate of three meters per day and the eighty meters of the "Heroes and Martyrs of Los Molinos" leg was completed in four weeks.

It was now the beginning of June 1990, and the deadline for completion imposed by the National Directorate was only six weeks away. Three new arrivals joined the team to make a total of eighteen diggers, plus four above ground in the household staff, or a total of twenty-two people crowded into the cramped safe house. Through months of close-quarters living and hard-won experience underground, the entire team now functioned like a well-oiled machine. The dirt moved steadily back from the tunnel face in three one-man carts, was hoisted to the surface and hauled away in the truck. Huge amounts of high-calorie food arrived regularly to be prepared by Paloma and María and dispensed to the hungry crew.

Armando calculated that the tunnel had reached the rear corner of the patio belonging to Pavilion 1-A and a course correction was now required to steer it beneath Patios 1-A and 1-B and into the patio area of Pavilion 2-A. Leg No. 4—a short stretch of only thirteen meters—veered to the left and was christened, "Hasta la victoria, siempre" (Until victory, always), from a celebrated phrase by Che Guevara. It was made necessary to avoid digging beneath the two pavilions themselves. This leg was accomplished in five days, and Armando set the final course to bring the tunnel beneath the patio of 2-A to its exit point in the no-man's-land beside the MRTA pavilion.

With the new *compañeros*, we now had two shifts of nine workers in each team—Antonio recalls—but the digging conditions continued to be difficult. When the electricity went off there was no ventilation, only emergency lighting, and the heat was always stifling. Under those conditions we discovered that we could make the best progress by working twenty-four hours a day, including Sundays, and dividing the team into two shifts of twelve hours each. That way, each team got twelve hours or more of rest after completing its quota, and everyone was fresh and motivated when they started work again. We also decided we could reduce the dimensions of the tunnel on the last leg to one meter high by seventy centimeters wide, and this enabled us to start progressing at the rate of five meters a day.

The final stretch was christened "Tupac Amaru, libertador" (Tupac Amaru, liberator), and Armando estimated its length at somewhere between sixty and seventy-five meters. Halfway through its excavation he instructed the diggers to start sloping the tunnel toward the surface at the rate of one meter's rise for each three meters advanced.

June drew to an end, and the digging slowed as the tunnel penetrated another patch of almost cement-like sand. It was also made more difficult because the mine cars were unusable on the upward slope, and the dirt-filled sacks had to be hauled down to level ground before being loaded into the carts.

Antonio was digging at the tunnel face late one afternoon when he dropped his crowbar and pressed his ear to the sandy wall.

"Ricardito," he called to one of the haulers, "go get Armando and tell him to bring his stethoscope. I can hear the *bombo*."

~

The MRTA musical group in Canto Grande had achieved professional quality after practicing together daily over a period of nearly two years. The instruments were a motley collection: two guitars, two *quenas* (the Andean shepherd's bamboo flute), a *charanga* or five-string soprano guitar, various percussion instruments, and a large *bombo* drum whose deep throbbing tone set the beat for the musicians and the choral group.

Initially, they had practiced in the corridor of the fourth floor of their pavilion, preparing concerts which they presented in the patio on visitors' days. During the past few months, however, on instructions passed along from Armando, they had started giving daily concerts in the patio for the entertainment of all the prison inmates. The musicians and the twelve-man choral group assembled along the wall that separated the patio from the triangular patch of no-man's-land and started playing and singing punctually at 5 P.M. The *bombo* drum rested on the cement floor of the patio, and its deep bass note reverberated through the earth, providing a subterranean sonar beacon to guide the tunnelers to their final exit point.

Armando pressed past Antonio and applied his stethoscope to different points at the face and sides of the tunnel.

"I can even hear the guitars and the voices," he told Antonio. "They're singing the MRTA hymn. They are right on schedule, and we are right on course."

There were other surface noises that carried down to the tunnel. The world soccer championship play-offs were under way in Italy, and prisoners and guards alike clustered around every television set in Canto Grande. Because of the frequent blackouts, the Republican guards had brought a gasoline generator into the central patio so they could follow the matches even when the power failed. During these periods, the throbbing of the gasoline motor provided another directional point of reference for the diggers.

Armando planned to bring the tunnel to the surface under the patio of Pavilion 2-A and he expected to find himself somewhere beneath the concrete paving which covered the entire patio. Then, using the paving as the tunnel overhead, he intended to dig horizontally from that point either toward the ready-made exit of the women's latrine or toward the natural dirt surface of the no-man's-land between Pavilion 1-B and 2-A, whichever was closer.

The next two days were spent probing upward at a thirty-degree angle, and Armando approved a reduction in the dimensions to a square excavation measuring seventy by seventy centimeters. On the third day, the diggers discovered to their dismay that the hard, compacted sand they had been tunneling through was gradually giving way to a looser mixture of sand and earth that came showering down every time they raked the overhead with their crowbars. Jaime called Armando to the tunnel face and demonstrated the problem to him.

"This is the most dangerous terrain we've struck so far," he worried. "We could have a cave-in at any minute. Don't you think we should start timbering again?"

Armando inspected the overhead carefully with his flashlight.

"We should have anticipated this," he said thoughtfully. "We're very close to the surface now, and we're running into the loose earth fill that was bulldozed when the prison was under construction. The tunnel is too small and the slope is too steep for timbering, so we'll have to keep tunneling upward and hope for the best."

The earth around them was now a mixture of dirt and sand that had not been compacted by centuries of rain and compression. The digger at the tunnel face was ordered to tie a rope around his waist as a safety precaution, so that in case of a cave-in his companions could pull him out by brute force before he smothered.

It was Sunday, a visitors' day and the final day of the world soccer championship. Digging was proceeding around the clock, and Antonio's group came on duty at 4 P.M.

The leader of the previous team warned me that the earth was soft and no longer sandy—he told us.—There was also a shortage of sacks by then because many of them had been torn on protruding rocks now that the tunnel dimensions were so much smaller. When I reached the tunnel face I found the situation really frightening. All I had to do was scratch overhead and the earth came showering down. The worst of it was that we estimated we were still at least eight meters underground, and that's a lot of dirt hanging over one's head. We also had the fixed idea that we were going to come up under the concrete layer of the patio floor and would have to tunnel horizontally from there.

I happened to be the one who was digging when it happened. The noise above me was louder than ever, and I even thought I could hear footsteps, when suddenly the earth caved in over my head. I threw myself backward into the tunnel so I wouldn't be buried. But strangely enough, the quantity of earth that came down wasn't very great, and when it stopped I inched forward and found myself looking up at a dim round light. I couldn't see very well, and at first I didn't understand what had happened. I shone my flashlight upward, then turned it off, and I began to realize I was looking up at the sky. It was 6:30, twilight time, and the light was dim. I could hear the murmur of voices overhead, but it wasn't until a current of fresh air began to flow against my face that it suddenly dawned on me that we'd finally reached our goal: the Canto Grande tunnel was open from end to end.

18

Sources and Resources of Zapatism

Michael Lowy

The revolutionary tradition of Mexico received a rejuvenating jolt in the early hours of January 1, 1994, when a ragtag army made up of members of various ethnic groups native to Chiapas seized five of the main highland towns of the state. They demanded justice and the overthrow of the president of the republic, Carlos Salinas de Gortari. The rebels identified themselves as the Zapatista National Liberation Army (EZLN). Acting with textbooklike precision, the EZLN posted its list of demands and after a brief and bloody confrontation with the army withdrew into its jungle hideout. This latest uprising by a largely Latin American indigenous group captured the world's attention and imagination. As a result, the true nature of the Chiapas rebellion has become the object of a multitude of arguments. It has been variously defined as an indigenous rebellion, a reformist uprising, a modern revolution, and a postmodern revolution. Regardless of the final consensus reached by academicians, the Chiapas uprising has served to dramatize the plight of some of the most exploited and neglected peoples of the continent. Michael Lowy, the research director in sociology at the National Center of Scientific Research in Paris and the author of The Marxism of Che Guevara *and* On Changing the World, *provides a comprehensive, incisive, and precise understanding of the ideological roots of the EZLN and the ideological and practical considerations that contributed to its gestation.*

We are living in a time when the world is disenchanted. Now more than ever before, capitalism, in its neoliberal form, has reduced all social relations, all values, all qualities to the status of commodities. This is a realm of universal quantification, commercialization, monetarization. This is an age when all human feelings are drowned in what Marx, in the Communist Manifesto, called "the icy water of egotistical calculation."

From *Monthly Review* 49, no. 10 (March 1998): 1–4. © 1997 by Monthly Review Press. Reprinted by permission of the Monthly Review Press Foundation.

Zapatism, a movement opposed to neoliberalism, seeks, on a modest scale, to re-enchant the world. (I am borrowing this idea from Yvon Le Bot's 1997 book *Le Rêve zapatiste* [*The Zapatista Dream*], but giving it a slightly different interpretation.) It is a movement freighted with magic, with myths, utopias, poetry, romanticism, enthusiasms, and wild hopes, with "mysticism" (in the sense that Charles Peguy used the word, in opposition to "politics"),[1] and with faith. It is also full of insolence, humor, irony, and self-irony. There is no contradiction in that: as Lukacs wrote in *The Theory of the Novel*, irony is the mysticism of times without a god. . . .[2]

This ability to reinvent the re-enchantment of the world is no doubt one of the reasons why Zapatism is so fascinating to people far beyond the mountains of Chiapas.

What is Zapatism composed of? It is a subtle mixture, an alchemistic fusion, an explosive cocktail made up of several ingredients, several traditions, each of them indispensable, each of them present in the final product. Or rather, it is a carpet made of threads of different colors, old and new, interwoven in a wonderful design whose secret is known only to the Mayan Indians.

The first thread, the first tradition is Guevarism-Marxism in its Latin American revolutionary form. The original core of the Zapatista National Liberation Army (EZLN) was Guevarist. Of course, the evolution of the movement has taken it far from its beginnings, but the uprising of January 1994 and the very spirit of the EZLN retain elements of this heritage: the importance of armed struggle, the organic link between the armed forces and the peasantry, the rifle as a material expression of an exploited people's distrust of their oppressors, the readiness to risk one's life for the emancipation of one's brothers. We are a long way from the Bolivian adventure of 1967 but close to the revolutionary ethic of which Che was the incarnation.

The second thread, and doubtless the most direct, is of course the legacy of Emiliano Zapata. It is the uprising of the peasants and indigenous people, the *Ejercito del Sur* as an army of the masses, the uncompromising struggle against the powerful that does not seek to seize power, the agrarian program for the redistribution of land, and the community organization of peasant life (what Adolfo Gilly called the "commune of Morelos"). But at the same time, it is Zapata the internationalist, who, in a famous letter of February 1918, hailed the Russian Revolution, emphasizing "the visible analogy, the obvious parallelism, the absolute parity" between it and the agrarian revolution in Mexico. "Both of them," he wrote, "are directed against what Tolstoy called 'the great crime,' against the infamous usurpation of the earth, which, belonging to all, like the water and the air, has been monopolized by a few powerful men, supported by the strength of armies and the iniquity of laws."

"Land and Liberty" remains the central slogan of the new Zapatistas, who are continuing a revolution "interrupted" (as Gilly put it in the title of his beautiful book)[3] in 1919, by the assassination of Zapata in Chinameca.

A thread that the Zapatistas don't talk much about is liberation theology. Yet it is hard to imagine that their movement could have had such an impact in Chiapas had it not been for the work accomplished by Msgr. Samuel Ruiz and his thousands of catechists ever since the 1970s—the work of raising consciousness in the indigenous communities and of encouraging them to organize to struggle for their rights. Of course, that work had no revolutionary tendency and rejected all violence, whereas the dynamics of the EZLN were to be entirely different. It is nonetheless true that in the indigenous communities the thinking of many Zapatistas— including some of the most prominent—was basically molded by liberation theology, by a religious faith that chose a commitment to the self-emancipation of the poor.

Perhaps the most important thread is the Mayan culture of the native people of Chiapas, with its magical relation to nature, its community solidarity, its resistance to neoliberal modernization. Zapatism harks back to a community tradition of the past, a precapitalist, premodern, pre-Columbian tradition. The Peruvian Marxist José Carlos Mariátegui spoke, not without some exaggeration, of the "communism of the Incas." In the same spirit, one can speak of the "communism of the Mayas." Is that romanticism? Perhaps. But without the magic hammer of revolutionary romanticism, how are we to break the bars of what Max Weber called the steel cage in which capitalist modernity has confined us?

The EZLN is heir to five centuries of native resistance to the Conquest, to "civilization" and "modernity." It is no coincidence that the Zapatista uprising was originally planned for 1992, the fifth centenary of the Conquest, and that at that time crowds of indigenous people occupied San Cristóbal de las Casas and tore down the statue of the Conquistador Diego de Mazariegos, the hated symbol of their despoliation and enslavement.

The last, most recent thread, added to the others after January 1994, consists of the democratic demands made by Mexican civil society, by that vast network of unions, neighborhood associations, women's, students', and ecologists' associations, of Leftist parties—Cardenists, Trotskyists, anarchists, and many other "ists"—of associations of debtors, peasants, and indigenous communities that have risen up throughout Mexico to support the demands of the Zapatistas: democracy, dignity, justice.

There are many things one can criticize about the Zapatistas—for example, I don't understand why they did not issue a call to vote for Cardenas in the last elections. But we must grant them one tremendous virtue: in these gloomy closing years of the century, in this time of triumphant neoliberalism, of rampant commercialism, of galloping cynicism, of a politics of politicians, they have succeeded in making people dream in Chiapas, in Mexico, and in places all over the planet. They are re-enchanters of the world.

Notes

1. That sense is perhaps best summed up in Peguy's own definition of the two terms: "la mystique républicaine, c'était quand on mourait pour la République, la politique républicaine, c'est le présent qu'on en vit." (Republican mysticism meant dying for the Republic; republican politics at present means living off it.) From the pamphlet "Notre Jeunesse" (1910) in Charles Peguy, *Oeuvres en prose complètes* (Paris: Gallimard, 1992), Vol. III, p. 156.

2. "The writer's irony is a negative mysticism to be found in times without a god." From Georg Lukacs, *The Theory of the Novel* (1920), translated from the German by Anna Bostock (Cambridge, Massachusetts: MIT Press, 1971), p. 90.

3. An expanded version of Adolfo Gilly's *La Revolución interrumpida* (1971) has been translated from the Spanish by Patrick Camiller under the title *The Mexican Revolution* (London: N.L.B., 1983).

19

End of an Era

Herbert Braun

Of the countries where insurgent movements are still active, Colombia holds the rather dubious distinction of having lived the better part of this century in a state of permanent and endemic warfare and of being home to the longest-running unsuccessful guerrilla movement on the continent and perhaps in the world. Of the surviving groups, the National Libera- tion Army (ELN), headed by Spanish-born priest Manuel Pérez, is one of the most visible. Founded in 1965, the ELN, at the close of the twentieth century, is estimated to have nearly four thousand members and to be worth somewhere in the neighborhood of $12.5 million, money obtained mostly from kidnappings and quota collections. Latin American historian Herbert "Tico" Braun, author of The Assassination of Gaitán, *was unwit- tingly drawn into the political drama of Colombia when his brother-in- law, Jacobo "Jake" Gambini, was kidnapped by the ELN. As the brother-in-law of the victim, Braun was one of the people chosen to nego- tiate with the guerrillas. After extorting a ransom from the family, the ELN, fearing that Gambini would starve himself to death, freed him to rejoin his family in the United States. Years later, Braun recounted this painful experience in* Our Guerrillas, Our Sidewalks, *from which "Tico" and "Postscript" have been excerpted.*

Tico

Saturday, June 17, 1989

I'm sitting in [the University of Virginia's] Alderman Library with *El Tiempo*. A long article on the kidnappings glares up at me. The writer

From *Our Guerrillas, Our Sidewalks: A Journey into the Violence of Colom- bia* (Niwot: University Press of Colorado, 1994), 224–32. Reprinted by permis- sion of the University Press of Colorado.

seems to have done quite a bit of research. My eyes focus quickly on a
familiar name somewhere in the middle of the story. This time Jake's last
name is spelled correctly. I have the feeling that the journalist knows what
he is talking about, even though the dates are way off, the year is wrong,
and so, too, is the name of the company.

> In July 1987, the ELN kidnapped Jacobo Gambini, the president of
> General American Pipe, a petroleum company. The company refused to
> pay the *rescate*, and his body was found in a grave in Sabana de Torres.

For a split second I come to doubt what I know. We got him out. I
mean, he got himself out. Right? Right. He *is* alive.

Still, I almost believe the story and have to catch myself, even though
I know all about the way news gets into the newspapers.

That day back in July flashes in front of me, when I was sitting at the
Miami airport and I learned that he had been killed and his body mutilated and burned. Reading the news again makes it seem simply too real.
Too possible. The printed name. The information. For a tiny moment before I can gather my thoughts, he is dead. It ended as we had feared all
along.

I get up and take a walk through the library, then up to the fourth
floor and out. I need to inhale the fresh spring air.

After the relief comes anger. How the hell is anybody going to write
the history of Colombia for this period with those kinds of newspapers? I
thrust my arms into the air, oblivious of all those walking around me.

There is no objective truth to be had. We can't rely on anything. What
good is it all?

Then slowly I start to smile. I don't know quite why at first. I begin to
understand, and it seems all too fitting. We worked so hard to keep all this
secret.

Silence is the way to survive Colombia. His release didn't get into
the papers, and only our friends know what happened. There are only
rumors about.

The guerrillas know, of course. They were the only ones we were ever
really able to count on in Colombia during those months. Nobody else
could come to our aid. They even came to César afterward to ask about
Jake and see how he was doing. The guerrillas know, and they haven't
told anybody either. A few important higher-ups in the police know. They
aren't talking either. To them Jake is just another statistic. For all anybody knows, Jake is dead.

Yes! I like that. Nobody can harm him that way.

This is it! To be publicly dead and privately alive. This is indeed the
way to survive Colombia. To live life in total silence. No harm can come

that way.

The news in *El Tiempo* is just great, just what we need and want. Jake is dead. That way he can keep on living.

I am chuckling to myself as I walk briskly over to the cafeteria for a cup of coffee. Then as I sit down I begin to realize just how horrible I am feeling. Was I really laughing to myself just moments before? Now I am even finding it hard to breathe deeply.

I have come to the most terrible conclusion. It is everything that I am opposed to. To live in silence and walk our own path through life, only taking care of our own, that's exactly what I have always been most opposed to.

A public voice is what Gaitán fought for. He wanted everybody to be able to speak and be heard, to have a place and be accounted for. And Camilo, too. That's what Camilo was all about. And the guerrillas. Long ago, that's what they were fighting for.

Looking down into my cup of coffee, I realize that I am thinking about the guerrillas in much the same way as I have long thought about Gaitán and Camilo. They are dead. The guerrillas are also gone. They have lost themselves out there in the mountains during all these lonely years. Their voice has been drowned out in the violence of Colombia, in their violence. The guerrillas are dead, finished.

Something more begins to dawn on me. It feels like a tiny kernel of new knowledge. Is it making me look at Colombia in a completely different way, or does it just seem that way?

My thoughts run ahead of me. Suddenly I know that in Colombia we can live with the guerrillas, that we are at one with them. We understand them so well and so deeply precisely because they are kidnappers, because they take prominent members of society, because they come for us. And there is more. We can't blame them for what they do to us. Their actions are nothing more than a logical step, one that is so obvious and so easy.

Those who have become rich and powerful in Colombia, from coffee growers to cattle ranchers to cocaine barons, know that they have exerted their will on the countryside. They have taken the land of others, and when necessary, when those others fought back or did not move, they deprived them of life as well. And they have done it for so many decades out there, so often, and with such impunity that not even the government has done much to stop them. They have acted freely.

So the guerrillas and the kidnappings aren't a surprise to anyone. They are simply a form of payback. The guerrillas are dispensing a measure of raw justice by taking back some of the resources of those who are rich and powerful. And rarely do they kill those they take away. The guerrillas are now little more than an obvious and even inevitable reaction to all the violence in the countryside.

Retribution. That's what it is. After all, that's how the guerrillas see their actions, how they always refer to the kidnappings. And this is how we can easily understand them, whether we agree with what the guerrillas are doing or not. Savage capitalism and kidnappings are different sides of the same coin.

Retribution. That we can understand. That's why we accept the kidnappings so easily. We can tell one another to relax, for we can't react with moral outrage. On what grounds? We participate. It's not just that we don't have any choice but to negotiate with the guerrillas to get one of our own back. It's business, not politics and not morality.

Jake understands what the guerrillas are all about, no matter how much he disagrees with what they did to him. He even said that at one point, when he remarked on the poverty that rural people live in. He knows what leads people out there to become guerrillas. He has a good sense for why they took him.

And it doesn't much matter that he and many others like him are moral and honest people who have never taken anyone else's land. Were those thousands of people who lost their lands over the years, who lost their lives, not also moral and honest? And what have all the good people of Colombia done over the years to put a stop to the violence?

So we tell each other to accept reality when one of us is taken away. It's the world we have made, and we live in it, for we can survive it.

The old words ring in my ears. My words.

"Hey! Don't worry. This will end well. It always does. The guerrillas are responsible people. They have to maintain their image. You'll get him back. They will take care of him. Don't worry. Nothing is going to happen to him. Negotiate. Go ahead. It's only a business transaction."

The old words seem to have a whole new meaning to them.

Have I not thought about the kidnappings in these terms before? Is this really new knowledge that I have inside of me, or is it simply a deeper kind of understanding of what I have always known? I can't really tell.

Is this how Jake has always understood the kidnappings? Why he never bothered to get kidnapping insurance, figuring the insurance would come out being a larger expense than any ransom that might have to be paid?

No. Not him. Jake's different. If he ever thought about it like this, he certainly doesn't anymore. And he sure didn't act like his kidnapping was simply a business transaction when they had him. No. He's as different as can be. Jake sees it all in moral terms. I remember those words of his on my tape recorder, coming back to me again and again as I transcribed the interview.

"It's wrong," he said.

That is his view of it, plain and simple. Kidnapping is wrong. It is about the worst thing that can be done to a human being, such a terrible human action that it's hardly worth surviving. And Jake can't understand how the Colombian people go along with it, how they can still believe in the guerrillas.

What Jake understands is that nothing good can come from kidnapping. If the guerrillas think that they can kidnap people, that they have the right to treat a human being like that, then there's no telling what they will think they have the right to do once they have more influence, once they win and come to power. Evil can only beget evil.

Is this why I'm thinking of the guerrillas in the past tense? Because Jake has shown me how wrong they are? Is there now no difference between his ideas and mine? Does it make any difference that I see the kidnappings and all the violence of Colombia in terms of history, the past, and the growth of the market, of capitalism? Does it make any difference that I see the sidewalks and he simply walks on them? Am I saying anything more than he is? I can't tell.

Isn't his clear moral vision the really meaningful one?

I can't keep my mind from churning this idea around.

Doesn't he have the absolute truth?

Are all my ideas and all my historical knowledge just ways of messing up that truth? Am I simply trying to make something understandable that shouldn't be understandable? Maybe I am even making it acceptable, making it seem inevitable. Maybe this is why it always seemed so strangely easy for me, and for so many others in Colombia, to tell friends to relax when one of their own was kidnapped.

Am I trying to make the kidnappings seem less horrific than they are, less grotesque, by seeking to explain them?

Jake knew from the start that what was happening to him was wrong. Jake looked his kidnappers in the eye and said, "No, I'm not going to go along with this. It's wrong." His truth allowed him to act according to his principles. He was able to look at himself and decide that he wasn't going to be treated like a piece of meat, like a commodity, like something to be exchanged. His beliefs made it possible for him to look death in the face.

He's different. Jake does not live in silence. He has a public voice.

I don't know where to turn. At the very moment when I feel that I have learned so much more than ever before about Colombia, about the guerrillas and the kidnappings, even about history, my thoughts are crashing down all around me. I am beginning to doubt everything I know, the very ways in which I think, in which I was trained to think as a historian.

Am I just making the truth relative?

I don't have answers to my questions, or at least I don't want to reach any answers right now. I turn my mind quickly back to the past, to history, to all those years of guerrilla struggle. These thoughts seem more comfortable. It appears that I can do more with them.

What *would* have happened had Camilo not been killed out there? What would the history of Colombia look like had the guerrillas remained revolutionaries? Could we have lived with their politics? I don't think Jake could have, even had they not become kidnappers. Their politics violate his sense of freedom. Could I have lived with a revolution?

One thing is certain. Successful revolutionary guerrillas would have been something that the upper class of Colombia could not have lived with. The elite would have fought the guerrillas had they remained revolutionaries, instead of surviving next to them, as the rich have done for all these years. The elite understands that a successful revolution will eliminate them.

Which side would have won?

I sit here in the cafeteria in Charlottesville as in a daze, with my eyes tightly closed and my head in my hands, seeing circles, round forms with figures hovering around them, men talking and laughing, joking around those tiny round tables in the cafés. And that wonderful, rhythmic music from the corner record store is dancing around in my head.

I want to focus my mind, to think about politics. I want to listen to public voices.

But there aren't any left.

Postscript

Saturday, July 2, 1994

It's been six years since he was taken away. Much stays the same in Colombia. Much changes. It's quieter now.

Like many times before in our history, a public exhaustion sets in. The hemorrhaging takes its toll. During this year's presidential campaign, the Liberal and Conservative candidates do not talk much about either the guerrillas or the cocaine capitalists. Mainstream politicians are quiet. The election brings the lowest voter turnout in history. The people are not paying much attention to what little it is that the politicians might be saying. The people are quiet, trying to survive. As before, Colombians want to be left alone to work and to make something of their individual lives. The election is won by a calm and pragmatic Liberal economist with bullets still lodged in his body as constant reminders of the public violence that is being left behind. Colombia's long-standing democratic institutions survive and continue to exist next to the regional influences of the guerrillas and the economic power of the cocaine capitalists, neither of which seeks the overthrow of those institutions.

There is much loss of life. The homicide rate remains constant, although some claim that it is rising a bit in the cities. Many say that it continues to be the highest in the world. As before, most of those who kill know those they kill. The loud public violence among armed groups turns more quiet. The quiet private violence of daily life goes on. Those who kill are convinced that they will not be prosecuted even if they are caught. The judicial system remains paralyzed. Impunity is widespread.

One of the nation's beloved soccer stars on the national team is shot to death early in the morning as he leaves a restaurant with his fiancée. The gunmen inform him that they are displeased with his performance in a World Cup game against the United States as they pump twelve bullets into his body. Most people hope that the cocaine capitalists who lost many millions betting on the national team are responsible for the shooting. Crime caused by money seems more palatable than crime caused by crazed national fanaticism. But anybody can be responsible. The culture of violence knows no limits.

The economy grows at a rapid clip. Wealth is everywhere. Conspicuous consumption remains the order of the day. Our sidewalks are worse, although some are much improved through individual effort and private financial expense. The streets are packed with people going here and there, and the cafés are filled with men talking. Music is everywhere. The deep foundation for a high-rise building that is under construction a block from our home caves in. People and cars on the surrounding highways fall into the gigantic hole. Newspaper pictures taken from surrounding buildings show a bombed-out area, as though the city were at war. The surrounding sidewalks are gone, too.

The cocaine capitalists of Medellín help bring about the emerging calm by orchestrating a horrendous bombing and assassination campaign against civilians, the police, the media, and high government officials. The government fights back, freezing assets, impounding homes, and organizing elite hit squads to get the leaders. The years 1989 and 1990 bring the most deaths.

Four of the six presidential candidates in the 1990 election are shot to death. They are all men of the Left, including Luis Carlos Galán, the standard-bearer of the Liberal Party. One of these reformers, Carlos Pizarro, who is the last commander of the M-19 guerrillas, finds his bullet while he is high up in the air, sitting comfortably on a commercial airliner, as he tours the nation campaigning for the presidency. The killer knows that he, too, is to die before the plane lands.

The bullets come from the Right, from the violent cocaine capitalists, the paramilitary defense squads, their friends in the military and in government, or some combination of some or all of them. Two violent cocaine barons lose their lives. José Gonzalo Rodríguez Gacha is shot in 1989 along with his son. Pablo Escobar is shot in 1993 when he has only one bodyguard left to protect him. The threat from a violent Right is much diminished.

At Luis Carlos Galán's funeral, his young son hands the Liberal Party over to César Gaviria, a soft-spoken and pragmatic politician with nothing like the social vision of the deceased leader. Gaviria continues the pro-market policies of his predecessors while devoting little thought to social expenditures. And he oversees the writing of a new constitution. Although not many citizens seem to know what the renewed law means, or how their lives will be affected, few feel that the new charter is any worse than the previous one, which lasted for more than one hundred years. It might be better.

For the drug barons the document is a huge step forward, for it declares extradition to be illegal. An understanding exists that allows the government and the cocaine capitalists to survive together. The new entrepreneurs can stay in Colombia and work, but they are not to be politicians. Politics is to remain the domain of the traditional politicians. Led by astute investors from Cali, the cocaine capitalists quietly make money exporting commodities throughout the world. They sell heroin now, too. Their profits quietly underwrite the campaigns of the politicians.

The drug barons no longer need to spark the imagination. They still their own voices. With the violence from their Medellín counterparts out of the way, the New Right survives with silent ease. As before, Colombia has surrendered to the forces of the market, to the export of valuable goods.

After many of the M-19 guerrillas lose their lives in battle and it becomes obvious that a military victory will not be coming, the leaders decide to turn in their guns and turn into politicians. Many of the old guerrilla leaders lose their lives on the streets of the cities. After initial electoral gains in 1990, the Left is of little consequence, gaining only a few thousand votes here and there. It is quiet, barely managing to survive.

The guerrillas are still out there in the mountains, even though some have given up. Only those of us who are in some way directly affected by them pay much attention to what they are doing. The encounters between them and the military are few and far between. They avoid each other and survive. Their revolutionary voice has not returned. Our guerrillas rule over diverse regions of the nation.

In one round after another of peace negotiations with the government, the guerrillas assert that they do not engage in kidnappings. In 1991 at least 1,717 people were taken, far more than the 1,000 or so in 1988. "With many families reluctant to notify the police," reports the *New York Times* on August 16, 1992, "the real number could be much higher." A new organization lobbies for kidnap victims. Gabriel García Márquez and the nation's major intellectuals sign a written declaration opposing the kidnappings. The government sets up a new anti-kidnapping police unit. There is a law on the books that says that the government will freeze the assets of families that negotiate ransom settlements. The kidnappings continue. Statistics are hardly kept anymore. Nobody needs them. Nobody wants them.

The guerrillas keep their word, once again. They leave us alone. No one comes again. An eerie calm settles over the company in Sabana. Jake does not return to Colombia. He rises each morning by 4:00, as before. He spends hours on his rose garden. He cooks. He eats and diets. He's healthy. He seems unchanged.

Only his diary has stopped. A detailed journal of each day's events over almost thirty years comes to an end on that morning in June six years ago.

Mine begins.

Suggested Readings

With the exception of works on Sendero Luminoso and the EZLN, there are relatively few books and articles published after 1990 on the subject of guerrillas and revolutionary movements in Latin America.

Sources in English

Anderson, Jon Lee. *Che Guevara: A Revolutionary Life*. New York: Grove Press, 1997.

Asencio, Diego and Nancy. *Our Man Is Inside*. Boston: Little, Brown and Company, 1983.

Beals, Carleton. *Latin America: World in Revolution*. London: Abelard-Schuman, 1963.

Béjar, Hector. *Peru 1965: Notes on a Guerrilla Experience*. New York: Monthly Review Press, 1970.

Bonachea, Rolando E., and Nelsón P. Valdés, eds. *Cuba in Revolution*. New York: Doubleday and Company, 1972.

Braun, Herbert. *Our Guerrillas, Our Sidewalks: A Journey into the Violence of Colombia*. Niwot: University Press of Colorado, 1994.

Campbell, Leon G. "Ideology and Factionalism during the Great Rebellion, 1780–1782," in *Resistance and Consciousness in the Andean Peasant World, 18th to 20th Centuries*, edited by Steve J. Stern. Madison: University of Wisconsin Press, 1987.

———. "Women and the Great Rebellion in Peru, 1780–1783." *Americas* 42, no. 2 (October 1985): 163–96.

Carrigan, Ana. *The Palace of Justice: A Colombian Tragedy*. New York: Four Walls, Eight Windows, 1993.

Castañada, Jorge G. *Compañero: The Life and Death of Che Guevara*. Translated by Marina Castañeda. New York: Alfred A. Knopf, 1997.

———. *Utopia Unarmed: The Latin American Left after the Cold War*. New York: Vintage Books, 1995.

Chaliand, Gérard. *Revolution in the Third World*. Translated by Diana Johnstone. Harmondsworth, Middlesex, England: Penguin Books Ltd., 1977.

———, ed. *Guerrilla Strategies : An Historical Anthology from the Long March to Afghanistan*. Berkeley: University of California Press, 1982.

Chernick, Mark W. "Negotiated Settlement to Armed Conflict: Lessons from the Colombian Peace Process." *Journal of Inter-American Studies and World Affairs* 30, no. 4 (Winter 1988–89): 53–88.

Debray, Régis. *Revolution in the Revolution? Armed Struggle and Political Struggle in Latin America.* Translated by Bobbye Ortiz. 2d printing. New York: Monthly Review Press, 1967.

De Fronzo, James. *Revolutions and Revolutionary Movements.* Boulder, CO: Westview Press, 1991.

Deutschmann, David, ed. *Che Guevara and the Cuban Revolution: Writings and Speeches of Ernesto Che Guevara.* Sydney, Australia: Pathfinder, 1987.

Dix, Robert H. *Colombia: The Political Dimensions of Change.* New Haven, CT: Yale University Press, 1967.

Dunkerley, James. *Rebellion in the Veins: Political Struggle in Bolivia, 1952–1982.* London: Verso Editions, 1984.

Fairbairn, Geoffrey. *Revolutionary Guerrilla Warfare: The Countryside Version.* Harmondsworth, Middlesex, England: Penguin Books Ltd., 1974.

Fisher, Lillian Estelle. *The Last Inca Revolt, 1780–1783.* Norman: University of Oklahoma Press, 1966.

Gerassi, John, ed. *The Great Fear in Latin America.* London: Collier Macmillan Ltd., 1969.

———. *Revolutionary Priest: The Complete Writings and Messages of Camilo Torres.* New York: Random House, 1971.

Gil, Federico G. "The Kennedy-Johnson Years." In *United States Policy in Latin America: A Quarter Century of Crisis and Challenge, 1961–1986,* edited by John D. Martz. Lincoln: University of Nebraska Press, 1988.

Gilio, Maria Esther. *The Tupamaro Guerrillas.* Translated by Anne Edmonson. New York: Saturday Review Press, 1970.

Gillespie, Richard. *Soldiers of Peron: Argentina's Montoneros.* Oxford: Clarendon Press, 1982.

Gorriti Elenbogen, Gustavo. *The Shining Path: A History of the Millenarian War in Peru.* Translated by Robin Kirk. Chapel Hill: University of North Carolina Press, 1999.

Gott, Richard. *Guerrilla Movements in Latin America.* London: Thomas Nelson and Sons Ltd., 1970.

Guevara, Ernesto "Che". *The Bolivian Diary of Ernesto Che Guevara.* Edited by Mary-Alice Waters. New York: Pathfinder Press, 1994.

———. *Che Guevara Speaks: Selected Speeches and Writings.* Edited by George Lavan. New York: Pathfinder Press, 1982.

———. *Guerrilla Warfare.* Edited by Brian Loveman and Thomas M. Davies Jr. Lincoln: University of Nebraska Press, 1985.

Guzmán Bouvard, Marguerite. *Revolutionizing Motherhood: The Mothers of the Plaza de Mayo.* Wilmington, DE: Scholarly Resources, 1994.

Heinz, Wolfgang S. "Guerrillas, Political Violence and the Peace Process in Colombia." *Latin American Research Review* 24, no. 3 (1989): 249–58.

Hodges, Don Clark. *Argentina's "Dirty War": An Intellectual Biography.* Austin: University of Texas Press, 1991.

James, Daniel, ed. *The Complete Diaries of Che Guevara and Other Captured Documents.* New York: Stein and Day Publishers, 1968.

Katz, Friedrich, ed. *Riot, Rebellion and Revolution: Rural Social Conflict in Mexico.* Princeton, NJ: Princeton University Press, 1988.

Kohl, James, and John Litt, eds. *Urban Guerrilla Warfare in Latin America.* Cambridge, MA: MIT Press, 1974.

LaFeber, Walter. *Inevitable Revolutions: The United States in Central America.* New York: W. W. Norton & Company, 1993.

Laqueur, Walter. *Guerrilla: A Historical and Critical Study.* Boston: Little, Brown and Company, 1976.

———, ed. *The Guerrilla Reader: A Historical Anthology.* New York: New American Library, 1977.

Lartéguy, Jean. *The Guerrillas.* Translated by Stanley Hochman. New York: World Publishing Company, 1970.

McClintock, Cynthia. "Peru's Sendero Luminoso Rebellion: Origins and Trajectory." In *Power and Popular Protest: Latin America's Social Movements,* edited by Susan Eckstein, 61–101. Los Angeles: University of California Press, 1989.

———. "Sendero Luminoso: Peru's Maoist Guerrillas." *Problems of Communism* (September–October 1983): 19–34.

Mallin, Jay, ed. *Strategy for Conquest: Communist Documents on Guerrilla Warfare.* Coral Gables, FL: University of Miami Press, 1970.

Martic, Milos. *Insurrection: Five Schools of Revolutionary Thought.* New York: Dunellen Publishing Company, 1975.

Means, Philip Ainsworth. "The Rebellion of Tupac Amaru II, 1780–1781." *Hispanic American Historical Review* 2, no. 1 (February 1919): 1–25.

Millon, Robert P. *Zapata: The Ideology of a Peasant Revolutionary.* New York: International Publishers, 1969.

Palmer, David Scott, ed. *The Shining Path of Peru.* 2d ed. New York: St. Martin's Press, 1994.

Paret, Peter, and John W. Shy. *Guerrillas in the 1960s.* 4th ed. New York: Frederick A. Praeger Publishers, 1965.

Petras, James, and Maurice Zeitlin, eds. *Latin America: Reform or Revolution?* New York: Fawcett Books, 1968.

Phelan, John Leddy. *The People and the King: The Comunero Revolution in Colombia, 1781.* Madison: University of Wisconsin Press, 1978.

Porczecanski, Arturo C. *Uruguay's Tupamaros: The Urban Guerrilla.* New York: Praeger Publishers, 1973.

Quartim, João. *Dictatorship and Armed Struggle in Brazil.* Translated by David Fernbach. New York: Monthly Review Press, 1971.

Radu, Michael, and Vladimir Tismaneanu. *Latin American Revolutionaries: Groups, Goals, Methods.* Washington, DC: Pergamon-Brassey's International Defense Publishers, 1990.

Rodriguez, Frederick M. "Yanga's Revolt and the Growth of the Cimarrons." Master's thesis, DePaul University, 1972.

Rojas Sanford, Robinson. *The Murder of Allende and the End of the Chilean Way to Socialism.* New York: Harper and Row, 1976.

Ross, John. *Rebellion from the Roots: Indian Uprising in Chiapas.* Monroe, ME: Common Courage Press, 1995.

Sarkesian, Sam C., ed. *Revolutionary Guerrilla Warfare.* Chicago: Precedent Publishing, 1975.

Sigmund, Paul E. *The Overthrow of Allende and the Politics of Chile, 1964–1976.* Pittsburgh: University of Pittsburgh Press, 1977.

Spooner, Mary Helen. *Soldiers in a Narrowland: The Pinochet Regime in Chile.* Berkeley: University of California Press, 1994.

Stern, Steve J., ed. *Resistance, Rebellion, and Consciousness in the Andean Peasant World, 18th to 20th Centuries.* Madison: University of Wisconsin Press, 1987.

———. *Shining and Other Paths: War and Society in Peru, 1980–1995.* Durham: Duke University Press, 1998.

Strong, Simon. *Shining Path: The World's Deadliest Revolutionary Force.* London: HarperCollins Publishers, 1992.

Sun Tzu. *The Art of War.* Translated and with an introduction by Samuel B. Griffith. London: Oxford University Press, 1975.

Taber, Robert. *The War of the Flea: A Study of Guerrilla Warfare, Theory and Practice.* New York: Lyle Stuart, 1965.

Tarazona-Sevillano, Gabriela, with John B. Reuter. *Sendero Luminoso and the Threat of Narcoterrorism.* New York: Praeger, 1990.

Wickham-Crowley, Timothy P. *Guerrillas and Revolution in Latin America: A Comparative Study of Insurgents and Regimes since 1956.* Princeton: Princeton University Press, 1992.

Sources in Spanish

Bolo Hidalgo, Salomón. *Micaela Bastidas Puyacagua: La mujer más grande de América.* Lima: Private printing, 1976.

Camejo, Pedro Miguel. *La Guerrilla: Por qué fracasó como estrategia.* New York: Pathfinder Press, 1976.

Comité Central del Partido Comunista del Perú. *Bases de discusión del PCP*: "La Guerra Popular y los Instrumentos de la Revolución, El Partido, el Ejército y el Frente Unico." *El Diario*, Suplemento Especial 7 de enero 1988.

———. *¡Desarrollemos la Guerra de Guerrillas!* Perú: Ediciones Bandera Roja. 8 de setiembre 1981.

La crisis de los rehenes en el Peru: Base Tokio, el verano sangriento. Lima: Empresa Editorial *El Comercio*, 1997.

Degregori, Carlos Iván. *Ayacucho 1969–1979: El surgimiento de Sendero Luminoso.* Lima: Instituto de Estudios Peruanos, 1990.

———. *"Sendero Luminoso"*: I. *Los Hondos y mortales desencuentros.* II. *Lucha Armada y utopía autoritaria.* 6th ed. Lima: Instituto de Estudios Peruanos, 1988.

De la Puente, Luis. *El camino de la revolución, obras escogidas.* Lima: Ediciones Voz Rebelde-IV Epoca, 1976.

Gorriti Elenbogen, Gustavo. *Sendero: Historia de la Guerra Milenaria en el Perú.* Vol 1. Lima: Editorial Apoyo, 1990.

López, Jaime. *10 años de guerrillas en México 1964–1974.* 2d ed. Mexico D.F.: Editorial Posada, 1977.

Simón Munaro, Yehude. *Estado y guerrillas en el Perú de los '80.* Lima: Asociación Instituto de Estudios Estratégicos y Sociales, 1988.

Tello, María del Pilar. *Sobre el volcán: Diálogo sobre la subversión.* Lima: Centro de Estudios Latinoamericanos, 1989.

Vega, Juan José. *Micaela Bastidas y las heroínas tupamaristas.* Lima: Ediciones Universidad Nacional de Educación, 1971.

Suggested Films

These films are available in the United States, either subtitled or dubbed.

Alsino and the Condor (Nicaragua-Chile). 1982. Directed by Miguel Litín. The story of a boy who dreams of being able to fly but falls out of a tree and grows malformed. His participation in the FSLN guerrillas provides the best substitute for his dream, for in a sense only then can he be capable of flying.

Burn! (Italy-USA). 1970. Director Guillo Pontecorvo uses an imaginary nineteenth-century Caribbean island to depict the struggle waged by its people to gain independence from Portugal only to succumb to English imperialism.

Fire in the Mind: Revolutions and Revolutionaries (USA). 1993. Part of *The Americas* series, this documentary looks at revolutionary movements in El Salvador and Peru.

No Habrá Mas Penas ni Olvido (Funny dirty little war) (Argentina). 1983. A civil war in a rural Argentine village started as the result of conflicts between *peronistas* and people accused of being Communists.

In Women's Hands: The Changing Role of Women (USA). 1993. Part of *The Americas* series, this documentary examines changes among Chilean women of every social class and how they organized during the Pinochet dictatorship to create better living conditions for their families.

Las Madres de la Plaza de Mayo (Argentina). 1985. Poignant documentary about the efforts of the relatives of the *desaparecidos* to obtain justice from the authorities.

The Last Supper (Cuba). 1976. Directed by Tomás Gutiérrez Alea. The story of a slave rebellion in the eighteenth century. During a reenactment of the Last Supper, the slaves are forced to realize their condition of bondage and some of them choose to struggle.

La Vida Es una Sola (Peru-Norway). 1994. Explores the effects of the violence inflicted on the people of the Sierras by the Peruvian army and the Shining Path guerrillas.

Los de Abajo (Mexico). Based on Mariano Azuela's novel, the film is a revealing chronicle of the violent and passionate emotions unchained by the Mexican Revolution.

Missing (USA). 1982. French director Constantin Costa Gravas is a one-man campaign against authoritarian regimes. This film was based on the killing of journalist Charles Horman in the aftermath of the 1973 coup and the involvement of U.S. officials in the cover-up.

The Official Story (Argentina). 1986. The story of a sheltered Argentine woman who unknowingly has adopted the stolen child of a couple of *desaparecidos*.

The People of the Shining Path (Peru-England). 1992. One of the most complete documentaries about the Shining Path and its work among the masses in the early 1990s.

Salvador (USA). 1986. Directed by Oliver Stone. Story of a photojournalist in El Salvador at the height of the guerrilla offensive in 1980.

School of the Americas/Assassins (USA). 1994. Short documentary examining the role that U.S. training has played in contributing to the creation of Dirty War warriors among the Latin American military.

Search for the Disappeared (USA). Somber documentary on attempts to identify remains from mass graves from the time of the Dirty War.

State of Siege (Chile-France). 1973. Constantin Costa Gravas's version of the kidnapping and execution of USAID agent Daniel Mitrione by the Tupamaros.

Under Fire (USA). 1983. An American photographer is caught in Nicaragua during the final FSLN offensive and contributes to keeping a myth alive through the use of trick photography. The film reenacts the cold-blooded shooting of ABC-TV reporter Bill Stewart.

The Uprising (Germany-Nicaragua-Chile). 1979. Based on a novel by Chilean Antonio Skarmeta, this film is a story of the conflicts encountered by a Nicaraguan National Guard soldier who must decide where his loyalty lies.

Viva Mexico (USA-USSR). An unfinished documentary about the Mexican Revolution partially financed by Upton Sinclair and directed by Sergei Eisenstein in the 1920s.

Viva Zapata (USA). 1952. Depiction of Emiliano Zapata's rise to prominence as a revolutionary leader, based on a screenplay by John Steinbeck.